I0003651

Amazon Simple Queue Service Developer Guide

A catalogue record for this book is available from the Hong Kong Public Libraries.

Published in Hong Kong by Samurai Media Limited.

Email: info@samuraimedia.org

ISBN 9789888408559

Copyright 2018 Amazon Web Services, Inc. and/or its affiliates.
Minor modifications for publication Copyright 2018 Samurai Media Limited.

This book is licensed under the Creative Commons Attribution-ShareAlike 4.0 International Public License.

Background Cover Image by https://www.flickr.com/people/webtreatsetc/

Contents

What is Amazon Simple Queue Service?   **11**
    What Are the Main Benefits of Amazon SQS? 11
    How Is Amazon SQS Different from Amazon MQ or Amazon SNS? 11
    What Type of Queue Do I Need? 11
    How Can I Get Started with Amazon SQS? 12
    We Want to Hear from You 12

New and Frequently Viewed Amazon SQS Topics   **13**
    Amazon Simple Queue Service Developer Guide 13
    Amazon Simple Queue Service API Reference 13

Setting Up Amazon SQS   **13**
    Step 1: Create an AWS Account 13
    Step 2: Create an IAM User 13
    Step 3: Get Your Access Key ID and Secret Access Key 14
    Step 4: Get Ready to Use the Example Code 15
    Next Steps 15

Getting Started with Amazon SQS   **16**
    Prerequisites 16
    Step 1: Create a Queue 16
    Step 2: Send a Message 16
    Step 3: Receive and Delete Your Message 19
    Step 4: Delete Your Queue 22
    Next Steps 23

Amazon SQS Tutorials   **24**

Tutorials: Creating Amazon SQS Queues   **25**

Tutorial: Creating an Amazon SQS Queue   **26**
    AWS Management Console 26
    AWS SDK for Java 27
       To create a standard queue 27
       To create a FIFO queue 27
    AWS CloudFormation 28

Tutorial: Creating an Amazon SQS Queue with Server-Side Encryption (SSE)   **30**
    AWS Management Console 30
    AWS SDK for Java 31

Tutorial: Listing All Amazon SQS Queues in a Region   **34**
    AWS Management Console 34
    AWS SDK for Java 34

Tutorial: Adding Permissions to an Amazon SQS Queue   **36**
    AWS Management Console 36

Tutorial: Adding, Updating, and Removing Cost Allocation Tags for an Amazon SQS Queue   **39**
    AWS Management Console 39
    AWS SDK for Java 39
       To add, update, and remove tags from a queue 40

Tutorials: Sending Messages to Amazon SQS Queues   **41**

Tutorial: Sending a Message to an Amazon SQS Queue   **42**
AWS Management Console 42
AWS SDK for Java 44
    To send a message to a standard queue 44
    To send a message to a FIFO queue 44

Tutorial: Sending a Message with Attributes to an Amazon SQS Queue   **46**
AWS Management Console 46
AWS SDK for Java 49
    To send a message with attributes to a queue 49

Tutorial: Sending a Message with a Timer to an Amazon SQS Queue   **52**
AWS Management Console 52
AWS SDK for Java 54
    To send a message with a timer to a queue 54

Tutorial: Receiving and Deleting a Message from an Amazon SQS Queue   **55**
AWS Management Console 55
AWS SDK for Java 59
    To receive and delete a message from a standard queue 59
    To receive and delete a message from a FIFO queue 60

Tutorial: Subscribing an Amazon SQS Queue to an Amazon SNS Topic   **61**
AWS Management Console 61

Tutorial: Purging Messages from an Amazon SQS Queue   **64**
AWS Management Console 64

Tutorial: Deleting an Amazon SQS Queue   **66**
AWS Management Console 66
AWS SDK for Java 67

Tutorials: Configuring Amazon SQS Queues   **68**

Tutorial: Configuring Server-Side Encryption (SSE) for an Existing Amazon SQS Queue   **69**
AWS Management Console 69
AWS SDK for Java 70

Tutorial: Configuring Long Polling for an Amazon SQS Queue   **72**
AWS Management Console 72
AWS SDK for Java 72
    To configure long polling for a queue 72
    To configure long polling for a queue and send, receive, and delete a message 74

Tutorial: Configuring an Amazon SQS Dead-Letter Queue   **75**
AWS Management Console 75
AWS SDK for Java 76
    To configure a dead-letter queue 76
    To configure a dead-letter queue and send, receive, and delete a message 78

Tutorial: Configuring Visibility Timeout for an Amazon SQS Queue   **79**
AWS Management Console 79
AWS SDK for Java 79
    To configure visibility timeout for a queue 79

To configure visibility timeout for a single message or multiple messages and send, receive, and
delete messages 81

Tutorial: Configuring an Amazon SQS Delay Queue **83**
AWS Management Console 83
AWS SDK for Java 83
To configure a delay queue 83
To configure a delay queue and send, receive, and delete messages 85

How Amazon SQS Works **86**

Basic Amazon SQS Architecture **87**
Distributed Queues 87
Message Lifecycle 87

Amazon SQS Standard Queues **89**
Message Ordering 89
At-Least-Once Delivery 89
Consuming Messages Using Short Polling 89

Working Java Example for Standard Queues **91**
Prerequisites 91
SQSSimpleJavaClientExample.java 91

Amazon SQS FIFO (First-In-First-Out) Queues **94**
Message Ordering 94
Key Terms 95
FIFO Delivery Logic 95
Exactly-Once Processing 96
Moving from a Standard Queue to a FIFO Queue 96
Compatibility 97

Working Java Example for FIFO Queues **98**
Prerequisites 98
SQSFIFOJavaClientExample.java 98

Amazon SQS Queue and Message Identifiers **102**

Identifiers for Amazon SQS Standard and FIFO Queues **103**
Queue Name and URL 103
Message ID 103
Receipt Handle 103

Additional Identifiers for Amazon SQS FIFO Queues **104**
Message Deduplication ID 104
Message Group ID 104
Sequence Number 104

Amazon SQS Message Attributes **105**
Message Attribute Components 105
Message Attribute Data Types 105
Calculating the MD5 Message Digest for Message Attributes 106
Overview 106
To encode a single Amazon SQS message attribute 106

Resources Required to Process Amazon SQS Messages **108**

Amazon SQS Cost Allocation Tags   **109**

Amazon SQS Long Polling   **110**
Differences Between Long and Short Polling 110

Amazon SQS Dead-Letter Queues   **111**
How Do Dead-Letter Queues Work? 111
What are the Benefits of Dead-Letter Queues? 112
How Do Different Queue Types Handle Message Failure? 112
     Standard Queues 112
     FIFO Queues 112
When Should I Use a Dead-Letter Queue? 112
Troubleshooting Dead-Letter Queues 113
     Viewing Messages using the AWS Management Console Might Cause Messages to be Moved to a
       Dead-Letter Queue 113
     The `NumberOfMessagesSent` and `NumberOfMessagesReceived` for a Dead-Letter Queue Don't
       Match 113

Amazon SQS Visibility Timeout   **114**
Inflight Messages 115
Setting the Visibility Timeout 115
Changing the Visibility Timeout for a Message 115
Terminating the Visibility Timeout for a Message 116

Amazon SQS Delay Queues   **117**

Amazon SQS Message Timers   **118**

Managing Large Amazon SQS Messages Using Amazon S3   **119**

Working Java Example for Using Amazon S3 for Large Amazon SQS Messages   **120**
Prerequisites 120
SQSExtendedClientExample.java 120

Working with JMS and Amazon SQS   **124**

Prerequisites   **125**

Getting Started with the Amazon SQS Java Messaging Library   **126**
Creating a JMS Connection 126
Creating an Amazon SQS Queue 126
     To create a standard queue 126
     To create a FIFO queue 127
Sending Messages Synchronously 127
Receiving Messages Synchronously 128
Receiving Messages Asynchronously 129
Using Client Acknowledge Mode 130
Using Unordered Acknowledge Mode 130

Using the Amazon SQS Java Message Service (JMS) Client with Other Amazon SQS Clients132

Working Java Example for Using JMS with Amazon SQS Standard Queues   **133**
ExampleConfiguration.java 133
TextMessageSender.java 135
SyncMessageReceiver.java 136
AsyncMessageReceiver.java 138

SyncMessageReceiverClientAcknowledge.java 139
SyncMessageReceiverUnorderedAcknowledge.java 142
SpringExampleConfiguration.xml 145
SpringExample.java 146
ExampleCommon.java 148

Supported JMS 1.1 Implementations   **150**
Supported Common Interfaces 150
Supported Message Types 150
Supported Message Acknowledgment Modes 150
JMS-Defined Headers and Reserved Properties 150
    For Sending Messages 150
    For Receiving Messages 150

Best Practices for Amazon SQS   **152**

Recommendations for Amazon SQS Standard and FIFO (First-In-First-Out) Queues **153**

Working with Amazon SQS Messages   **154**
Processing Messages in a Timely Manner 154
Handling Request Errors 154
Setting Up Long Polling 154
Capturing Problematic Messages 155
Setting Up Dead-Letter Queue Retention 155
Avoiding Inconsistent Message Processing 155
Implementing Request-Response Systems 155

Reducing Amazon SQS Costs   **156**
Batching Message Actions 156
Using the Appropriate Polling Mode 156

Moving from an Amazon SQS Standard Queue to a FIFO Queue   **157**

Additional Recommendations for Amazon SQS FIFO Queues   **158**

Using the Amazon SQS Message Deduplication ID   **159**
Providing the Message Deduplication ID 159
Enabling Deduplication for a Single-Producer/Consumer System 159
Designing for Outage Recovery Scenarios 159

Using the Amazon SQS Message Group ID   **160**
Interleaving Multiple Ordered Message Groups 160
Avoiding Processing Duplicates in a Multiple-Producer/Consumer System 160

Using the Amazon SQS Receive Request Attempt ID   **161**

Amazon SQS Limits   **162**
Limits Related to Queues 162
Limits Related to Messages 162
Limits Related to Policies 162

Monitoring, Logging, and Automating Amazon SQS Queues   **163**

Monitoring Amazon SQS Queues Using CloudWatch   **164**

Access CloudWatch Metrics for Amazon SQS   **165**
Amazon SQS Console 165

Amazon CloudWatch Console 165
AWS Command Line Interface 166
CloudWatch API 166

Setting CloudWatch Alarms for Amazon SQS Metrics   **168**

Available CloudWatch Metrics for Amazon SQS   **171**
Amazon SQS Metrics 171
Dimensions for Amazon SQS Metrics 172

Logging Amazon SQS Actions Using AWS CloudTrail   **173**
Amazon SQS Information in CloudTrail 173
Understanding Amazon SQS Log File Entries 173
    AddPermission 174
    CreateQueue 174
    DeleteQueue 175
    RemovePermission 175
    SetQueueAttributes 176

Automating Notifications from AWS Services to Amazon SQS using CloudWatch Events   **178**

Amazon SQS Security   **179**

Authentication and Access Control for Amazon SQS   **180**
Authentication 180
Access Control 181

Overview of Managing Access Permissions to Your Amazon Simple Queue Service Resource **182**
Amazon Simple Queue Service Resource and Operations 182
Understanding Resource Ownership 183
Managing Access to Resources 183
    Identity-Based Policies (IAM Policies and Amazon SQS Policies) 183
    Resource-Based Policies 185
Specifying Policy Elements: Actions, Effects, Resources, and Principals 185
Specifying Conditions in a Policy 186

Using Identity-Based (IAM) Policies for Amazon SQS   **187**
Using Amazon SQS and IAM Policies 187
Permissions Required to Use the Amazon SQS Console 189
AWS-Managed (Predefined) Policies for Amazon SQS 189

Basic Amazon SQS Policy Examples   **190**
Example 1: Allow a User to Create Queues 190
Example 2: Allow Developers to Write Messages to a Shared Queue 190
Example 3: Allow Managers to Get the General Size of Queues 191
Example 4: Allow a Partner to Send Messages to a Specific Queue 191

Advanced Amazon SQS Policy Examples   **192**
Example 1: Grant One Permission to One AWS Account 192
Example 2: Grant Two Permissions to One AWS Account 192
Example 3: Grant All Permissions to Two AWS Accounts 193
Example 4: Grant Cross-Account Permissions to a Role and a User Name 193
Example 5: Grant a Permission to All Users 194
Example 6: Grant a Time-Limited Permission to All Users 194
Example 7: Grant All Permissions to All Users in a CIDR Range 195
Example 8: Whitelist and Blacklist Permissions for Users in Different CIDR Ranges 195

Using Custom Policies with the Amazon SQS Access Policy Language   **197**

Amazon SQS Access Control Architecture   **198**

Amazon SQS Access Control Process Workflow   **199**

Amazon SQS Access Policy Language Key Concepts   **200**

Amazon SQS Access Policy Language Evaluation Logic   **201**

Relationships Between Explicit and Default Denials in the Amazon SQS Access Policy Language   **204**

Custom Amazon SQS Access Policy Language Examples   **206**
Example 1: Give Permission to One Account 206
Example 2: Give Permission to One or More Accounts 206
Example 3: Give Permission to Requests from Amazon EC2 Instances 207
Example 4: Deny Access to a Specific Account 207

Using Temporary Security Credentials   **209**
Prerequisites 209
To call an Amazon SQS Query API action using temporary security credentials 209

Amazon SQS API Permissions: Actions and Resource Reference   **211**

Protecting Data Using Server-Side Encryption (SSE) and AWS KMS   **212**
What Does SSE for Amazon SQS Encrypt? 213
Key Terms 213
How Does the Data Key Reuse Period Work? 214
How Do I Estimate My AWS KMS Usage Costs? 214
    Example 1: Calculating the Number of AWS KMS API Calls for 2 Principals and 1 Queue . . . 215
    Example 2: Calculating the Number of AWS KMS API Calls for Multiple Producers and Consumers and 2 Queues 215
What AWS KMS Permissions Do I Need to Use SSE for Amazon SQS? 215
    Example 1: Allow a User to Send Single or Batched Messages to a Queue with SSE 215
    Example 2: Allow a User to Receive Messages from a Queue with SSE 216
    Example 3: Enable Compatibility between AWS Services Such as Amazon CloudWatch Events, Amazon S3, and Amazon SNS and Queues with SSE 216
Errors 217

Working with Amazon SQS APIs   **218**

Making Query API Requests   **219**
Constructing an Endpoint 219
Making a GET Request 219
Making a POST Request 220

Authenticating Requests   **221**
Basic Authentication Process with HMAC-SHA 221
Part 1: The Request from the User 222
Part 2: The Response from AWS 223

Interpreting Responses   **224**
Successful Response Structure 224
Error Response Structure 224

Amazon SQS Batch Actions   **226**

Enabling Client-Side Buffering and Request Batching   **227**

    Using AmazonSQSBufferedAsyncClient 227

    Configuring AmazonSQSBufferedAsyncClient 228

Increasing Throughput using Horizontal Scaling and Action Batching   **231**

    Horizontal Scaling 231

    Action Batching 232

    Working Java Example for Single-Operation and Batch Requests 232

       Prerequisites 232

       SimpleProducerConsumer.java 233

       Monitoring Volume Metrics from the Example Run 240

Related Amazon SQS Resources   **242**

Amazon SQS Release Notes   **243**

Amazon SQS Document History   **248**

AWS Glossary   **254**

What is Amazon Simple Queue Service?

Amazon Simple Queue Service (Amazon SQS) offers a secure, durable, and available hosted queue that lets you integrate and decouple distributed software systems and components. Amazon SQS offers common constructs such as dead-letter queues and cost allocation tags. It provides a generic web services API and it can be accessed by any programming language that the AWS SDK supports.

Amazon SQS supports both standard and FIFO queues. For more information, see What Type of Queue Do I Need?

Topics

- What Are the Main Benefits of Amazon SQS?
- How is Amazon SQS Different from Amazon MQ or Amazon SNS?
- What Type of Queue Do I Need?
- How Can I Get Started with Amazon SQS?
- We Want to Hear from You

What Are the Main Benefits of Amazon SQS?

- **Security** – You control who can send messages to and receive messages from an Amazon SQS queue. Server-side encryption (SSE) lets you transmit sensitive data by protecting the contents of messages in queues using keys managed in AWS Key Management Service (AWS KMS).
- **Durability** – To ensure the safety of your messages, Amazon SQS stores them on multiple servers. Standard queues support at-least-once message delivery, and FIFO queues support exactly-once message processing.
- **Availability** – Amazon SQS uses redundant infrastructure to provide highly-concurrent access to messages and high availability for producing and consuming messages.
- **Scalability** – Amazon SQS can process each buffered request independently, scaling transparently to handle any load increases or spikes without any provisioning instructions.
- **Reliability** – Amazon SQS locks your messages during processing, so that multiple producers can send and multiple consumers can receive messages at the same time.
- **Customization** – Your queues don't have to be exactly alike—for example, you can set a default delay on a queue. You can store the contents of messages larger than 256 KB using Amazon Simple Storage Service (Amazon S3) or Amazon DynamoDB, with Amazon SQS holding a pointer to the Amazon S3 object, or you can split a large message into smaller messages.

How Is Amazon SQS Different from Amazon MQ or Amazon SNS?

Amazon SQS and Amazon SNS are queue and topic services that are highly scalable, simple to use, and don't require you to set up message brokers. We recommend these services for new applications that can benefit from nearly unlimited scalability and simple APIs.

Amazon MQ is a managed message broker service that provides compatibility with many popular message brokers. We recommend Amazon MQ for migrating applications from existing message brokers that rely on compatibility with APIs such as JMS or protocols such as AMQP, MQTT, OpenWire, and STOMP.

What Type of Queue Do I Need?

Standard Queue	FIFO Queue
Available in all regions. **Unlimited Throughput** – Standard queues support a nearly unlimited number of transactions per second (TPS) per action. **At-Least-Once Delivery** – A message is delivered at least once, but occasionally more than one copy of a message is delivered. **Best-Effort Ordering** – Occasionally, messages might be delivered in an order different from which they were sent.	Available in the US East (N. Virginia), US East (Ohio), US West (Oregon), and EU (Ireland) Regions.High Throughput – By default, FIFO queues support up to 3,000 messages per second with batching. To request a limit increase, file a support request. FIFO queues support up to 300 messages per second (300 send, receive, or delete operations per second) without batching.**Exactly-Once Processing** – A message is delivered once and remains available until a consumer processes and deletes it. Duplicates aren't introduced into the queue.**First-In-First-Out Delivery** – The order in which messages are sent and received is strictly preserved.

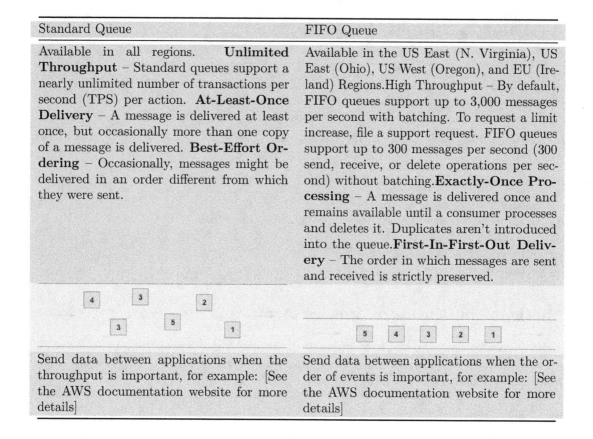

Standard Queue	FIFO Queue
Send data between applications when the throughput is important, for example: [See the AWS documentation website for more details]	Send data between applications when the order of events is important, for example: [See the AWS documentation website for more details]

How Can I Get Started with Amazon SQS?

- To create your first queue with Amazon SQS and send, receive, and delete a message, see Getting Started with Amazon SQS.
- To discover the functionality and architecture of Amazon SQS, see How Amazon SQS Works.
- To find out the guidelines and caveats that will help you make the most of Amazon SQS, see Best Practices for Amazon SQS.
- To learn about Amazon SQS actions, see the *Amazon Simple Queue Service API Reference*.
- To learn about Amazon SQS AWS CLI commands, see Amazon SQS in the *AWS CLI Command Reference*.

We Want to Hear from You

We welcome your feedback. To contact us, visit the Amazon SQS Discussion Forum.

New and Frequently Viewed Amazon SQS Topics

Latest update: May 4, 2018

Amazon Simple Queue Service Developer Guide

New Topics on Service Features	Most Frequently Viewed Topics
[See the AWS documentation website for more details]	[See the AWS documentation website for more details]

Amazon Simple Queue Service API Reference

New Topics on Service Features	Most Frequently Viewed Topics
[See the AWS documentation website for more details]	[See the AWS documentation website for more details]

Setting Up Amazon SQS

Before you can use Amazon SQS for the first time, you must complete the following steps.

Step 1: Create an AWS Account

To access any AWS service, you first need to create an AWS account, an Amazon.com account that can use AWS products. You can use your AWS account to view your activity and usage reports and to manage authentication and access.

To avoid using your AWS account root user for Amazon SQS actions, it is a best practice to create an IAM user for each person who needs administrative access to Amazon SQS.

To set up a new account

1. Open https://aws.amazon.com/, and then choose **Create an AWS Account. Note**
   This might be unavailable in your browser if you previously signed into the AWS Management Console. In that case, choose **Sign in to a different account**, and then choose **Create a new AWS account**.

2. Follow the online instructions.

   Part of the sign-up procedure involves receiving a phone call and entering a PIN using the phone keypad.

Step 2: Create an IAM User

To create an IAM user for yourself and add the user to an Administrators group

1. Use your AWS account email address and password to sign in as the *AWS account root user* to the IAM console at https://console.aws.amazon.com/iam/. **Note**
   We strongly recommend that you adhere to the best practice of using the **Administrator** IAM user below and securely lock away the root user credentials. Sign in as the root user only to perform a few account and service management tasks.

2. In the navigation pane of the console, choose **Users**, and then choose **Add user**.

3. For **User name**, type **Administrator**.

4. Select the check box next to **AWS Management Console access**, select **Custom password**, and then type the new user's password in the text box. You can optionally select **Require password reset** to force the user to create a new password the next time the user signs in.

5. Choose **Next: Permissions**.

6. On the **Set permissions for user** page, choose **Add user to group**.

7. Choose **Create group**.

8. In the **Create group** dialog box, type **Administrators**.

9. For **Filter**, choose **Job function**.

10. In the policy list, select the check box for **AdministratorAccess**. Then choose **Create group**.

11. Back in the list of groups, select the check box for your new group. Choose **Refresh** if necessary to see the group in the list.

12. Choose **Next: Review** to see the list of group memberships to be added to the new user. When you are ready to proceed, choose **Create user**.

You can use this same process to create more groups and users, and to give your users access to your AWS account resources. To learn about using policies to restrict users' permissions to specific AWS resources, go to Access Management and Example Policies.

Step 3: Get Your Access Key ID and Secret Access Key

To use Amazon SQS actions (for example, using Java or through the AWS Command Line Interface), you need an access key ID and a secret access key.

Note
The access key ID and secret access key are specific to AWS Identity and Access Management. Don't confuse them with credentials for other AWS services, such as Amazon EC2 key pairs.

To get the access key ID and secret access key for an IAM user

Access keys consist of an access key ID and secret access key, which are used to sign programmatic requests that you make to AWS. If you don't have access keys, you can create them from the AWS Management Console. We recommend that you use IAM access keys instead of AWS account root user access keys. IAM lets you securely control access to AWS services and resources in your AWS account.

The only time that you can view or download the secret access keys is when you create the keys. You cannot recover them later. However, you can create new access keys at any time. You must also have permissions to perform the required IAM actions. For more information, see Permissions Required to Access IAM Resources in the *IAM User Guide*.

1. Open the IAM console.

2. In the navigation pane of the console, choose **Users**.

3. Choose your IAM user name (not the check box).

4. Choose the **Security credentials** tab and then choose **Create access key**.

5. To see the new access key, choose **Show**. Your credentials will look something like this:

   - Access key ID: AKIAIOSFODNN7EXAMPLE
   - Secret access key: wJalrXUtnFEMI/K7MDENG/bPxRfiCYEXAMPLEKEY

6. To download the key pair, choose **Download .csv file**. Store the keys in a secure location.

   Keep the keys confidential in order to protect your AWS account, and never email them. Do not share them outside your organization, even if an inquiry appears to come from AWS or Amazon.com. No one who legitimately represents Amazon will ever ask you for your secret key.

Related topics

- What Is IAM? in the *IAM User Guide*
- AWS Security Credentials in *AWS General Reference*

Step 4: Get Ready to Use the Example Code

This guide shows how to work with Amazon SQS using the AWS Management Console and using Java. If you want to use the example code, you must install the Java Standard Edition Development Kit and make some configuration changes to the example code.

You can write code in other programming languages. For more information, see the documentation of the AWS SDKs.

Note
You can explore Amazon SQS without writing code with tools such as the AWS Command Line Interface (AWS CLI) or Windows PowerShell. You can find AWS CLI examples in the Amazon SQS section of the *AWS CLI Command Reference*. You can find Windows PowerShell examples in the Amazon Simple Queue Service section of the *AWS Tools for PowerShell Cmdlet Reference*.

Next Steps

Now that you're prepared for working with Amazon SQS, can get started with managing Amazon SQS queues and messages using the AWS Management Console. You can also try the more advanced Amazon SQS tutorials.

Getting Started with Amazon SQS

This section helps you become more familiar with Amazon SQS by showing you how to manage queues and messages using the AWS Management Console.

Prerequisites

Before you begin, complete the steps in Setting Up Amazon SQS.

Step 1: Create a Queue

The first and most common Amazon SQS task is creating queues. In this tutorial you'll learn how to create and configure a queue.

1. Sign in to the Amazon SQS console.

2. Choose **Create New Queue.**

3. On the **Create New Queue** page, ensure that you're in the correct region and then type the **Queue Name. Note**
   The name of a FIFO queue must end with the `.fifo` suffix. FIFO queues are available in the US East (N. Virginia), US East (Ohio), US West (Oregon), and EU (Ireland) Regions.

4. **Standard** is selected by default. Choose **FIFO**.

5. To create your queue with the default parameters, choose **Quick-Create Queue.**

   Your new queue is created and selected in the queue list. **Note**
   When you create a queue, it can take a short time for the queue to propagate throughout Amazon SQS..

   The **Queue Type** column helps you distinguish standard queues from FIFO queues at a glance. For a FIFO queue, the **Content-Based Deduplication** column displays whether you have enabled exactly-once processing.

	Name	Queue Type	Content-Based Deduplication	Messages Available	Messages in Flight	Created
	MyQueue	Standard Queue	N/A	0	0	2016-12-07 13:42:47 GMT-08:00
	MyQueue.fifo	FIFO Queue	Disabled	0	0	2016-12-07 13:42:55 GMT-08:00

   Your queue's **Name**, **URL**, and **ARN** are displayed on the **Details** tab.

Name: MyQueue.fifo

URL: https://sqs.us-west-2.amazonaws.com//MyQueue.fifo

ARN: arn:aws:sqs:us-west-2::MyQueue.fifo

Step 2: Send a Message

After you create your queue, you can send a message to it. The following example shows sending a message to an existing queue.

1. From the queue list, select the queue that you've created.

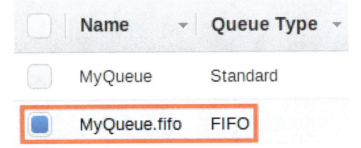

2. From **Queue Actions**, select **Send a Message**.

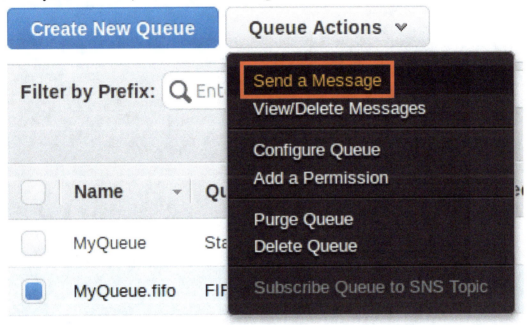

The **Send a Message to** *QueueName* dialog box is displayed.

The following example shows the **Message Group ID** and **Message Deduplication ID** parameters specific to FIFO queues (content-based deduplication is disabled).

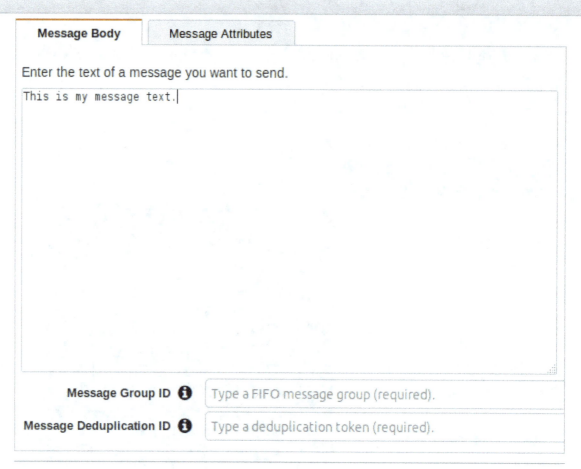

Send a Message to MyQueue.fifo   ✕

Message Body	Message Attributes

Enter the text of a message you want to send.

This is my message text.

Message Group ID ℹ️ Type a FIFO message group (required).

Message Deduplication ID ℹ️ Type a deduplication token (required).

Cancel   **Send Message**

3. To send a message to a FIFO queue, type the **Message Body**, the **Message Group ID** MyMessageGroupId1234567890, and the **Message Deduplication ID** MyMessageDeduplicationId1234567890, and then choose **Send Message**. For more information, see FIFO Delivery Logic. **Note**
The message group ID is always required. However, if content-based deduplication is enabled, the message deduplication ID is optional.

Message Group ID ℹ️ MyMessageGroupId1234567890

Message Deduplication ID ℹ️ MyMessageDeduplicationId1234567890

Cancel   **Send Message**

Your message is sent and the **Send a Message to** *QueueName* dialog box is displayed, showing the attributes of the sent message.

The following example shows the **Sequence Number** attribute specific to FIFO queues.

Send a Message to MyQueue.fifo

Your message has been sent and is ready to be received.

Note: It may take up to 60 seconds for the *Messages Available* column to update.

Sent Message Attributes:

Message Identifier: 78fa2441-04c9-4873-9390-

MD5 of Body: 6a1559560f67c5e7a7d5d8

Sequence Number: 188259190627

4. Choose **Close**.

Step 3: Receive and Delete Your Message

After you send a message into a queue, you can consume it (retrieve it from the queue). When you request a message from a queue, you can't specify which message to get. Instead, you specify the maximum number of messages (up to 10) that you want to get.

In this tutorial you'll learn how to receive and delete a message.

1. From the queue list, select the queue that you have created.

2. From **Queue Actions**, select **View/Delete Messages**.

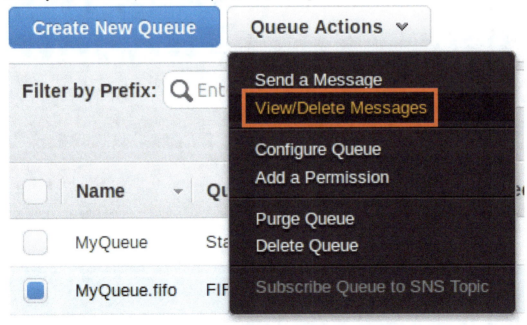

The **View/Delete Messages in** *QueueName* dialog box is displayed. **Note**
The first time you take this action, an information screen is displayed. To hide the screen, check the **Don't show this again** checkbox.

3. Choose **Start Polling for messages**.

Amazon SQS begins to poll the messages in the queue. The dialog box displays a message from the queue. A progress bar at the bottom of the dialog box displays the status of the message's visibility timeout.

The following example shows the **Message Group ID**, **Message Deduplication ID**, and **Sequence Number** columns specific to FIFO queues.

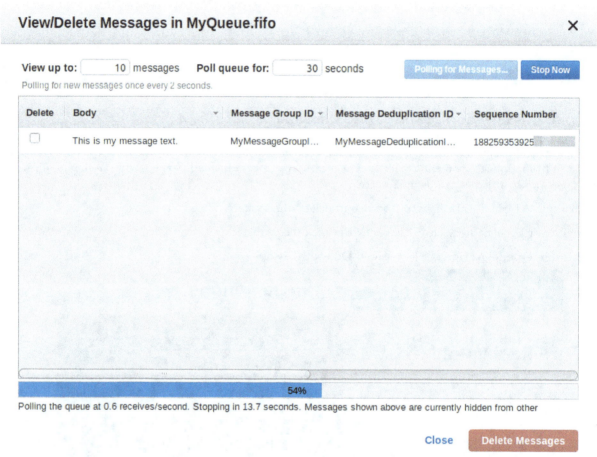

4. *Before* the visibility timeout expires, select the message that you want to delete and then choose **Delete** *1* **Message**.

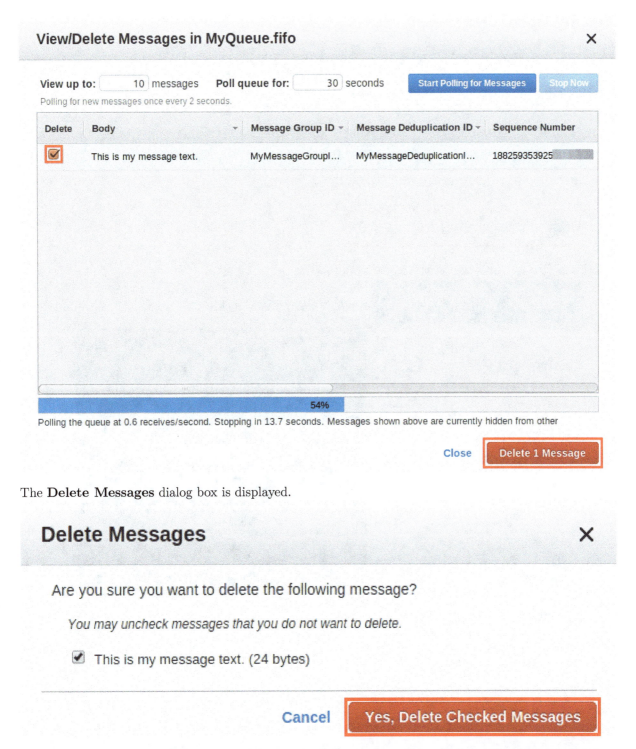

The **Delete Messages** dialog box is displayed.

5. Confirm that the message you want to delete is checked and choose **Yes, Delete Checked Messages**.

The selected message is deleted.

When the progress bar is filled in, the visibility timeout expires and the message becomes visible to consumers.

6. Select **Close**.

Step 4: Delete Your Queue

If you don't use an Amazon SQS queue (and don't foresee using it in the near future), it is a best practice to delete it from Amazon SQS. In this tutorial you'll learn how to delete a queue.

1. From the queue list, select the queue that you have created.

2. From **Queue Actions**, select **Delete Queue**.

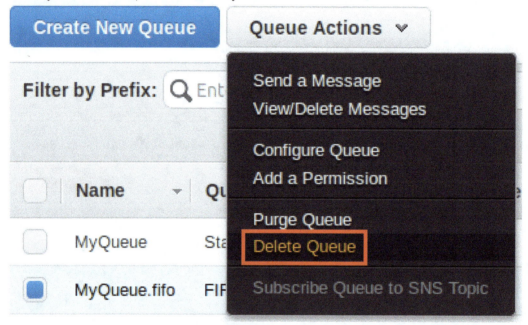

The **Delete Queues** dialog box is displayed.

3. Choose **Yes, Delete Queue**.

The queue is deleted.

Next Steps

Now that you've created a queue and learned how to send, receive, and delete messages and how to delete a queue, you might want to try the following:

- Enable server-side encryption (SSE) for a new queue or configure SSE for an existing queue.
- Add permissions to a queue.
- Add, update, or remove tags for a queue.
- Configure long polling for a queue.
- Send a message with attributes.
- Send a message with a timer.
- Configure a dead-letter queue.
- Configure visibility timeout for a queue.
- Configure a delay queue.
- Subscribe a queue to an Amazon SNS topic.
- Purge a queue.
- Learn more about Amazon SQS workflows and processes: Read How Queues Work, Best Practices, and Limits. You can also explore the Amazon SQS Articles & Tutorials. If you ever have any questions, browse the Amazon SQS FAQs or participate in the Amazon SQS Developer Forums.
- Learn how to interact with Amazon SQS programmatically: Read Working with APIs and explore the Sample Code and Libraries and the developer centers:
  - Java
  - JavaScript
  - PHP
  - Python
  - Ruby
  - Windows & .NET
- Learn about keeping an eye on costs and resources in the Monitoring, Logging, and Automating Amazon SQS Queues section.
- Learn about protecting your data and access to it in the Security section.

Amazon SQS Tutorials

This guide shows how to work with Amazon SQS using the AWS Management Console and using Java. If you want to use the example code, you must install the Java Standard Edition Development Kit and make some configuration changes to the example code.

You can write code in other programming languages. For more information, see the documentation of the AWS SDKs.

Note
You can explore Amazon SQS without writing code with tools such as the AWS Command Line Interface (AWS CLI) or Windows PowerShell. You can find AWS CLI examples in the Amazon SQS section of the *AWS CLI Command Reference*. You can find Windows PowerShell examples in the Amazon Simple Queue Service section of the *AWS Tools for PowerShell Cmdlet Reference*.

Topics

- Creating Amazon SQS Queues
- Listing all Amazon SQS Queues in a Region
- Adding Permissions to an Amazon SQS Queue
- Adding, Updating, and Removing Tags from an Amazon SQS Queue
- Sending Messages to Amazon SQS Queues
- Receiving and Deleting a Message from an Amazon SQS Queue
- Subscribing an Amazon SQS Queue to an Amazon SNS Topic
- Purging Messages from an Amazon SQS Queue
- Deleting an Amazon SQS Queue
- Configuring Amazon SQS Queues

Tutorials: Creating Amazon SQS Queues

The following tutorials show how to create Amazon SQS queues in various ways.

Topics

- Creating an Amazon SQS Queue
- Creating an Amazon SQS Queue with SSE

Tutorial: Creating an Amazon SQS Queue

The first and most common Amazon SQS task is creating queues. In this tutorial you'll learn how to create and configure a queue.

Topics

- AWS Management Console
- AWS SDK for Java
- AWS CloudFormation

AWS Management Console

1. Sign in to the Amazon SQS console.

2. Choose **Create New Queue.**

3. On the **Create New Queue** page, ensure that you're in the correct region and then type the **Queue Name. Note**
   The name of a FIFO queue must end with the `.fifo` suffix. FIFO queues are available in the US East (N. Virginia), US East (Ohio), US West (Oregon), and EU (Ireland) Regions.

4. **Standard** is selected by default. Choose **FIFO**.

5. Create your queue.

   - To create your queue with the default parameters, choose **Quick-Create Queue**.

   - To configure your queue's parameters, choose **Configure Queue**. When you finish configuring the parameters, choose **Create Queue**. For more information about creating a queue with SSE, see Tutorial: Creating an Amazon SQS Queue with Server-Side Encryption (SSE).

   The following example shows the **Content-Based Deduplication** parameter specific to FIFO queues.

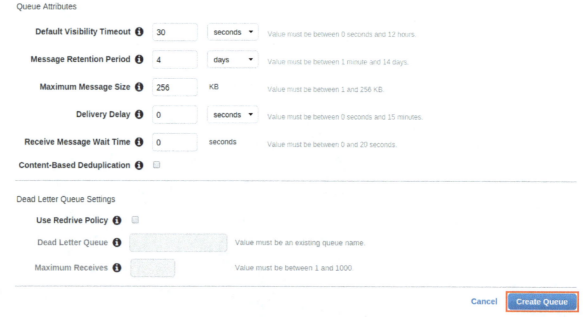

Your new queue is created and selected in the queue list. **Note**
When you create a queue, it can take a short time for the queue to propagate throughout Amazon SQS.

The **Queue Type** column helps you distinguish standard queues from FIFO queues at a glance. For a FIFO queue, the **Content-Based Deduplication** column displays whether you have enabled exactly-once processing.

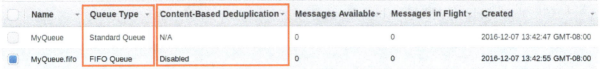

	Name	Queue Type	Content-Based Deduplication	Messages Available	Messages in Flight	Created
☐	MyQueue	Standard Queue	N/A	0	0	2016-12-07 13:42:47 GMT-08:00
☑	MyQueue.fifo	FIFO Queue	Disabled	0	0	2016-12-07 13:42:55 GMT-08:00

Your queue's **Name**, **URL**, and **ARN** are displayed on the **Details** tab.

Name: MyQueue.fifo

URL: https://sqs.us-west-2.amazonaws.com/   /MyQueue.fifo

ARN: arn:aws:sqs:us-west-2:   :MyQueue.fifo

AWS SDK for Java

Before you begin working with the example code, specify your AWS credentials. For more information, see Set up AWS Credentials and Region for Development in the *AWS SDK for Java Developer Guide*.

To create a standard queue

1. Copy the example program.

   The following section of the code creates the `MyQueue` queue:

```
1 // Create a queue
2 System.out.println("Creating a new SQS queue called MyQueue.\n");
3 final CreateQueueRequest createQueueRequest = new CreateQueueRequest("MyQueue");
4 final String myQueueUrl = sqs.createQueue(createQueueRequest).getQueueUrl();
```

2. Compile and run the example.

   The queue is created.

To create a FIFO queue

1. Copy the example program.

   The following section of the code creates the `MyFifoQueue.fifo` queue:

```
1  // Create a FIFO queue
2  System.out.println("Creating a new Amazon SQS FIFO queue called " + "MyFifoQueue.fifo.\n");
3  final Map<String, String> attributes = new HashMap<String, String>();
4
5  // A FIFO queue must have the FifoQueue attribute set to True
6  attributes.put("FifoQueue", "true");
7
8  // If the user doesn't provide a MessageDeduplicationId, generate a MessageDeduplicationId
       based on the content.
9  attributes.put("ContentBasedDeduplication", "true");
10
11 // The FIFO queue name must end with the .fifo suffix
12 final CreateQueueRequest createQueueRequest = new CreateQueueRequest("MyFifoQueue.fifo")
```

```
13          .withAttributes(attributes);
14 final String myQueueUrl = sqs.createQueue(createQueueRequest).getQueueUrl();
```

2. Compile and run the example.

   The queue is created.

AWS CloudFormation

You can use the AWS CloudFormation console and a JSON (or YAML) template to create an Amazon SQS
queue. For more information, see Working with AWS CloudFormation Templates and the `AWS::SQS::Queue`
Resource in the *AWS CloudFormation User Guide*.

1. Copy the following JSON code to a file named `MyQueue.json`. To create a standard queue, omit the
   `FifoQueue` and `ContentBasedDeduplication` properties. For more information on content-based deduplication, see Exactly-Once Processing. **Note**
   The name of a FIFO queue must end with the `.fifo` suffix. FIFO queues are available in the US East (N.
   Virginia), US East (Ohio), US West (Oregon), and EU (Ireland) Regions.

```
1  {
2      "AWSTemplateFormatVersion": "2010-09-09",
3      "Resources": {
4        "MyQueue": {
5          "Properties": {
6            "QueueName": "MyQueue.fifo",
7            "FifoQueue": true,
8            "ContentBasedDeduplication": true
9            },
10         "Type": "AWS::SQS::Queue"
11         }
12     },
13     "Outputs": {
14       "QueueName": {
15         "Description": "The name of the queue",
16         "Value": {
17           "Fn::GetAtt": [
18             "MyQueue",
19             "QueueName"
20           ]
21         }
22       },
23       "QueueURL": {
24         "Description": "The URL of the queue",
25         "Value": {
26           "Ref": "MyQueue"
27         }
28       },
29       "QueueARN": {
30         "Description": "The ARN of the queue",
31         "Value": {
32           "Fn::GetAtt": [
33             "MyQueue",
34             "Arn"
35           ]
36         }
```

```
37        }
38    }
39 }
```

2. Sign in to the AWS CloudFormation console, and then choose **Create Stack**.

3. On the **Select Template** page, choose **Upload a template to Amazon S3**, choose your `MyQueue.json` file, and then choose **Next**.

4. On the **Specify Details** page, type `MyQueue` for **Stack Name**, and then choose **Next**.

5. On the **Options** page, choose **Next**.

6. On the **Review** page, choose **Create**.

   AWS CloudFormation begins to create the `MyQueue` stack and displays the **CREATE_IN_PROGRESS** status. When the process is complete, AWS CloudFormation displays the **CREATE_COMPLETE** status.

7. (Optional) To display the name, URL, and ARN of the queue, choose the name of the stack and then on the next page expand the **Outputs** section.

Tutorial: Creating an Amazon SQS Queue with Server-Side Encryption (SSE)

Server-side encryption (SSE) for Amazon SQS is available in all commercial regions where Amazon SQS is available, except for the China Regions. You can enable SSE for a queue to protect its data. For more information about using SSE, see Protecting Data Using Server-Side Encryption (SSE) and AWS KMS .

Important
All requests to queues with SSE enabled must use HTTPS and Signature Version 4.

In this tutorial you'll learn how to create an Amazon SQS queue with SSE enabled. Although the example uses a FIFO queue, SSE works with both standard and FIFO queues.

Topics

- Create an Amazon SQS Queue with SSE Using the AWS Management Console
- Create an Amazon SQS Queue with SSE using the AWS SDK for Java

AWS Management Console

1. Sign in to the Amazon SQS console.

2. Choose **Create New Queue.**

3. On the **Create New Queue** page, ensure that you're in the correct region and then type the **Queue Name. Note**
The name of a FIFO queue must end with the `.fifo` suffix. FIFO queues are available in the US East (N. Virginia), US East (Ohio), US West (Oregon), and EU (Ireland) Regions.

4. **Standard** is selected by default. Choose **FIFO**.

5. Choose **Configure Queue**, and then choose **Use SSE**.

6. Specify the customer master key (CMK) ID. For more information, see Key Terms.

   For each CMK type, the **Description**, **Account**, and **Key ARN** of the CMK are displayed. **Important**
   If you aren't the owner of the CMK, or if you log in with an account that doesn't have the `kms:ListAliases` and `kms:DescribeKey` permissions, you won't be able to view information about the CMK on the Amazon SQS console.
   Ask the owner of the CMK to grant you these permissions. For more information, see the AWS KMS API Permissions: Actions and Resources Reference in the *AWS Key Management Service Developer Guide*.

   - The AWS managed CMK for Amazon SQS is selected by default.

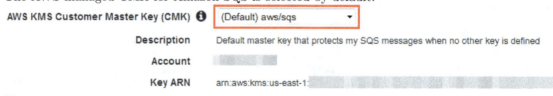

Note
Keep the following in mind:
If you don't specify a custom CMK, Amazon SQS uses the AWS managed CMK for Amazon SQS. For instructions on creating custom CMKs, see Creating Keys in the *AWS Key Management Service Developer Guide*. The first time you use the AWS Management Console to specify the AWS managed CMK for Amazon SQS for a queue, AWS KMS creates the AWS managed CMK for Amazon SQS. Alternatively, the first time you use the `SendMessage` or `SendMessageBatch` action on a queue with SSE enabled, AWS KMS creates the AWS managed CMK for Amazon SQS.

- To use a custom CMK from your AWS account, select it from the list.

AWS KMS Customer Master Key (CMK) ❶ | demo-key ▾

Description	A key for demonstrating the functionality of SSE in Amazon SQS.
Account	
Key ARN	arn:aws:kms:us-east-1:

Note

For instructions on creating custom CMKs, see Creating Keys in the *AWS Key Management Service Developer Guide*.

- To use a custom CMK ARN from your AWS account or from another AWS account, select **Enter an existing CMK ARN** from the list and type or copy the CMK.

AWS KMS Customer Master Key (CMK) ❶ | Enter an existing CMK ARN ▾

Enter a CMK ARN ❶ | arn:aws:kms:us-east-1:

7. (Optional) For **Data key reuse period**, specify a value between 1 minute and 24 hours. The default is 5 minutes. For more information, see How Does the Data Key Reuse Period Work?.

Data Key Reuse Period ❶ | 5 | minutes ▾ | This value must be between 1 minute and 24 hours.

8. Choose **Create Queue**.

Your new queue is created with SSE. The encryption status, alias of the CMK, **Description**, **Account**, **Key ARN**, and the **Data Key Reuse Period** are displayed on the **Encryption** tab.

Server-side encryption (SSE) is enabled. SSE lets you protect the contents of messages in Amazon SQS queues using keys managed in the AWS Key Management Service (AWS KMS). Learn more.

To modify the SSE parameters, choose **Queue Actions, Configure Queue**.

AWS KMS Customer Master Key (CMK) ❶ | alias/aws/sqs

Description	Default master key that protects my SQS messages when no other key is defined
Account	
Key ARN	
Data Key Reuse Period ❶	5 minutes

AWS SDK for Java

Before you begin working with the example code, specify your AWS credentials. For more information, see Set up AWS Credentials and Region for Development in the *AWS SDK for Java Developer Guide*.

Before you can use SSE, you must configure AWS KMS key policies to allow encryption of queues and encryption and decryption of messages. You must also ensure that the key policies of the customer master key (CMK) allow the necessary permissions. For more information, see What AWS KMS Permissions Do I Need to Use SSE for Amazon SQS?

1. Obtain the customer master key (CMK) ID. For more information, see Key Terms. **Note**
   Keep the following in mind:
   If you don't specify a custom CMK, Amazon SQS uses the AWS managed CMK for Amazon SQS. For instructions on creating custom CMKs, see Creating Keys in the *AWS Key Management Service Developer Guide*. The first time you use the AWS Management Console to specify the AWS managed CMK for Amazon SQS for a queue, AWS KMS creates the AWS managed CMK for Amazon SQS. Alternatively, the first time you use the `SendMessage` or `SendMessageBatch` action on a queue with SSE enabled, AWS KMS creates the AWS managed CMK for Amazon SQS.

2. To enable server-side encryption, specify the CMK ID by setting the `KmsMasterKeyId` attribute of the `[CreateQueue](http://docs.aws.amazon.com/AWSSimpleQueueService/latest`

/APIReference/API_CreateQueue.html) or [SetQueueAttributes](http://docs.aws.amazon.com/
AWSSimpleQueueService/latest/APIReference/API_SetQueueAttributes.html) action.

The following code example creates a new queue with SSE using the AWS managed CMK for Amazon SQS:

```
1  final AmazonSQS sqs = AmazonSQSClientBuilder.defaultClient();
2  final CreateQueueRequest createRequest = new CreateQueueRequest("MyQueue");
3  final Map<String, String> attributes = new HashMap<String, String>();
4
5  // Enable server-side encryption by specifying the alias ARN of the
6  // AWS managed CMK for Amazon SQS.
7  final String kmsMasterKeyAlias = "arn:aws:kms:us-east-2:123456789012:alias/aws/sqs";
8  attributes.put("KmsMasterKeyId", kmsMasterKeyAlias);
9
10 // (Optional) Specify the length of time, in seconds, for which Amazon SQS can reuse
11 attributes.put("KmsDataKeyReusePeriodSeconds", "60");
12
13 final CreateQueueResult createResult = client.createQueue(createRequest);
```

The following code example creates a new queue with SSE using a custom CMK:

```
1  final AmazonSQS sqs = AmazonSQSClientBuilder.defaultClient();
2  final CreateQueueRequest createRequest = new CreateQueueRequest("MyQueue");
3  final Map<String, String> attributes = new HashMap<String, String>();
4
5  // Enable server-side encryption by specifying the alias ARN of the custom CMK.
6  final String kmsMasterKeyAlias = "arn:aws:kms:us-east-2:123456789012:alias/MyAlias";
7  attributes.put("KmsMasterKeyId", kmsMasterKeyAlias);
8
9  // (Optional) Specify the length of time, in seconds, for which Amazon SQS can reuse
10 // a data key to encrypt or decrypt messages before calling AWS KMS again.
11 attributes.put("KmsDataKeyReusePeriodSeconds", "864000");
12
13 final CreateQueueResult createResult = client.createQueue(createRequest);
```

3. (Optional) Specify the length of time, in seconds, for which Amazon SQS can reuse a data key to encrypt or decrypt messages before calling AWS KMS again. Set the KmsDataKeyReusePeriodSeconds attribute of the [CreateQueue](http://docs.aws.amazon.com/AWSSimpleQueueService/latest/APIReference/API_CreateQueue.html) or [SetQueueAttributes](http://docs.aws.amazon.com/AWSSimpleQueueService/latest/APIReference/API_SetQueueAttributes.html) action. Possible values may be between 60 seconds (1 minute) and 86,400 seconds (24 hours). If you don't specify a value, the default value of 300 seconds (5 minutes) is used.

The first code example above sets the data key reuse time period to 60 seconds (1 minute). The second code example sets it to 86,400 seconds (24 hours). The following code example sets the data key reuse period to 60 seconds (1 minute):

```
1  // (Optional) Specify the length of time, in seconds, for which Amazon SQS can reuse
2  // a data key to encrypt or decrypt messages before calling AWS KMS again.
3  attributes.put("KmsDataKeyReusePeriodSeconds", "60");
```

For information about retrieving the attributes of a queue, see Examples in the *Amazon Simple Queue Service API Reference*.

To retrieve the CMK ID or the data key reuse period for a particular queue, use the KmsMasterKeyId and KmsDataKeyReusePeriodSeconds attributes of the [GetQueueAttributes](http://docs.aws.amazon.com/AWSSimpleQueueService/latest/APIReference/API_GetQueueAttributes.html) action.

For information about switching a queue to a different CMK with the same alias, see Updating an Alias in the *AWS Key Management Service Developer Guide.*

Tutorial: Listing All Amazon SQS Queues in a Region

When you create a queue, it can take a short time for the queue to propagate throughout Amazon SQS. In this tutorial you'll learn how to confirm your queue's existence by listing all queues in the current region.

Topics

- AWS Management Console
- AWS SDK for Java

AWS Management Console

1. Sign in to the Amazon SQS console.

2. Your queues in the current region are listed.

   The **Queue Type** column helps you distinguish standard queues from FIFO queues at a glance. For a FIFO queue, the **Content-Based Deduplication** column displays whether you have enabled exactly-once processing.

Name	Queue Type	Content-Based Deduplication	Messages Available	Messages in Flight	Created
MyQueue	Standard Queue	N/A	0	0	2016-12-07 13:42:47 GMT-08:00
MyQueue.fifo	FIFO Queue	Disabled	0	0	2016-12-07 13:42:55 GMT-08:00

   Your queue's **Name**, **URL**, and **ARN** are displayed on the **Details** tab.

   Name: MyQueue.fifo

   URL: https://sqs.us-west-2.amazonaws.com/▮▮▮▮▮▮▮/MyQueue.fifo

   ARN: arn:aws:sqs:us-west-2:▮▮▮▮▮▮▮:MyQueue.fifo

AWS SDK for Java

Before you begin working with the example code, specify your AWS credentials. For more information, see Set up AWS Credentials and Region for Development in the *AWS SDK for Java Developer Guide*.

Note
This action is identical for standard and FIFO queues.

1. Copy the standard queue example program or the FIFO queue example program.

   The following section of the code list all queues in the current region:

   ```
   1 // List queues
   2 System.out.println("Listing all queues in your account.\n");
   3 for (final String queueUrl : sqs.listQueues().getQueueUrls()) {
   4     System.out.println("  QueueUrl: " + queueUrl);
   5 }
   6 System.out.println();
   ```

2. Compile and run the example.

   All queues in the current region created using API version 2012-11-05 are listed. The response include the following items:

   - The unique *queue URL*.

- The *request ID* that Amazon SQS assigned to your request.

Tutorial: Adding Permissions to an Amazon SQS Queue

You can specify to whom you allow (or explicitly deny) the ability to interact with your queue in specific ways by adding permissions to a queue. The following example shows how to add the permission for anyone to get a queue's URL.

Note
An Amazon SQS policy can have a maximum of 7 actions.

AWS Management Console

1. Sign in to the Amazon SQS console.

2. From the queue list, select a queue.

3. From **Queue Actions**, select **Add a Permission**.

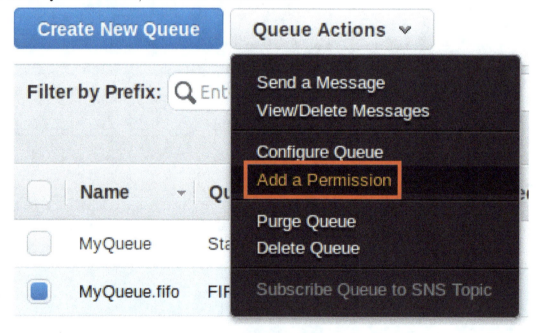

   The **Add a Permission** dialog box is displayed.

4. In this example, you allow anyone to get the queue's URL:

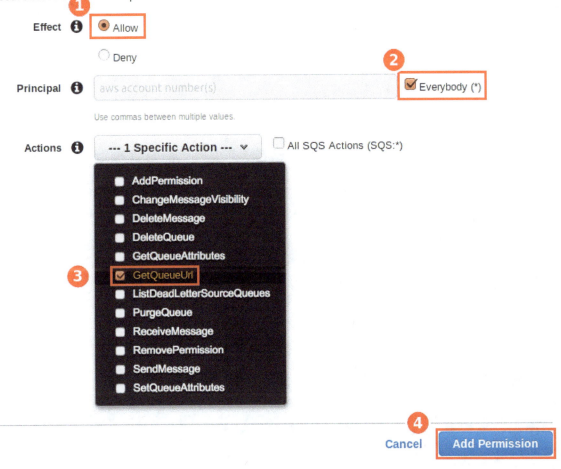

① Ensure that next to **Effect**, **Allow** is selected.

② Next to **Principal**, check the **Everybody** box.

③ From the **Actions** drop-down list, select **GetQueueUrl** box.

④ Choose **Add Permission**.

The permission is added to the queue.

Your queues's policy **Effect**, **Principals**, **Actions**, and **Conditions** are displayed on your queue's **Permissions** tab.

Add a Permission	**Edit Policy Document (Advanced)**		What's an SQS Queue Access Policy?	

Effect	Principals	Actions	Conditions	
Allow	• Everybody (*)	• SQS:GetQueueUrl	*None*	✏ ✖

Tutorial: Adding, Updating, and Removing Cost Allocation Tags for an Amazon SQS Queue

You can add cost allocation tags to your Amazon SQS queues to help organize and identify them. The following example show how to add, update, and remove tags for a queue. For a more information, see Amazon SQS Cost Allocation Tags.

Topics

- To Update or Remove a Tag Added to an Amazon SQS Queue Using the AWS Management Console
- AWS SDK for Java

AWS Management Console

The following steps assume that you already created an Amazon SQS queue.

1. Sign in to the Amazon SQS console.

2. From the queue list, select a queue.

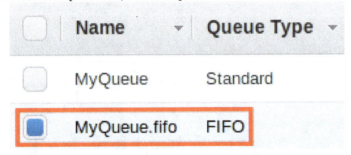

3. Choose the **Tags** tab.

   The tags added to the queue are listed.

4. Choose **Add/Edit Tags**.

5. Modify queue tags:

   - To add a tag, choose **Add New Tag**, enter a **Key** and **Value**, and then choose **Apply Changes**.
   - To update a tag, change its **Key** and **Value** and then choose **Apply Changes**.
   - To remove a tag, choose ✖ next to a key-value pair and then choose **Apply Changes**.

   The queue tag changes are applied.

AWS SDK for Java

Before you begin working with the example code, specify your AWS credentials. For more information, see Set up AWS Credentials and Region for Development in the *AWS SDK for Java Developer Guide*.

To add, update, and remove tags from a queue

1. Copy the example program for a standard queue or a FIFO queue.

2. To list the tags added to a queue, add the following code which uses the `ListQueueTags` action:

```
1  final ListQueueTagsRequest listQueueTagsRequest = new ListQueueTagsRequest(queueUrl);
2  final ListQueueTagsResult listQueueTagsResult = SQSClientFactory.newSQSClient()
3          .listQueueTags(listQueueTagsRequest);
4  System.out.println(String.format("ListQueueTags: \tTags for queue %s are %s.\n",
5          QUEUE_NAME, listQueueTagsResult.getTags()));
```

3. To add or update the values of the queue's tags using the tag's key, add the following code which uses the `TagQueue` action:

```
1  final Map<String, String> addedTags = new HashMap<>();
2  addedTags.put("Team", "Development");
3  addedTags.put("Priority", "Beta");
4  addedTags.put("Accounting ID", "456def");
5  final TagQueueRequest tagQueueRequest = new TagQueueRequest(queueUrl, addedTags);
6
7  System.out.println(String.format("TagQueue: \t\tAdd tags %s to queue %s.\n", addedTags,
       QUEUE_NAME));
8  SQSClientFactory.newSQSClient().tagQueue(tagQueueRequest);
```

4. To remove a tag from the queue using the tag's key, add the following code which uses the `UntagQueue` action:

```
1  final List<String> tagKeys = Arrays.asList("Accounting ID");
2  final UntagQueueRequest untagQueueRequest = new UntagQueueRequest(queueUrl, tagKeys);
3  System.out.println(String.format("UntagQueue: \tRemove tags %s from queue %s.\n", tagKeys,
       QUEUE_NAME));
4  SQSClientFactory.newSQSClient().untagQueue(untagQueueRequest);
```

5. Compile and run your program.

   The existing tags are listed, three are updated, and one tag is removed from the queue.

Tutorials: Sending Messages to Amazon SQS Queues

The following tutorials show how to send messages to Amazon SQS queues in various ways.

Topics

- Sending a Message to an Amazon SQS Queue
- Sending a Message with Attributes to an Amazon SQS Queue
- Sending a Message with a Timer to an Amazon SQS Queue

Tutorial: Sending a Message to an Amazon SQS Queue

After you create your queue, you can send a message to it. The following example shows sending a message to an existing queue.

Topics

- AWS Management Console
- AWS SDK for Java

AWS Management Console

1. Sign in to the Amazon SQS console.

2. From the queue list, select a queue.

3. From **Queue Actions**, select **Send a Message**.

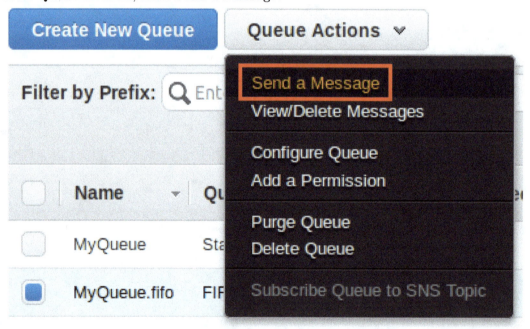

The **Send a Message to _QueueName_** dialog box is displayed.

The following example shows the **Message Group ID** and **Message Deduplication ID** parameters specific to FIFO queues (content-based deduplication is disabled).

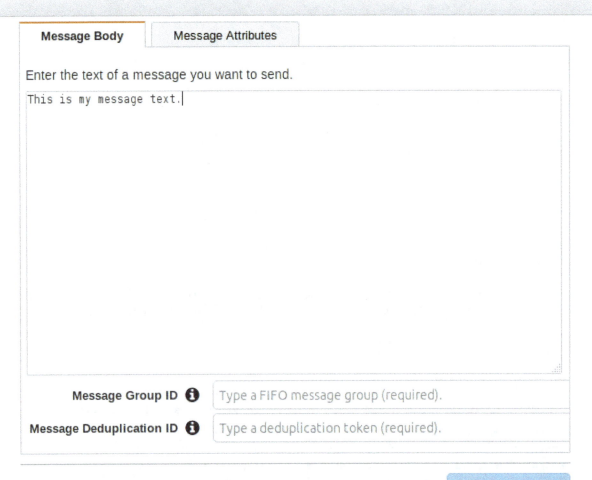

Send a Message to MyQueue.fifo   ✕

Message Body   Message Attributes

Enter the text of a message you want to send.

This is my message text.

Message Group ID ℹ️   Type a FIFO message group (required).

Message Deduplication ID ℹ️   Type a deduplication token (required).

Cancel   **Send Message**

4. To send a message to a FIFO queue, type the **Message Body**, the **Message Group ID** MyMessageGroupId1234567890, and the **Message Deduplication ID** MyMessageDeduplicationId1234567890, and then choose **Send Message**. For more information, see FIFO Delivery Logic. **Note** The message group ID is always required. However, if content-based deduplication is enabled, the message deduplication ID is optional.

Message Group ID ℹ️   MyMessageGroupId1234567890

Message Deduplication ID ℹ️   MyMessageDeduplicationId1234567890

Cancel   **Send Message**

Your message is sent and the **Send a Message to** *QueueName* dialog box is displayed, showing the attributes of the sent message.

The following example shows the **Sequence Number** attribute specific to FIFO queues.

Send a Message to MyQueue.fifo

Your message has been sent and is ready to be received.

Note: It may take up to 60 seconds for the *Messages Available* column to update.

Sent Message Attributes:

Message Identifier: 78fa2441-04c9-4873-9390-

MD5 of Body: 6a1559560f67c5e7a7d5d8

Sequence Number: 188259190627

5. Choose **Close**.

AWS SDK for Java

Before you begin working with the example code, specify your AWS credentials. For more information, see Set up AWS Credentials and Region for Development in the *AWS SDK for Java Developer Guide*.

To send a message to a standard queue

1. Copy the example program.

   The following section of the code sends the `This is my message text.` message to your queue:

```
1 // Send a message
2 System.out.println("Sending a message to MyQueue.\n");
3 sqs.sendMessage(new SendMessageRequest(myQueueUrl, "This is my message text."));
```

2. Compile and run the example.

   The message is sent to the queue. The response includes the following items:

   - The message ID Amazon SQS assigns to the message.
   - An MD5 digest of the message body, used to confirm that Amazon SQS received the message correctly (for more information, see RFC1321).
   - The *request ID* that Amazon SQS assigned to your request.

To send a message to a FIFO queue

1. Copy the example program.

   The following section of the code sends the `This is my message text.` message to your queue:

```
1 // Send a message
2 System.out.println("Sending a message to MyFifoQueue.fifo.\n");
3 final SendMessageRequest sendMessageRequest = new SendMessageRequest(myQueueUrl, "This is
    my message text.");
4
5 // When you send messages to a FIFO queue, you must provide a non-empty MessageGroupId.
6 sendMessageRequest.setMessageGroupId("messageGroup1");
7
```

```
 8 // Uncomment the following to provide the MessageDeduplicationId
 9 //sendMessageRequest.setMessageDeduplicationId("1");
10 final SendMessageResult sendMessageResult = sqs.sendMessage(sendMessageRequest);
11 final String sequenceNumber = sendMessageResult.getSequenceNumber();
12 final String messageId = sendMessageResult.getMessageId();
13 System.out.println("SendMessage succeed with messageId " + messageId + ", sequence number "
       + sequenceNumber
14          + "\n");
```

2. Compile and run the example.

   The message is sent to your queue.

Tutorial: Sending a Message with Attributes to an Amazon SQS Queue

You can include structured metadata (such as timestamps, geospatial data, signatures, and identifiers) with messages using *message attributes*. In this tutorial you'll learn how to send a message with attributes to an existing queue. For more information, see Amazon SQS Message Attributes.

For a more detailed explanation of sending messages to standard and FIFO queues, see Tutorial: Sending a Message to an Amazon SQS Queue.

Topics

- AWS Management Console
- AWS SDK for Java

AWS Management Console

1. Sign in to the Amazon SQS console.

2. From the queue list, select a queue.

3. From **Queue Actions**, select **Send a Message**.

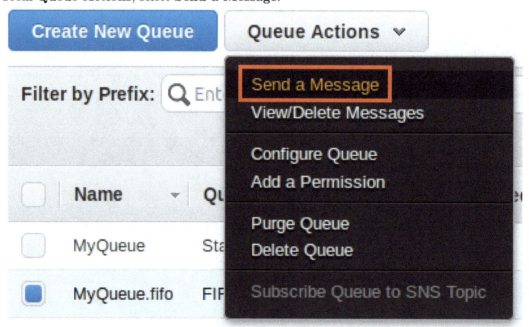

The **Send a Message to** *QueueName* dialog box is displayed.

The following example shows the **Message Group ID** and **Message Deduplication ID** parameters specific to FIFO queues (content-based deduplication is disabled).

Send a Message to MyQueue.fifo   ✕

| Message Body | Message Attributes |

Enter the text of a message you want to send.

```
This is my message text.|
```

Message Group ID 🛈   `Type a FIFO message group (required).`

Message Deduplication ID 🛈   `Type a deduplication token (required).`

                                                         Cancel   **Send Message**

4. To send a message to a FIFO queue, type the **Message Body**, the **Message Group ID** `MyMessageGroupId1234567890`, and the **Message Deduplication ID** `MyMessageDeduplicationId1234567890`, and then choose **Message Attributes**.

Send a Message to MyQueue.fifo   ✕

| Message Body | **Message Attributes** |

Name [   ]

Type [String   ▾] [(Custom Type: Optional)   ]

Value [   ]

Enter a string value.

[**Add Attribute**]   **What is Message Attribute?**

Name	Type	Values

Cancel   **Send Message**

5. Define the message attribute parameters. For more information, see Message Attribute Components and Message Attribute Data Types.

   1. For the message attribute **Name** type `MyMessageAttribute`.

   2. For the message attribute data **Type**, select **Number** and type `byte` for the optional custom type.

   3. For the message attribute **Value**, type 24.

Choose **Add Attribute**.

The attribute is added to the message as **Number.byte**.

Name	Type	Values	
MyMessage…	Number.byte	[24]	✖

You can modify the value before sending the message. To delete the attribute, choose .

6. When you finish adding attributes to the message, choose **Send Message**.

Your message is sent and the **Send a Message to** *QueueName* dialog box is displayed, showing the attributes of the sent message.

The following example shows the **MD5 of Message Attributes** specific to your custom message attribute and the **Sequence Number** attribute specific to FIFO queues.

Send a Message to MyQueue.fifo

Your message has been sent and is ready to be received.

Note: It may take up to 60 seconds for the *Messages Available* column to update.

Sent Message Attributes:

Message Identifier: dea890ef-d9ba-43e1-9e86-badcb6a5ad92

MD5 of Body: 6a1559560f67c5e7a7d5d838bf0272ee

MD5 of Message Attributes: c7e128fff5069b1f485828551d66084a

Sequence Number: 18836602484391663616

7. Choose **Close**.

AWS SDK for Java

Before you begin working with the example code, specify your AWS credentials. For more information, see Set up AWS Credentials and Region for Development in the *AWS SDK for Java Developer Guide*.

To send a message with attributes to a queue

1. Copy the standard queue example program or the FIFO queue example program.

2. To define an attribute for a message, add the following code which uses the [MessageAttributeValue](http://docs.aws.amazon.com/AWSSimpleQueueService/latest/APIReference/API_MessageAttributeValue.html) data type. For more information, see Message Attribute Components and Message Attribute Data Types. **Note**
   The AWS SDK for Java automatically calculates the message body and message attribute checksums and compares them with the data which Amazon SQS returns. For more information, see the *AWS SDK for Java Developer Guide* and Calculating the MD5 Message Digest for Message Attributes for other programming languages.

[String]

This example defines a `String` attribute named `Name` with the value `Jane`.

```
1 final Map<String, MessageAttributeValue> messageAttributes = new HashMap<>();
2 messageAttributes.put("Name", new MessageAttributeValue()
3         .withDataType("String")
4         .withStringValue("Jane"));
```

[Number]

This example defines a `Number` attribute named `AccurateWeight` with the value 230.000000000000000001.

```
1 final Map<String, MessageAttributeValue> messageAttributes = new HashMap<>();
2 messageAttributes.put("AccurateWeight", new MessageAttributeValue()
3         .withDataType("Number")
4         .withStringValue("230.000000000000000001"));
```

[Binary]

This example defines a `Binary` attribute named `ByteArray` with the value of an uninitialized 10-byte array.

```
1 final Map<String, MessageAttributeValue> messageAttributes = new HashMap<>();
2 messageAttributes.put("ByteArray", new MessageAttributeValue()
3         .withDataType("Binary")
4         .withBinaryValue(ByteBuffer.wrap(new byte[10])));
```

[String (Custom)]

This example defines the custom attribute `String.EmployeeId` named `EmployeeId` with the value ABC123456.

```
1 final Map<String, MessageAttributeValue> messageAttributes = new HashMap<>();
2 messageAttributes.put("EmployeeId", new MessageAttributeValue()
3         .withDataType("String.EmployeeId")
4         .withStringValue("ABC123456"));
```

[Number (Custom)]

This example defines the custom attribute `Number.AccountId` named `AccountId` with the value 0023456.

```
1 final Map<String, MessageAttributeValue> messageAttributes = new HashMap<>();
2 messageAttributes.put("AccountId", new MessageAttributeValue()
3         .withDataType("Number.AccountId")
4         .withStringValue("000123456"));
```

Note
Because the base data type is Number, the [ReceiveMessage](http://docs.aws.amazon.com/AWSSimpleQueueService/latest/APIReference/API_ReceiveMessage.html) action returns 123456.

[Binary (Custom)]

This example defines the custom attribute `Binary.JPEG` named `ApplicationIcon` with the value of an uninitialized 10-byte array.

```
1 final Map<String, MessageAttributeValue> messageAttributes = new HashMap<>();
2 messageAttributes.put("ApplicationIcon", new MessageAttributeValue()
3         .withDataType("Binary.JPEG")
4         .withBinaryValue(ByteBuffer.wrap(new byte[10])));
```

---

1. Replace the section of the code that sends the message with the following:

```
1 // Send a message with an attribute
2 final SendMessageRequest sendMessageRequest = new SendMessageRequest();
3 sendMessageRequest.withMessageBody("This is my message text.");
4 sendMessageRequest.withQueueUrl(myQueueUrl);
5 sendMessageRequest.withMessageAttributes(messageAttributes);
6 sqs.sendMessage(sendMessageRequest);
```

Important

If you send a message to a FIFO queue, make sure that the **sendMessage** method executes *after* you provide the message group ID.

If you use the [SendMessageBatch](http://docs.aws.amazon.com/AWSSimpleQueueService/latest/APIReference/API_SendMessageBatch.html) action instead of [SendMessage](http://docs.aws.amazon.com/AWSSimpleQueueService/latest/APIReference/API_SendMessage.html), you must specify message attributes for each individual message in the batch.

1. Compile and run the example.

   The message is sent to the queue. The response includes the following items:

   - The message ID Amazon SQS assigns to the message.
   - An MD5 digest of the message body, used to confirm that Amazon SQS received the message correctly (for more information, see RFC1321).
   - An MD5 digest of the message attributes, used to confirm that Amazon SQS received the message attributes correctly.
   - The *request ID* that Amazon SQS assigned to your request.

Tutorial: Sending a Message with a Timer to an Amazon SQS Queue

Message timers let you specify an initial invisibility period for a message added to a queue. For example, if you send a message with a 45-second timer, the message isn't visible to consumers for its first 45 seconds in the queue. The default is 0 seconds. In this tutorial you'll learn how to send a message with a timer to an existing queue. For more information, see Amazon SQS Message Timers.

Note
FIFO queues don't support timers on individual messages.

For a more detailed explanation of sending messages to standard and FIFO queues, see Tutorial: Sending a Message to an Amazon SQS Queue.

Topics

- AWS Management Console
- AWS SDK for Java

AWS Management Console

1. Sign in to the Amazon SQS console.

2. From the queue list, select a queue.

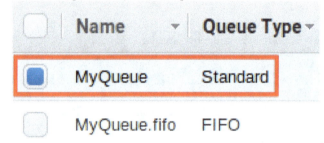

3. From **Queue Actions**, select **Send a Message**.

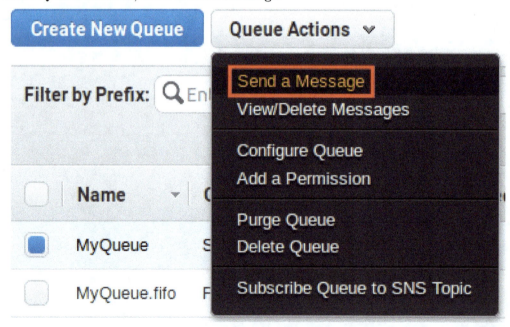

The **Send a Message to** *QueueName* dialog box is displayed.

4. To send a message to a standard queue, type the **Message Body**, choose **Delay delivery of this message by** and type a value, for example 60 seconds.

5. Choose **Send Message**.

   Your message is sent and the **Send a Message to** *QueueName* dialog box is displayed, showing the attributes of the sent message.

Send a Message to MyQueue

Your message has been sent and will be ready to be received in 1 minutes.

Note: It may take up to 60 seconds for the *Messages Delayed* attribute to update.

Sent Message Attributes:

Message Identifier: 9853f772-b99d-437c-9904-a5a932549a87

MD5 of Body: 6a1559560f67c5e7a7d5d838bf0272ee

6. Choose **Close**.

AWS SDK for Java

Before you begin working with the example code, specify your AWS credentials. For more information, see Set up AWS Credentials and Region for Development in the *AWS SDK for Java Developer Guide.*

To send a message with a timer to a queue

1. Copy the standard queue example program.

2. Change the **main** method signature to the following:

```
1 public static void main(String[] args) throws InterruptedException
```

3. Replace the section of the code that sends the message with the following:

```
1 // Send a message with a 5-second timer.
2 System.out.println("Sending a message with a 5-second timer to MyQueue.\n");
3 SendMessageRequest request = new SendMessageRequest(myQueueUrl, "This is my message text.")
    ;
4 request.setDelaySeconds(5);
5 sqs.sendMessage(request);
6
7 // Wait for 10 seconds.
8 System.out.println("Waiting for 10 seconds.");
9 Thread.sleep(10000L);
```

4. Compile and run the example.

The message is sent to the queue. The response includes the following items:

- The message ID Amazon SQS assigns to the message.
- An MD5 digest of the message body, used to confirm that Amazon SQS received the message correctly (for more information, see RFC1321).
- The *request ID* that Amazon SQS assigned to your request.

Tutorial: Receiving and Deleting a Message from an Amazon SQS Queue

After you send a message into a queue, you can consume it from the queue. When you request a message from a queue, you can't specify which message to get. Instead, you specify the maximum number of messages (up to 10) that you want to get.

Note

Because Amazon SQS is a distributed system, a queue with very few messages might display an empty response to a receive request. In this case, you can rerun the request to get your message. Depending on your application's needs, you might have to use short or long polling to receive messages.

Amazon SQS doesn't automatically delete a message after receiving it for you, in case you don't successfully receive the message (for example, the consumers can fail or lose connectivity). To delete a message, you must send a separate request which acknowledges that you no longer need the message because you've successfully received and processed it.

In this tutorial you'll learn how to receive and delete a message.

Topics

- AWS Management Console
- AWS SDK for Java

AWS Management Console

1. Sign in to the Amazon SQS console.

2. From the queue list, select a queue.

3. From **Queue Actions**, select **View/Delete Messages**.

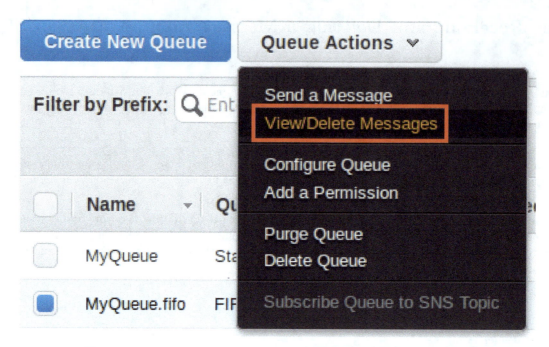

The **View/Delete Messages in** *QueueName* dialog box is displayed. **Note**
The first time you take this action, an information screen is displayed. To hide the screen, check the **Don't show this again** checkbox.

4. Choose **Start Polling for messages.**

Amazon SQS begins to poll the messages in the queue. The dialog box displays a message from the queue. A progress bar at the bottom of the dialog box displays the status of the message's visibility timeout.

The following example shows the **Message Group ID**, **Message Deduplication ID**, and **Sequence Number** columns specific to FIFO queues.

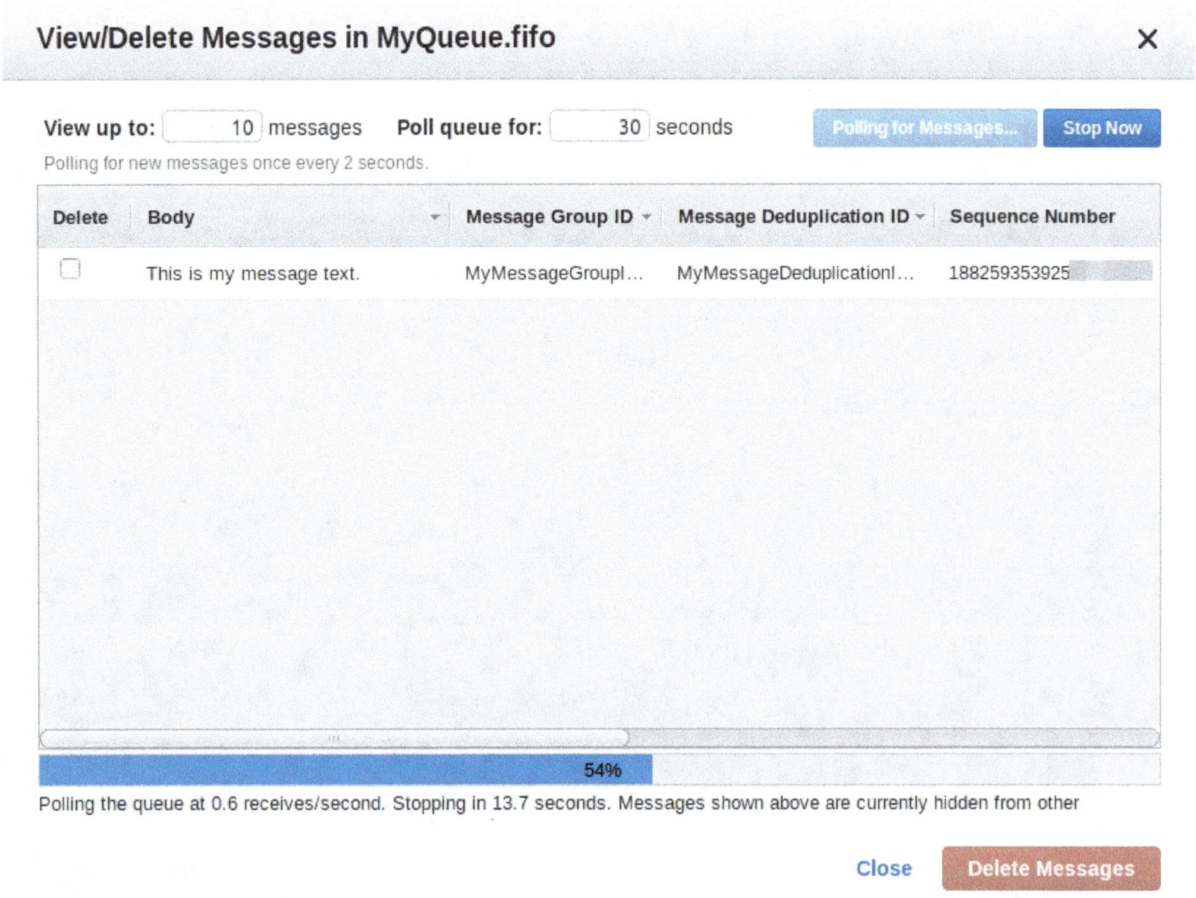

View/Delete Messages in MyQueue.fifo   ✕

View up to: [10] messages   **Poll queue for:** [30] seconds   Polling for Messages... | Stop Now

Polling for new messages once every 2 seconds.

Delete	Body	▾	Message Group ID ▾	Message Deduplication ID ▾	Sequence Number
☐	This is my message text.		MyMessageGroupI...	MyMessageDeduplicationI...	188259353925

54%

Polling the queue at 0.6 receives/second. Stopping in 13.7 seconds. Messages shown above are currently hidden from other

Close   Delete Messages

5. *Before* the visibility timeout expires, select the message that you want to delete and then choose **Delete *1* Message**.

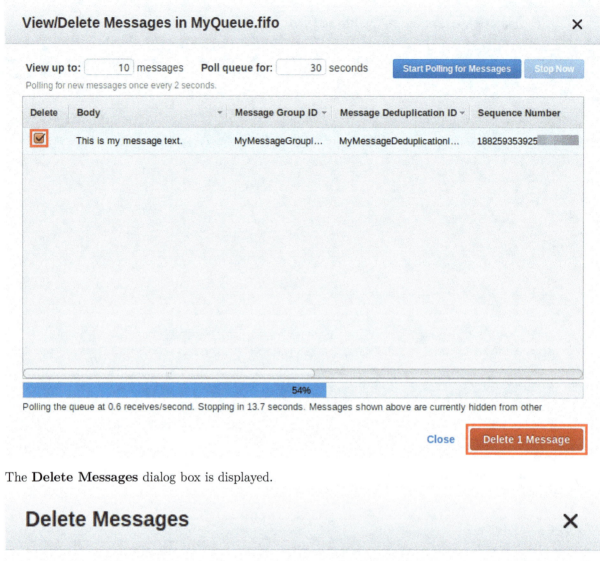

The **Delete Messages** dialog box is displayed.

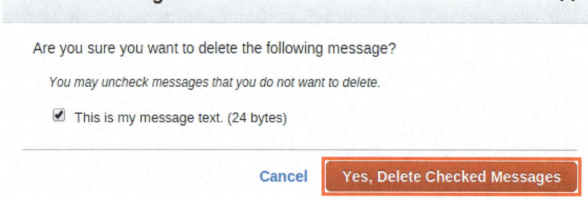

6. Confirm that the message you want to delete is checked and choose **Yes, Delete Checked Messages**.

The selected message is deleted.

When the progress bar is filled in, the visibility timeout expires and the message becomes visible to consumers.

7. Select **Close**.

AWS SDK for Java

To specify the message to delete, provide the receipt handle that Amazon SQS returned when you received the message. You can delete only one message per action. To delete an entire queue, you must use the `DeleteQueue` action. (You can delete an entire queue even if the queue has messages in it.)

Note

If you don't have the receipt handle for the message, you can call the `ReceiveMessage` action to receive the message again. Each time you receive the message, you get a different receipt handle. Use the latest receipt handle when using the `DeleteMessage` action. Otherwise, your message might not be deleted from the queue.

Before you begin working with the example code, specify your AWS credentials. For more information, see Set up AWS Credentials and Region for Development in the *AWS SDK for Java Developer Guide*.

To receive and delete a message from a standard queue

1. Copy the example program.

   The following section of the code receives a message from your queue:

```java
// Receive messages
System.out.println("Receiving messages from MyQueue.\n");
final ReceiveMessageRequest receiveMessageRequest = new ReceiveMessageRequest(myQueueUrl);
final List<Message> messages = sqs.receiveMessage(receiveMessageRequest).getMessages();
for (final Message message : messages) {
    System.out.println("Message");
    System.out.println("  MessageId:     " + message.getMessageId());
    System.out.println("  ReceiptHandle: " + message.getReceiptHandle());
    System.out.println("  MD5OfBody:     " + message.getMD5OfBody());
    System.out.println("  Body:          " + message.getBody());
    for (final Entry<String, String> entry : message.getAttributes().entrySet()) {
        System.out.println("Attribute");
        System.out.println("  Name:  " + entry.getKey());
        System.out.println("  Value: " + entry.getValue());
    }
}
System.out.println();
```

   The following section of the code deletes the message:

```java
// Delete the message
System.out.println("Deleting a message.\n");
final String messageReceiptHandle = messages.get(0).getReceiptHandle();
sqs.deleteMessage(new DeleteMessageRequest(myQueueUrl, messageReceiptHandle));
```

2. Compile and run the example.

   The queue is polled and returns 0 or more messages. The example prints the following items:

   - The message ID that you received when you sent the message to the queue.
   - The receipt handle that you later use to delete the message.
   - An MD5 digest of the message body (for more information, see RFC1321).
   - The message body.
   - The *request ID* that Amazon SQS assigned to your request

   If no messages are received in this particular call, the response includes only the request ID.

   The message is deleted. The response includes the request ID that Amazon SQS assigned to your request.

To receive and delete a message from a FIFO queue

1. Copy the example program.

   The following section of the code receives a message from your queue:

```
1  // Receive messages
2  System.out.println("Receiving messages from MyFifoQueue.fifo.\n");
3  final ReceiveMessageRequest receiveMessageRequest = new ReceiveMessageRequest(myQueueUrl);
4
5  // Uncomment the following to provide the ReceiveRequestDeduplicationId
6  //receiveMessageRequest.setReceiveRequestAttemptId("1");
7  final List<Message> messages = sqs.receiveMessage(receiveMessageRequest).getMessages();
8  for (final Message message : messages) {
9      System.out.println("Message");
10     System.out.println("  MessageId:     " + message.getMessageId());
11     System.out.println("  ReceiptHandle: " + message.getReceiptHandle());
12     System.out.println("  MD5OfBody:     " + message.getMD5OfBody());
13     System.out.println("  Body:          " + message.getBody());
14     for (final Entry<String, String> entry : message.getAttributes().entrySet()) {
15         System.out.println("Attribute");
16         System.out.println("  Name:  " + entry.getKey());
17         System.out.println("  Value: " + entry.getValue());
18     }
19 }
20 System.out.println();
```

   The following section of the code deletes the message:

```
1  // Delete the message
2  System.out.println("Deleting the message.\n");
3  final String messageReceiptHandle = messages.get(0).getReceiptHandle();
4  sqs.deleteMessage(new DeleteMessageRequest(myQueueUrl, messageReceiptHandle));
```

2. Compile and run the example.

   The message is received and deleted.

Tutorial: Subscribing an Amazon SQS Queue to an Amazon SNS Topic

You can subscribe one or more Amazon SQS queues to an Amazon SNS topic from a list of topics available for the selected queue. Amazon SQS manages the subscription and any necessary permissions. When you publish a message to a topic, Amazon SNS sends the message to every subscribed queue. For more information about Amazon SNS, see What is Amazon Simple Notification Service? in the *Amazon Simple Notification Service Developer Guide.*

In this tutorial you'll learn how to subscribe an existing Amazon SQS queue to an existing Amazon SNS topic.

Note
Amazon SNS isn't currently compatible with FIFO queues.
For information about using Amazon SNS with encrypted Amazon SQS queues, see Example 3: Enable Compatibility between AWS Services Such as Amazon CloudWatch Events, Amazon S3, and Amazon SNS and Queues with SSE.
When you subscribe an Amazon SQS queue to an Amazon SNS topic, Amazon SNS uses HTTPS to forward messages to Amazon SQS.

AWS Management Console

1. Sign in to the Amazon SQS console.

2. From the list of queues, choose the queue (or queues) to which you want to subscribe an Amazon SNS topic.

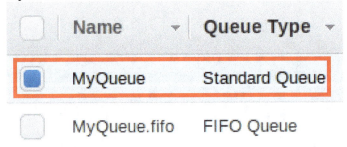

3. From **Queue Actions**, select **Subscribe Queue to SNS Topic** (or **Subscribe Queues to SNS Topic**).

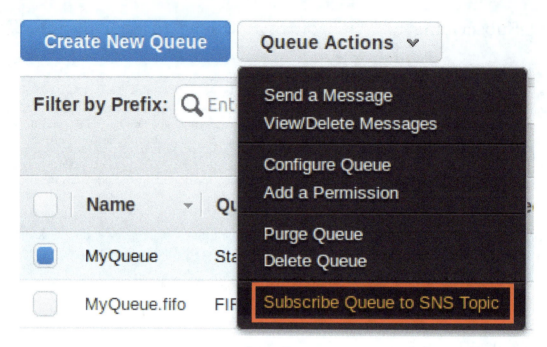

The **Subscribe to a Topic** dialog box is displayed.

4. From the **Choose a Topic** drop-down list, select an Amazon SNS topic to which you want to subscribe your queue (or queues), select the **Topic Region** (optional), and then choose **Subscribe**.

Note

Typing a different **Topic ARN** is useful when you want to subscribe a queue to an Amazon SNS topic from an AWS account other than the one you used to create your Amazon SQS queue.

This is also useful if the Amazon SNS topic isn't listed in the **Choose a Topic** drop-down list.

The **Topic Subscription Result** dialog box is displayed.

5. Review the list of Amazon SQS queues that are subscribed to the Amazon SNS topic and choose **OK**.

Topic Subscription Result

Successfully subscribed the following queue to the SNS topic MyTopic. Permission to receive SNS notifications was added to the queue.

- MyQueue

The queue is subscribed to the topic. **Note**
If your Amazon SQS queue and Amazon SNS topic are in different AWS accounts, the owner of the topic must first confirm the subscription. For more information, see Confirm the Subscription in the *Amazon Simple Notification Service Developer Guide*.
To list your subscriptions, unsubscribe from topics, and delete topics, use the Amazon SNS console. For more information, see Clean Up.

To verify the results of the subscription, you can publish to the topic and then view the message that the topic sends to the queue. For more information, see Sending Amazon SNS Messages to Amazon SQS Queues in the *Amazon Simple Notification Service Developer Guide*.

Tutorial: Purging Messages from an Amazon SQS Queue

If you don't want to delete an Amazon SQS queue but need to delete all the messages from it, you can purge the queue. In this tutorial you'll learn how to purge a queue.

Important
When you purge a queue, you can't retrieve any messages deleted from it.
The message deletion process takes up to 60 seconds. We recommend waiting for 60 seconds regardless of your queue's size.

AWS Management Console

1. Sign in to the Amazon SQS console.

2. From the queue list, select a queue.

3. From **Queue Actions**, select **Purge Queue**.

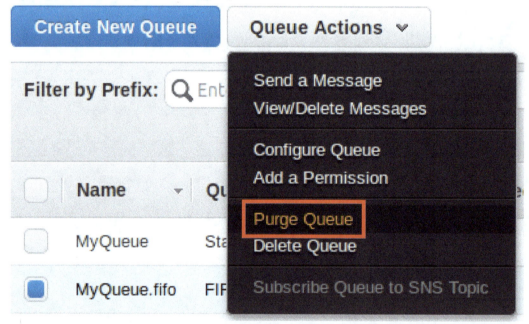

The **Purge Queues** dialog box is displayed.

Purge Queues   ✕

Are you **sure** you want to purge the following queue (removing all the messages left in it)?

- MyQueue.fifo - contains no messages.

Cancel   **Yes, Purge Queue**

4. Choose **Yes, Purge Queue**.

All messages are purged from the queue.

The **Purge Queues** confirmation dialog box is displayed.

Purge Queues   ✕

Your purge queue request for the following queue has been sent and is in progress.

Note: It may take up to 60 seconds for the message deletion process to complete.

- MyQueue.fifo

5. Choose **OK**.

Tutorial: Deleting an Amazon SQS Queue

If you don't use an Amazon SQS queue (and don't foresee using it in the near future), it is a best practice to delete it from Amazon SQS. In this tutorial you'll learn how to delete a queue.

Note
You can delete a queue even when it isn't empty. If you want to delete the messages in a queue but not the queue itself, you can purge the queue.
By default, a queue retains a message for four days after it is sent. You can configure a queue to retain messages for up to 14 days.

Topics

- AWS Management Console
- AWS SDK for Java

AWS Management Console

1. Sign in to the Amazon SQS console.

2. From the queue list, select a queue.

3. From **Queue Actions**, select **Delete Queue**.

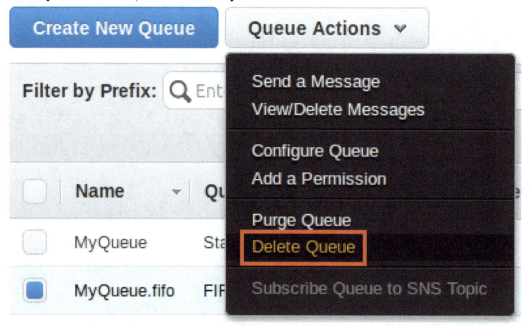

The **Delete Queues** dialog box is displayed.

Delete Queues   ✕

Are you **sure** you want to delete the following queue, and any messages left in it?

- MyQueue.fifo - contains no messages.

Cancel   Yes, Delete Queue

4. Choose **Yes, Delete Queue**.

   The queue is deleted.

AWS SDK for Java

Before you begin working with the example code, specify your AWS credentials. For more information, see Set up AWS Credentials and Region for Development in the *AWS SDK for Java Developer Guide*.

Note
This action is identical for standard and FIFO queues.

1. Copy the standard queue example program or the FIFO queue example program.

   The following section of the code deletes the queue:

```
1  // Delete the queue
2  System.out.println("Deleting the test queue.\n");
3  sqs.deleteQueue(new DeleteQueueRequest(myQueueUrl));
```

2. Compile and run the example.

   The queue is deleted.

Tutorials: Configuring Amazon SQS Queues

The following tutorials show how to configure Amazon SQS queues in various ways.

Topics

- Configuring SSE for an Existing Amazon SQS Queue
- Configuring Long Polling for an Amazon SQS queue
- Configuring an Amazon SQS Dead-Letter Queue
- Configuring Visibility Timeout for an Amazon SQS Queue
- Configuring an Amazon SQS Delay Queue

Tutorial: Configuring Server-Side Encryption (SSE) for an Existing Amazon SQS Queue

Server-side encryption (SSE) for Amazon SQS is available in all commercial regions where Amazon SQS is available, except for the China Regions. You can enable SSE for a queue to protect its data. For more information about using SSE, see Protecting Data Using Server-Side Encryption (SSE) and AWS KMS .

Important
All requests to queues with SSE enabled must use HTTPS and Signature Version 4.
When you disable SSE, messages remain encrypted. You must receive and decrypt a message to view its contents.

In this tutorial you'll learn how to enable, disable, and configure SSE for an existing Amazon SQS queue.

Topics

- Configure SSE for an Amazon SQS Queue Using the AWS Management Console
- Configure SSE for an Amazon SQS Queue Using the AWS SDK for Java

AWS Management Console

1. Sign in to the Amazon SQS console.

2. From the queue list, select a queue.

3. From **Queue Actions**, select **Configure Queue**.

   The **Configure *QueueName*** dialog box is displayed.

4. To enable or disable SSE, use the **Use SSE** check box.

5. Specify the customer master key (CMK) ID. For more information, see Key Terms.

For each CMK type, the **Description**, **Account**, and **Key ARN** of the CMK are displayed. **Important** If you aren't the owner of the CMK, or if you log in with an account that doesn't have the `kms:ListAliases` and `kms:DescribeKey` permissions, you won't be able to view information about the CMK on the Amazon SQS console.

Ask the owner of the CMK to grant you these permissions. For more information, see the AWS KMS API Permissions: Actions and Resources Reference in the *AWS Key Management Service Developer Guide*.

- To use the AWS managed CMK for Amazon SQS, select it from the list.

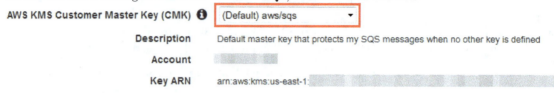

Note

Keep the following in mind:

If you don't specify a custom CMK, Amazon SQS uses the AWS managed CMK for Amazon SQS. For instructions on creating custom CMKs, see Creating Keys in the *AWS Key Management Service Developer Guide*. The first time you use the AWS Management Console to specify the AWS managed CMK for Amazon SQS for a queue, AWS KMS creates the AWS managed CMK for Amazon SQS. Alternatively, the first time you use the `SendMessage` or `SendMessageBatch` action on a queue with SSE enabled, AWS KMS creates the AWS managed CMK for Amazon SQS.

- To use a custom CMK from your AWS account, select it from the list.

Note

For instructions on creating custom CMKs, see Creating Keys in the *AWS Key Management Service Developer Guide*.

- To use a custom CMK ARN from your AWS account or from another AWS account, select **Enter an existing CMK ARN** from the list and type or copy the CMK.

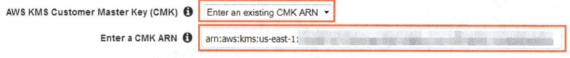

6. (Optional) For **Data key reuse period**, specify a value between 1 minute and 24 hours. The default is 5 minutes. For more information, see How Does the Data Key Reuse Period Work?.

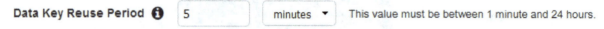

7. Choose **Save Changes**.

Your changes are applied to the queue.

AWS SDK for Java

Before you begin working with the example code, specify your AWS credentials. For more information, see Set up AWS Credentials and Region for Development in the *AWS SDK for Java Developer Guide*.

Before you can use SSE, you must configure AWS KMS key policies to allow encryption of queues and encryption and decryption of messages. You must also ensure that the key policies of the customer master key (CMK) allow the necessary permissions. For more information, see What AWS KMS Permissions Do I Need to Use SSE for Amazon SQS?

1. Obtain the customer master key (CMK) ID. For more information, see Key Terms. **Note**
   Keep the following in mind:
   If you don't specify a custom CMK, Amazon SQS uses the AWS managed CMK for Amazon SQS. For instructions on creating custom CMKs, see Creating Keys in the *AWS Key Management Service Developer Guide*. The first time you use the AWS Management Console to specify the AWS managed CMK for Amazon SQS for a queue, AWS KMS creates the AWS managed CMK for Amazon SQS. Alternatively, the first time you use the SendMessage or SendMessageBatch action on a queue with SSE enabled, AWS KMS creates the AWS managed CMK for Amazon SQS.

2. To enable server-side encryption, specify the CMK ID by setting the KmsMasterKeyId attribute of the [CreateQueue](http://docs.aws.amazon.com/AWSSimpleQueueService/latest /APIReference/API_CreateQueue.html) or [SetQueueAttributes](http://docs.aws.amazon.com/ AWSSimpleQueueService/latest/APIReference/API_SetQueueAttributes.html) action.

   The following code example enables SSE for an existing queue using the AWS managed CMK for Amazon SQS:

```
1 final SetQueueAttributesRequest setAttributesRequest = new SetQueueAttributesRequest();
2 setAttributesRequest.setQueueUrl(queueUrl);
3
4 // Enable server-side encryption by specifying the alias ARN of the
5 // AWS managed CMK for Amazon SQS.
6 final String kmsMasterKeyAlias = "arn:aws:kms:us-east-2:123456789012:alias/aws/sqs";
7 attributes.put("KmsMasterKeyId", kmsMasterKeyAlias);
8
9 final SetQueueAttributesResult setAttributesResult = client.setQueueAttributes(
    setAttributesRequest);
```

   To disable server-side encryption for an existing queue, set the KmsMasterKeyId attribute to an empty string using the SetQueueAttributes action. **Important**
   null isn't a valid value for KmsMasterKeyId.

3. (Optional) Specify the length of time, in seconds, for which Amazon SQS can reuse a data key to encrypt or decrypt messages before calling AWS KMS. Set the KmsDataKeyReusePeriodSeconds attribute of the [CreateQueue](http://docs.aws.amazon.com/AWSSimpleQueueService/latest /APIReference/API_CreateQueue.html) or [SetQueueAttributes](http://docs.aws.amazon.com/ AWSSimpleQueueService/latest/APIReference/API_SetQueueAttributes.html) action. Possible values may be between 60 seconds (1 minute) and 86,400 seconds (24 hours). If you don't specify a value, the default value of 300 seconds (5 minutes) is used.

   The following code example sets the data key reuse period to 60 seconds (1 minute):

```
1 // (Optional) Specify the length of time, in seconds, for which Amazon SQS can reuse
2 // a data key to encrypt or decrypt messages before calling AWS KMS again.
3 attributes.put("KmsDataKeyReusePeriodSeconds", "60");
```

For information about retrieving the attributes of a queue, see Examples in the *Amazon Simple Queue Service API Reference*.

To retrieve the CMK ID or the data key reuse period for a particular queue, use the KmsMasterKeyId and KmsDataKeyReusePeriodSeconds attributes of the [GetQueueAttributes](http://docs.aws.amazon.com/ AWSSimpleQueueService/latest/APIReference/API_GetQueueAttributes.html) action.

For information about switching a queue to a different CMK with the same alias, see Updating an Alias in the *AWS Key Management Service Developer Guide*.

Tutorial: Configuring Long Polling for an Amazon SQS Queue

Long polling helps reduce the cost of using Amazon SQS by eliminating the number of empty responses (when there are no messages available for a `[ReceiveMessage](http://docs.aws.amazon.com/AWSSimpleQueueService/latest/APIReference/API_ReceiveMessage.html)` request) and false empty responses (when messages are available but aren't included in a response). In this tutorial you'll learn how to configure long polling for an Amazon SQS queue. For more information, see Amazon SQS Long Polling.

Topics

- Configure Long Polling for an Existing Amazon SQS Queue Using the AWS Management Console
- AWS SDK for Java

AWS Management Console

1. Sign in to the Amazon SQS console.

2. Choose **Create New Queue.**

3. On the **Create New Queue** page, ensure that you're in the correct region and then type the **Queue Name. Note**
   The name of a FIFO queue must end with the `.fifo` suffix. FIFO queues are available in the US East (N. Virginia), US East (Ohio), US West (Oregon), and EU (Ireland) Regions.

4. **Standard** is selected by default. Choose **FIFO**.

5. Choose **Configure Queue**.

6. For **Receive Message Wait Time**, type a number between 1 and 20.

Receive Message Wait Time ❶	5	seconds	Value must be between 0 and 20 seconds.

   Note
   Setting the value to 0 configures *short polling*. For more information, see Differences Between Long and Short Polling.

7. Choose **Create Queue**.

   Your new queue is configured to use long polling, created, and selected in the queue list. **Note**
   When you create a queue, it can take a short time for the queue to propagate throughout Amazon SQS.

AWS SDK for Java

Before you begin working with the example code, specify your AWS credentials. For more information, see Set up AWS Credentials and Region for Development in the *AWS SDK for Java Developer Guide*.

To configure long polling for a queue

Prerequisites

Add the `aws-java-sdk-sqs.jar` package to your Java class path. The following example shows this dependency in a Maven project `pom.xml` file.

```
1  <dependencies>
2      <dependency>
3          <groupId>com.amazonaws</groupId>
4          <artifactId>aws-java-sdk-sqs</artifactId>
```

```
5        <version><replaceable>LATEST</replaceable></version>
6      </dependency>
7  </dependencies>
```

SQSLongPollingExample.java

The following example Java code creates a standard queue and configures long polling for it.

```
1  /*
2   * Copyright 2010-2018 Amazon.com, Inc. or its affiliates. All Rights Reserved.
3   *
4   * Licensed under the Apache License, Version 2.0 (the "License").
5   * You may not use this file except in compliance with the License.
6   * A copy of the License is located at
7   *
8   *  https://aws.amazon.com/apache2.0
9   *
10  * or in the "license" file accompanying this file. This file is distributed
11  * on an "AS IS" BASIS, WITHOUT WARRANTIES OR CONDITIONS OF ANY KIND, either
12  * express or implied. See the License for the specific language governing
13  * permissions and limitations under the License.
14  *
15  */
16
17  import com.amazonaws.AmazonClientException;
18  import com.amazonaws.AmazonServiceException;
19  import com.amazonaws.services.sqs.AmazonSQS;
20  import com.amazonaws.services.sqs.AmazonSQSClientBuilder;
21  import com.amazonaws.services.sqs.model.CreateQueueRequest;
22  import com.amazonaws.services.sqs.model.QueueAttributeName;
23
24  import java.util.Scanner;
25
26  public class SQSLongPollingExample {
27      public static void main(String[] args) {
28
29          final Scanner input = new Scanner(System.in);
30
31          System.out.print("Enter the queue name: ");
32          final String queueName = input.nextLine();
33
34          System.out.print("Enter the ReceiveMessage wait time (1-20 seconds): ");
35          final String receiveMessageWaitTime = input.nextLine();
36
37          /*
38           * Create a new instance of the builder with all defaults (credentials
39           * and region) set automatically. For more information, see
40           * Creating Service Clients in the AWS SDK for Java Developer Guide.
41           */
42          final AmazonSQS sqs = AmazonSQSClientBuilder.defaultClient();
43
44          try {
45              // Create a queue with long polling.
46              final CreateQueueRequest createQueueRequest = new CreateQueueRequest()
47                  .withQueueName(queueName)
```

```
48              .addAttributesEntry(QueueAttributeName.ReceiveMessageWaitTimeSeconds
49                      .toString(), receiveMessageWaitTime);
50          sqs.createQueue(createQueueRequest);
51
52          System.out.println("Created queue " + queueName + " with " +
53                  "ReceiveMessage wait time set to " + receiveMessageWaitTime +
54                  " seconds.");
55
56      } catch (final AmazonServiceException ase) {
57          System.out.println("Caught an AmazonServiceException, which means " +
58                  "your request made it to Amazon SQS, but was " +
59                  "rejected with an error response for some reason.");
60          System.out.println("Error Message:    " + ase.getMessage());
61          System.out.println("HTTP Status Code: " + ase.getStatusCode());
62          System.out.println("AWS Error Code:   " + ase.getErrorCode());
63          System.out.println("Error Type:       " + ase.getErrorType());
64          System.out.println("Request ID:       " + ase.getRequestId());
65      } catch (final AmazonClientException ace) {
66          System.out.println("Caught an AmazonClientException, which means " +
67                  "the client encountered a serious internal problem while " +
68                  "trying to communicate with Amazon SQS, such as not " +
69                  "being able to access the network.");
70          System.out.println("Error Message: " + ace.getMessage());
71      }
72  }
73 }
```

To configure long polling for a queue and send, receive, and delete a message

1. Copy the example program for a standard queue or a FIFO queue.

2. Retrieve the queue's URL:

```
1 final String queueUrl = sqs.getQueueUrl(queueName).getQueueUrl();
```

3. Use the `SetQueueAttributesRequest` action to configure long polling for an existing queue:

```
1 final SetQueueAttributesRequest setQueueAttributesRequest = new SetQueueAttributesRequest()
2      .withQueueUrl(queueUrl)
3      .addAttributesEntry("ReceiveMessageWaitTimeSeconds", "20");
4 sqs.setQueueAttributes(setQueueAttributesRequest);
```

4. Use the `ReceiveMessageRequest` action to configure the long polling for a message receipt:

```
1 final ReceiveMessageRequest receive_request = new ReceiveMessageRequest()
2      .withQueueUrl(queueUrl)
3      .withWaitTimeSeconds(20);
4 sqs.receiveMessage(receive_request);
```

5. Compile and run your program.

The long-polling for your queue is configured.

Tutorial: Configuring an Amazon SQS Dead-Letter Queue

A dead-letter queue is a queue that other (source) queues can target for messages that can't be processed (consumed) successfully. In this tutorial you'll learn how to create an Amazon SQS source queue and to configure a second queue as a dead-letter queue for it. For more information, see Amazon SQS Dead-Letter Queues.

Important
The dead-letter queue of a FIFO queue must also be a FIFO queue. Similarly, the dead-letter queue of a standard queue must also be a standard queue.

Topics

- AWS Management Console
- AWS SDK for Java

AWS Management Console

1. Sign in to the Amazon SQS console.

2. Choose **Create New Queue.**

3. On the **Create New Queue** page, ensure that you're in the correct region and then type the **Queue Name. Note**
   The name of a FIFO queue must end with the `.fifo` suffix. FIFO queues are available in the US East (N. Virginia), US East (Ohio), US West (Oregon), and EU (Ireland) Regions.

4. **Standard** is selected by default. Choose **FIFO**.

5. Choose **Configure Queue**.

6. In this example, you enable the redrive policy for your new queue, set the `MyDeadLetterQueue.fifo` queue as the dead-letter queue, and set the number of maximum receives to 50.

1 To configure the dead-letter queue, choose **Use Redrive Policy**.

2 Enter the name of the existing **Dead Letter Queue** to which you want sources queues to send messages.

3 To configure the number of times that a message can be received before being sent to a dead-letter queue, set **Maximum Receives** to a value between 1 and 1,000. **Note**
The **Maximum Receives** setting applies only to individual messages.

④ Choose **Create Queue**.

Your new queue is configured to use a dead-letter queue, created, and selected in the queue list. **Note** When you create a queue, it can take a short time for the queue to propagate throughout Amazon SQS.

Your queue's **Maximum Receives** and **Dead Letter Queue** ARN are displayed on the **Redrive Policy** tab.

Maximum Receives 50

Dead Letter Queue arn:aws:sqs:us-east-2:⬛⬛⬛⬛⬛⬛⬛⬛:MyDeadLetterQueue.fifo

AWS SDK for Java

Before you begin working with the example code, specify your AWS credentials. For more information, see Set up AWS Credentials and Region for Development in the *AWS SDK for Java Developer Guide*.

To configure a dead-letter queue

Prerequisites

Add the `aws-java-sdk-sqs.jar` package to your Java class path. The following example shows this dependency in a Maven project `pom.xml` file.

```
1 <dependencies>
2     <dependency>
3         <groupId>com.amazonaws</groupId>
4         <artifactId>aws-java-sdk-sqs</artifactId>
5         <version><replaceable>LATEST</replaceable></version>
6     </dependency>
7 </dependencies>
```

SQSDeadLetterQueueExample.java

The following example Java code creates two standard queues and configures one queue to act as a source queue for the other—a dead-letter queue.

```
1  /*
2   * Copyright 2010-2018 Amazon.com, Inc. or its affiliates. All Rights Reserved.
3   *
4   * Licensed under the Apache License, Version 2.0 (the "License").
5   * You may not use this file except in compliance with the License.
6   * A copy of the License is located at
7   *
8   *  https://aws.amazon.com/apache2.0
9   *
10  * or in the "license" file accompanying this file. This file is distributed
11  * on an "AS IS" BASIS, WITHOUT WARRANTIES OR CONDITIONS OF ANY KIND, either
12  * express or implied. See the License for the specific language governing
13  * permissions and limitations under the License.
14  *
15  */
16
17 import com.amazonaws.AmazonClientException;
18 import com.amazonaws.AmazonServiceException;
```

```java
19  import com.amazonaws.services.sqs.AmazonSQS;
20  import com.amazonaws.services.sqs.AmazonSQSClientBuilder;
21  import com.amazonaws.services.sqs.model.GetQueueAttributesRequest;
22  import com.amazonaws.services.sqs.model.GetQueueAttributesResult;
23  import com.amazonaws.services.sqs.model.QueueAttributeName;
24  import com.amazonaws.services.sqs.model.SetQueueAttributesRequest;
25
26  import java.util.Scanner;
27
28  public class SQSDeadLetterQueueExample {
29      public static void main(String[] args) {
30
31          final Scanner input = new Scanner(System.in);
32
33          System.out.print("Enter the source queue name: ");
34          final String sourceQueueName = input.nextLine();
35
36          System.out.print("Enter the dead-letter queue name: ");
37          final String deadLetterQueueName = input.nextLine();
38
39          /*
40           * Create a new instance of the builder with all defaults (credentials
41           * and region) set automatically. For more information, see
42           * Creating Service Clients in the AWS SDK for Java Developer Guide.
43           */
44          final AmazonSQS sqs = AmazonSQSClientBuilder.defaultClient();
45
46          try {
47              // Create a source queue.
48              sqs.createQueue(sourceQueueName);
49
50              // Create a dead-letter queue.
51              sqs.createQueue(deadLetterQueueName);
52
53              // Get the dead-letter queue ARN.
54              final String deadLetterQueueUrl = sqs.getQueueUrl(deadLetterQueueName)
55                      .getQueueUrl();
56              final GetQueueAttributesResult deadLetterQueueAttributes = sqs.getQueueAttributes(
57                      new GetQueueAttributesRequest(deadLetterQueueUrl)
58                              .withAttributeNames("QueueArn"));
59              final String deadLetterQueueArn = deadLetterQueueAttributes.getAttributes().get("
                  QueueArn");
60
61              // Set the dead letter queue for the source queue using the redrive policy.
62              final String sourceQueueUrl = sqs.getQueueUrl(sourceQueueName)
63                      .getQueueUrl();
64              final SetQueueAttributesRequest request = new SetQueueAttributesRequest()
65                      .withQueueUrl(sourceQueueUrl)
66                      .addAttributesEntry(QueueAttributeName.RedrivePolicy.toString(),
67                          "{\"maxReceiveCount\":\"5\", \"deadLetterTargetArn\":\""
68                              + deadLetterQueueArn + "\"}");
69              sqs.setQueueAttributes(request);
70
71              System.out.println("Set queue " + sourceQueueName + " as source queue " +
```

```
72              "for dead-letter queue " + deadLetterQueueName + ".");
73
74          } catch (final AmazonServiceException ase) {
75              System.out.println("Caught an AmazonServiceException, which means " +
76                      "your request made it to Amazon SQS, but was " +
77                      "rejected with an error response for some reason.");
78              System.out.println("Error Message:    " + ase.getMessage());
79              System.out.println("HTTP Status Code: " + ase.getStatusCode());
80              System.out.println("AWS Error Code:   " + ase.getErrorCode());
81              System.out.println("Error Type:       " + ase.getErrorType());
82              System.out.println("Request ID:       " + ase.getRequestId());
83          } catch (final AmazonClientException ace) {
84              System.out.println("Caught an AmazonClientException, which means " +
85                      "the client encountered a serious internal problem while " +
86                      "trying to communicate with Amazon SQS, such as not " +
87                      "being able to access the network.");
88              System.out.println("Error Message: " + ace.getMessage());
89          }
90      }
91  }
```

To configure a dead-letter queue and send, receive, and delete a message

1. Copy the example program for a standard queue or a FIFO queue.

2. Set a string that contains JSON-formatted parameters and values for the `RedrivePolicy` queue attribute:

```
1  final String redrivePolicy =
2          "{\"maxReceiveCount\":\"5\", \"deadLetterTargetArn\":\"arn:aws:sqs:us-east
              -2:123456789012:MyDeadLetterQueue\"}";
```

3. Use the `CreateQueue` or `SetQueueAttributesRequest` action to configure the `RedrivePolicy` queue attribute:

```
1  final SetQueueAttributesRequest queueAttributes = new SetQueueAttributesRequest();
2  final Map<String,String> attributes = new HashMap<String,String>();
3  attributes.put("RedrivePolicy", redrivePolicy);
4  queueAttributes.setAttributes(attributes);
5  queueAttributes.setQueueUrl(myQueueUrl);
6  sqs.setQueueAttributes(queueAttributes);
```

4. Compile and run your program.

   The dead-letter queue is configured.

Tutorial: Configuring Visibility Timeout for an Amazon SQS Queue

Immediately after a message is received, it remains in the queue. To prevent other consumers from processing the message again, Amazon SQS sets a *visibility timeout*, a period of time during which Amazon SQS prevents other consumers from receiving and processing the message. The default visibility timeout for a message is 30 seconds. The maximum is 12 hours. In this tutorial you'll learn how to configure visibility timeout for a queue using the AWS Management Console and for single or multiple messages using the AWS SDK for Java. For more information, see Amazon SQS Visibility Timeout.

Note

You can use the AWS Management Console to configure visibility timeout only for queues, not for single or multiple messages. To do this, you must use one of the AWS SDKs. For more information, see the second Java example code below.

Topics

- AWS Management Console
- AWS SDK for Java

AWS Management Console

1. Sign in to the Amazon SQS console.

2. Choose **Create New Queue.**

3. On the **Create New Queue** page, ensure that you're in the correct region and then type the **Queue Name. Note**
   The name of a FIFO queue must end with the `.fifo` suffix. FIFO queues are available in the US East (N. Virginia), US East (Ohio), US West (Oregon), and EU (Ireland) Regions.

4. **Standard** is selected by default. Choose **FIFO.**

5. Choose **Configure Queue.**

6. In this example, you set the default visibility timeout to 1 minute.

   Default Visibility Timeout ❶ | 1 | | minutes ▼ | Value must be between 0 seconds and 12 hours.

7. Choose **Create Queue.**

   Your new queue is configured to use a 1-minute visibility timeout, created, and selected in the queue list.
   Note
   When you create a queue, it can take a short time for the queue to propagate throughout Amazon SQS.

   Your queue's **Default Visibility Timeout** is displayed on the **Details** tab.

   Default Visibility Timeout: 1 minutes

AWS SDK for Java

Before you begin working with the example code, specify your AWS credentials. For more information, see Set up AWS Credentials and Region for Development in the *AWS SDK for Java Developer Guide.*

To configure visibility timeout for a queue

Prerequisites

Add the `aws-java-sdk-sqs.jar` package to your Java class path. The following example shows this dependency in a Maven project `pom.xml` file.

```xml
<dependencies>
    <dependency>
        <groupId>com.amazonaws</groupId>
        <artifactId>aws-java-sdk-sqs</artifactId>
        <version><replaceable>LATEST</replaceable></version>
    </dependency>
</dependencies>
```

SQSVisibilityTimeoutExample.java

The following example Java code creates a standard queue and sets the visibility timeout for it to 1 minute.

```java
/*
 * Copyright 2010-2018 Amazon.com, Inc. or its affiliates. All Rights Reserved.
 *
 * Licensed under the Apache License, Version 2.0 (the "License").
 * You may not use this file except in compliance with the License.
 * A copy of the License is located at
 *
 *  https://aws.amazon.com/apache2.0
 *
 * or in the "license" file accompanying this file. This file is distributed
 * on an "AS IS" BASIS, WITHOUT WARRANTIES OR CONDITIONS OF ANY KIND, either
 * express or implied. See the License for the specific language governing
 * permissions and limitations under the License.
 *
 */

    import com.amazonaws.AmazonClientException;
    import com.amazonaws.AmazonServiceException;
    import com.amazonaws.services.sqs.AmazonSQS;
    import com.amazonaws.services.sqs.AmazonSQSClientBuilder;
    import com.amazonaws.services.sqs.model.CreateQueueRequest;
    import com.amazonaws.services.sqs.model.QueueAttributeName;
    import com.amazonaws.services.sqs.model.SetQueueAttributesRequest;

    import java.util.Scanner;

    public class SQSVisibilityTimeoutExample {
        public static void main(String[] args) {

            final Scanner input = new Scanner(System.in);

            System.out.print("Enter the queue name: ");
            final String queueName = input.nextLine();

            System.out.print("Enter the visibility timeout in seconds " +
                    "(0 seconds to 12 hours): ");
            final String visibilityTimeout = input.nextLine();

            /*
             * Create a new instance of the builder with all defaults (credentials
```

```
41        * and region) set automatically. For more information, see
42        * Creating Service Clients in the AWS SDK for Java Developer Guide.
43        */
44        final AmazonSQS sqs = AmazonSQSClientBuilder.defaultClient();
45
46        try {
47            // Create a queue.
48            final CreateQueueRequest createQueueRequest = new CreateQueueRequest()
49                    .withQueueName(queueName);
50            sqs.createQueue(createQueueRequest);
51
52            // Set the visibility timeout for the queue.
53            final String queueUrl = sqs.getQueueUrl(queueName)
54                    .getQueueUrl();
55            final SetQueueAttributesRequest request = new SetQueueAttributesRequest()
56                    .withQueueUrl(queueUrl)
57                    .addAttributesEntry(QueueAttributeName.VisibilityTimeout
58                            .toString(), visibilityTimeout);
59            sqs.setQueueAttributes(request);
60
61            System.out.println("Created queue " + queueName + " with " +
62                    "visibility timeout set to " + visibilityTimeout +
63                    " seconds.");
64
65        } catch (final AmazonServiceException ase) {
66            System.out.println("Caught an AmazonServiceException, which means " +
67                    "your request made it to Amazon SQS, but was " +
68                    "rejected with an error response for some reason.");
69            System.out.println("Error Message:    " + ase.getMessage());
70            System.out.println("HTTP Status Code: " + ase.getStatusCode());
71            System.out.println("AWS Error Code:   " + ase.getErrorCode());
72            System.out.println("Error Type:       " + ase.getErrorType());
73            System.out.println("Request ID:       " + ase.getRequestId());
74        } catch (final AmazonClientException ace) {
75            System.out.println("Caught an AmazonClientException, which means " +
76                    "the client encountered a serious internal problem while " +
77                    "trying to communicate with Amazon SQS, such as not " +
78                    "being able to access the network.");
79            System.out.println("Error Message: " + ace.getMessage());
80        }
81    }
82 }
```

To configure visibility timeout for a single message or multiple messages and send, receive, and delete messages

1. Copy the example program for a standard queue or a FIFO queue.

2. To configure visibility timeout for a single message, pass the queue URL, the message receipt handle, and the visibility timeout value in seconds.

```
1 // Get the message receipt handle.
2 String receiptHandle = sqs.receiveMessage(myQueueUrl)
3         .getMessages()
4         .get(0)
```

```
5          .getReceiptHandle();
6
7  // Pass the queue URL, the message receipt handle, and the visibility timeout value.
8  sqs.changeMessageVisibility(myQueueUrl, receiptHandle, timeoutValue);
```

3. To configure visibility timeout for multiple messages (for example, if you want to set different timeout values for different messages), create an **ArrayList**, add messages to it with the visibility timeout value in seconds, and then pass the queue URL and the **ArrayList** of messages.

```
1  // Create an ArrayList for batched messages.
2  List<ChangeMessageVisibilityBatchRequestEntry> entries =
3          new ArrayList<ChangeMessageVisibilityBatchRequestEntry>();
4
5  // Add the first message to the ArrayList with a visibility timeout value.
6  entries.add(new ChangeMessageVisibilityBatchRequestEntry(
7          "uniqueMessageId123", sqs.receiveMessage(myQueueUrl)
8          .getMessages()
9          .get(0)
10         .getReceiptHandle())
11         .withVisibilityTimeout(timeoutValue));
12
13 // Add the second message to the ArrayList with a different timeout value.
14 entries.add(new ChangeMessageVisibilityBatchRequestEntry(
15         "uniqueMessageId456", sqs.receiveMessage(myQueueUrl)
16         .getMessages()
17         .get(0)
18         .getReceiptHandle())
19         .withVisibilityTimeout(timeoutValue + 60));
20
21 sqs.changeMessageVisibilityBatch(myQueueUrl, entries);
```

4. Compile and run your program.

   The visibility timeout for a single message or multiple messages is configured.

Tutorial: Configuring an Amazon SQS Delay Queue

Delay queues let you postpone the delivery of new messages to a queue for a number of seconds. If you create a delay queue, any messages that you send to the queue remain invisible to consumers for the duration of the delay period. The minimum delay for a queue is 0 seconds. The maximum is 15 minutes. In this tutorial you'll learn how to configure a delay queue using the AWS Management Console or using the AWS SDK for Java. For more information, see Amazon SQS Delay Queues.

Topics

- AWS Management Console
- AWS SDK for Java
- To configure a delay queue and send, receive, and delete messages

AWS Management Console

1. Sign in to the Amazon SQS console.

2. Choose **Create New Queue.**

3. On the **Create New Queue** page, ensure that you're in the correct region and then type the **Queue Name. Note**
   The name of a FIFO queue must end with the `.fifo` suffix. FIFO queues are available in the US East (N. Virginia), US East (Ohio), US West (Oregon), and EU (Ireland) Regions.

4. **Standard** is selected by default. Choose **FIFO**.

5. Choose **Configure Queue**.

6. In this example, you set the delivery delay to 1 minute.

Delivery Delay 🛈	60	seconds ▾	Value must be between 0 seconds and 15 minutes.

7. Choose **Create Queue**.

   Your new queue is configured to use a 1-minute delay, created, and selected in the queue list. **Note**
   When you create a queue, it can take a short time for the queue to propagate throughout Amazon SQS.

   Your queue's **Delivery Delay** is displayed on the **Details** tab.

   ## Delivery Delay: 1 minutes

AWS SDK for Java

Before you begin working with the example code, specify your AWS credentials. For more information, see Set up AWS Credentials and Region for Development in the *AWS SDK for Java Developer Guide*.

To configure a delay queue

Prerequisites

Add the `aws-java-sdk-sqs.jar` package to your Java class path. The following example shows this dependency in a Maven project `pom.xml` file.

```xml
1 <dependencies>
2     <dependency>
3         <groupId>com.amazonaws</groupId>
4         <artifactId>aws-java-sdk-sqs</artifactId>
5         <version><replaceable>LATEST</replaceable></version>
6     </dependency>
7 </dependencies>
```

SQSDelayQueueExample.java

The following example Java code creates a standard queue and sets the delay for it to 1 minute.

```java
1  /*
2   * Copyright 2010-2018 Amazon.com, Inc. or its affiliates. All Rights Reserved.
3   *
4   * Licensed under the Apache License, Version 2.0 (the "License").
5   * You may not use this file except in compliance with the License.
6   * A copy of the License is located at
7   *
8   *  https://aws.amazon.com/apache2.0
9   *
10  * or in the "license" file accompanying this file. This file is distributed
11  * on an "AS IS" BASIS, WITHOUT WARRANTIES OR CONDITIONS OF ANY KIND, either
12  * express or implied. See the License for the specific language governing
13  * permissions and limitations under the License.
14  *
15  */
16
17      import com.amazonaws.AmazonClientException;
18      import com.amazonaws.AmazonServiceException;
19      import com.amazonaws.services.sqs.AmazonSQS;
20      import com.amazonaws.services.sqs.AmazonSQSClientBuilder;
21      import com.amazonaws.services.sqs.model.CreateQueueRequest;
22      import com.amazonaws.services.sqs.model.QueueAttributeName;
23      import com.amazonaws.services.sqs.model.SetQueueAttributesRequest;
24
25      import java.util.Scanner;
26
27      public class SQSDelayQueueExample {
28          public static void main(String[] args) {
29
30              final Scanner input = new Scanner(System.in);
31
32              System.out.print("Enter the queue name: ");
33              final String queueName = input.nextLine();
34
35              System.out.print("Enter the delay in seconds (0 seconds to 15 minutes): ");
36              final String queueDelay = input.nextLine();
37
38              /*
39               * Create a new instance of the builder with all defaults (credentials
40               * and region) set automatically. For more information, see
41               * Creating Service Clients in the AWS SDK for Java Developer Guide.
42               */
43              final AmazonSQS sqs = AmazonSQSClientBuilder.defaultClient();
```

```
44
45          try {
46              // Create a queue.
47              final CreateQueueRequest createQueueRequest = new CreateQueueRequest()
48                      .withQueueName(queueName);
49              sqs.createQueue(createQueueRequest);
50
51              // Set the delay for the queue.
52              final String queueUrl = sqs.getQueueUrl(queueName)
53                      .getQueueUrl();
54              final SetQueueAttributesRequest request = new SetQueueAttributesRequest()
55                      .withQueueUrl(queueUrl)
56                      .addAttributesEntry(QueueAttributeName.DelaySeconds
57                              .toString(), queueDelay);
58              sqs.setQueueAttributes(request);
59
60              System.out.println("Created queue " + queueName + " with " +
61                      "delay set to " + queueDelay + " seconds.");
62
63          } catch (final AmazonServiceException ase) {
64              System.out.println("Caught an AmazonServiceException, which means " +
65                      "your request made it to Amazon SQS, but was " +
66                      "rejected with an error response for some reason.");
67              System.out.println("Error Message:    " + ase.getMessage());
68              System.out.println("HTTP Status Code: " + ase.getStatusCode());
69              System.out.println("AWS Error Code:   " + ase.getErrorCode());
70              System.out.println("Error Type:       " + ase.getErrorType());
71              System.out.println("Request ID:       " + ase.getRequestId());
72          } catch (final AmazonClientException ace) {
73              System.out.println("Caught an AmazonClientException, which means " +
74                      "the client encountered a serious internal problem while " +
75                      "trying to communicate with Amazon SQS, such as not " +
76                      "being able to access the network.");
77              System.out.println("Error Message: " + ace.getMessage());
78          }
79      }
80  }
```

To configure a delay queue and send, receive, and delete messages

1. Copy the example program for a standard queue or a FIFO queue.

2. To configure a delay queue, pass the delay value in seconds.

```
1 // Set the delay for the queue.
2 final String queueUrl = sqs.getQueueUrl(queueName).getQueueUrl();
3 final SetQueueAttributesRequest request = new SetQueueAttributesRequest()
4       .withQueueUrl(queueUrl)
5       .addAttributesEntry(QueueAttributeName.DelaySeconds.toString(), queueDelay);
6 sqs.setQueueAttributes(request);
```

3. Compile and run your program.

   The visibility timeout for a single message or multiple messages is configured.

How Amazon SQS Works

This section describes the types of Amazon SQS queues and their basic properties. It also describes the identifiers of queues and messages, and various queue and message management workflows.

Topics

- Basic Amazon SQS Architecture
- Amazon SQS Standard Queues
- Amazon SQS FIFO (First-In-First-Out) Queues
- Amazon SQS Queue and Message Identifiers
- Amazon SQS Message Attributes
- Resources Required to Process Amazon SQS Messages
- Amazon SQS Cost Allocation Tags
- Amazon SQS Long Polling
- Amazon SQS Dead-Letter Queues
- Amazon SQS Visibility Timeout
- Amazon SQS Delay Queues
- Amazon SQS Message Timers
- Managing Large Amazon SQS Messages Using Amazon S3
- Working with JMS and Amazon SQS

Basic Amazon SQS Architecture

Learn about the parts of a distributed messaging system and the lifecycle of an Amazon SQS message, from creation to deletion.

This section outlines the parts of a distributed messaging system and explains the lifecycle of an Amazon SQS message.

Distributed Queues

There are three main parts in a distributed messaging system: the components of your distributed system, your queue (distributed on Amazon SQS servers), and the messages in the queue.

In the following scenario, your system has several components that send messages to the queue and receive messages from the queue. The queue (which holds messages A through E) redundantly stores the messages across multiple Amazon SQS servers.

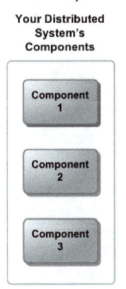

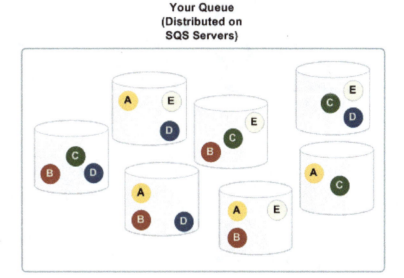

Message Lifecycle

The following scenario describes the lifecycle of an Amazon SQS message in a queue, from creation to deletion.

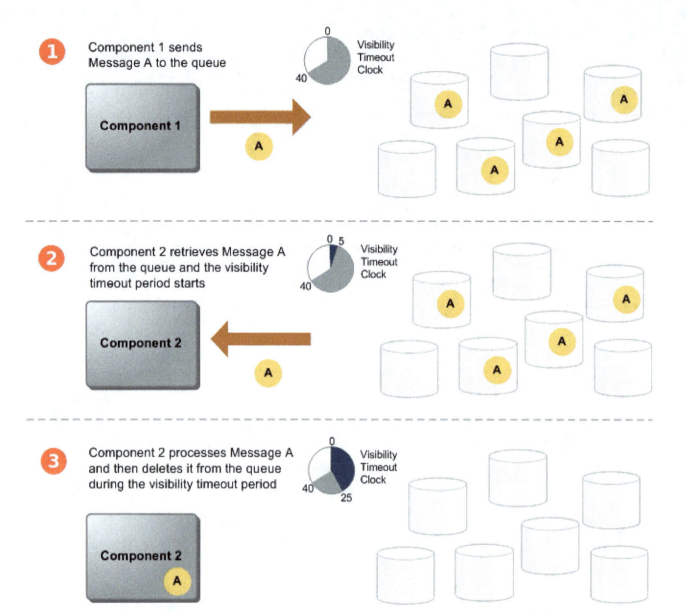

① A producer (component 1) sends message A to a queue, and the message is distributed across the Amazon SQS servers redundantly.

② When a consumer (component 2) is ready to process messages, it consumes messages from the queue, and message A is returned. While message A is being processed, it remains in the queue and isn't returned to subsequent receive requests for the duration of the visibility timeout.

③ The consumer (component 2) deletes message A from the queue to prevent the message from being received and processed again when the visibility timeout expires.

Note
Amazon SQS automatically deletes messages that have been in a queue for more than maximum message retention period. The default message retention period is 4 days. However, you can set the message retention period to a value from 60 seconds to 1,209,600 seconds (14 days) using the [SetQueueAttributes](http://docs.aws.amazon.com/AWSSimpleQueueService/latest/APIReference/API_SetQueueAttributes.html) action.

Amazon SQS Standard Queues

Amazon SQS offers *standard* as the default queue type. Standard queues support a nearly unlimited number of transactions per second (TPS) per action. Standard queues support at-least-once message delivery. However, occasionally (because of the highly distributed architecture that allows nearly unlimited throughput), more than one copy of a message might be delivered out of order. Standard queues provide best-effort ordering which ensures that messages are generally delivered in the same order as they're sent. For information on creating standard queues with or without server-side encryption using the AWS Management Console, the AWS SDK for Java (and the [CreateQueue](http://docs.aws.amazon.com/AWSSimpleQueueService/latest/APIReference/API_CreateQueue.html) action), or AWS CloudFormation, see Tutorial: Creating an Amazon SQS Queue and Tutorial: Creating an Amazon SQS Queue with Server-Side Encryption (SSE).

You can use standard message queues in many scenarios, as long as your application can process messages that arrive more than once and out of order, for example:

- **Decouple live user requests from intensive background work** – Let users upload media while resizing or encoding it.
- **Allocate tasks to multiple worker nodes** – Process a high number of credit card validation requests.
- **Batch messages for future processing** – Schedule multiple entries to be added to a database.

For best practices of working with standard queues, see Recommendations for Amazon SQS Standard and FIFO (First-In-First-Out) Queues .

Topics

- Message Ordering
- At-Least-Once Delivery
- Consuming Messages Using Short Polling
- Working Java Example for Standard Queues

Message Ordering

A standard queue makes a best effort to preserve the order of messages, but more than one copy of a message might be delivered out of order. If your system requires that order be preserved, we recommend using a *FIFO (First-In-First-Out) queue* or adding sequencing information in each message so you can reorder the messages when they're received.

At-Least-Once Delivery

Amazon SQS stores copies of your messages on multiple servers for redundancy and high availability. On rare occasions, one of the servers that stores a copy of a message might be unavailable when you receive or delete a message.

If this occurs, the copy of the message isn't deleted on that unavailable server, and you might get that message copy again when you receive messages. Design your applications to be *idempotent* (they should not be affected adversely when processing the same message more than once).

Consuming Messages Using Short Polling

The process of consuming messages from a queue depends on whether you use short polling (the default behavior) or long polling. For more information about long polling, see Amazon SQS Long Polling.

When you consume messages from a queue using short polling, Amazon SQS samples a subset of its servers (based on a weighted random distribution) and returns messages from only those servers. Thus, a particular receive request might not return all of your messages. However, if you have fewer than 1,000 messages in your queue, a subsequent request will return your messages. If you keep consuming from your queues, Amazon SQS samples all of its servers, and you receive all of your messages.

The following diagram shows the short-polling behavior of messages returned from a standard queue after one of your system components makes a receive request. Amazon SQS samples several of its servers (in gray) and returns messages A, C, D, and B from these servers. Message E isn't returned for this request, but is returned for a subsequent request.

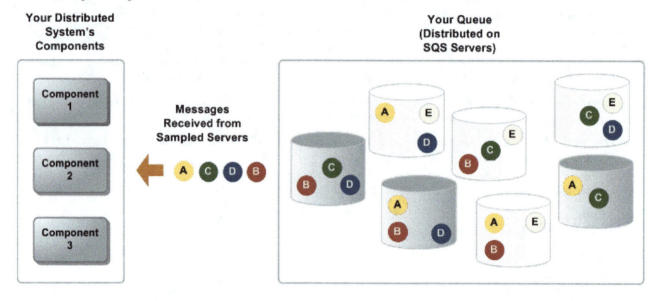

Working Java Example for Standard Queues

Learn about Amazon SQS standard queue functionality using the provided Maven prerequisites and example Java code.

Prerequisites

Add the `aws-java-sdk-sqs.jar` package to your Java class path. The following example shows this dependency in a Maven project `pom.xml` file.

```
1 <dependencies>
2     <dependency>
3         <groupId>com.amazonaws</groupId>
4         <artifactId>aws-java-sdk-sqs</artifactId>
5         <version><replaceable>LATEST</replaceable></version>
6     </dependency>
7 </dependencies>
```

SQSSimpleJavaClientExample.java

The following example Java code creates a queue and sends, receives, and deletes a message.

```
1  /*
2   * Copyright 2010-2018 Amazon.com, Inc. or its affiliates. All Rights Reserved.
3   *
4   * Licensed under the Apache License, Version 2.0 (the "License").
5   * You may not use this file except in compliance with the License.
6   * A copy of the License is located at
7   *
8   *  https://aws.amazon.com/apache2.0
9   *
10  * or in the "license" file accompanying this file. This file is distributed
11  * on an "AS IS" BASIS, WITHOUT WARRANTIES OR CONDITIONS OF ANY KIND, either
12  * express or implied. See the License for the specific language governing
13  * permissions and limitations under the License.
14  *
15  */
16
17 import com.amazonaws.AmazonClientException;
18 import com.amazonaws.AmazonServiceException;
19 import com.amazonaws.services.sqs.AmazonSQS;
20 import com.amazonaws.services.sqs.AmazonSQSClientBuilder;
21 import com.amazonaws.services.sqs.model.*;
22
23 import java.util.List;
24 import java.util.Map.Entry;
25
26 /**
27  * This sample demonstrates how to make basic requests to Amazon SQS using the
28  * AWS SDK for Java.
29  * <p>
30  * Prerequisites: You must have a valid Amazon Web Services developer account,
31  * and be signed up to use Amazon SQS. For more information about Amazon SQS,
```

```
32    * see https://aws.amazon.com/sqs
33    * <p>
34    * Make sure that your credentials are located in ~/.aws/credentials
35    */
36   public class SQSSimpleJavaClientExample {
37       public static void main(String[] args) {
38           /*
39            * Create a new instance of the builder with all defaults (credentials
40            * and region) set automatically. For more information, see
41            * [Creating Service Clients](http://docs.aws.amazon.com/sdk-for-java/v1/developer-guide
                  /creating-clients.html) in the AWS SDK for Java Developer Guide.
42            */
43           final AmazonSQS sqs = AmazonSQSClientBuilder.defaultClient();
44
45           System.out.println("===============================================");
46           System.out.println("Getting Started with Amazon SQS Standard Queues");
47           System.out.println("===============================================\n");
48
49           try {
50               // Create a queue.
51               System.out.println("Creating a new SQS queue called MyQueue.\n");
52               final CreateQueueRequest createQueueRequest =
53                       new CreateQueueRequest("MyQueue");
54               final String myQueueUrl = sqs.createQueue(createQueueRequest)
55                       .getQueueUrl();
56
57               // List all queues.
58               System.out.println("Listing all queues in your account.\n");
59               for (final String queueUrl : sqs.listQueues().getQueueUrls()) {
60                   System.out.println("  QueueUrl: " + queueUrl);
61               }
62               System.out.println();
63
64               // Send a message.
65               System.out.println("Sending a message to MyQueue.\n");
66               sqs.sendMessage(new SendMessageRequest(myQueueUrl,
67                       "This is my message text."));
68
69               // Receive messages.
70               System.out.println("Receiving messages from MyQueue.\n");
71               final ReceiveMessageRequest receiveMessageRequest =
72                       new ReceiveMessageRequest(myQueueUrl);
73               final List<Message> messages = sqs.receiveMessage(receiveMessageRequest)
74                       .getMessages();
75               for (final Message message : messages) {
76                   System.out.println("Message");
77                   System.out.println("  MessageId:     "
78                           + message.getMessageId());
79                   System.out.println("  ReceiptHandle: "
80                           + message.getReceiptHandle());
81                   System.out.println("  MD5OfBody:     "
82                           + message.getMD5OfBody());
83                   System.out.println("  Body:          "
84                           + message.getBody());
```

```
85          for (final Entry<String, String> entry : message.getAttributes()
86                  .entrySet()) {
87              System.out.println("Attribute");
88              System.out.println("  Name:  " + entry
89                      .getKey());
90              System.out.println("  Value: " + entry
91                      .getValue());
92          }
93      }
94      System.out.println();
95
96      // Delete the message.
97      System.out.println("Deleting a message.\n");
98      final String messageReceiptHandle = messages.get(0).getReceiptHandle();
99      sqs.deleteMessage(new DeleteMessageRequest(myQueueUrl,
100             messageReceiptHandle));
101
102     // Delete the queue.
103     System.out.println("Deleting the test queue.\n");
104     sqs.deleteQueue(new DeleteQueueRequest(myQueueUrl));
105 } catch (final AmazonServiceException ase) {
106     System.out.println("Caught an AmazonServiceException, which means " +
107             "your request made it to Amazon SQS, but was " +
108             "rejected with an error response for some reason.");
109     System.out.println("Error Message:    " + ase.getMessage());
110     System.out.println("HTTP Status Code: " + ase.getStatusCode());
111     System.out.println("AWS Error Code:   " + ase.getErrorCode());
112     System.out.println("Error Type:       " + ase.getErrorType());
113     System.out.println("Request ID:       " + ase.getRequestId());
114 } catch (final AmazonClientException ace) {
115     System.out.println("Caught an AmazonClientException, which means " +
116             "the client encountered a serious internal problem while " +
117             "trying to communicate with Amazon SQS, such as not " +
118             "being able to access the network.");
119     System.out.println("Error Message: " + ace.getMessage());
120     }
121 }
122 }
```

Amazon SQS FIFO (First-In-First-Out) Queues

FIFO queues are available in the US East (N. Virginia), US East (Ohio), US West (Oregon), and EU (Ireland) Regions. FIFO queues have all the capabilities of the standard queue. For information on creating FIFO queues with or without server-side encryption using the AWS Management Console, the AWS SDK for Java (and the [CreateQueue](http://docs.aws.amazon.com/AWSSimpleQueueService/latest/APIReference/API_CreateQueue.html) action), or AWS CloudFormation, see Tutorial: Creating an Amazon SQS Queue and Tutorial: Creating an Amazon SQS Queue with Server-Side Encryption (SSE).

FIFO (First-In-First-Out) queues are designed to enhance messaging between applications when the order of operations and events is critical, or where duplicates can't be tolerated, for example:

- Ensure that user-entered commands are executed in the right order.
- Display the correct product price by sending price modifications in the right order.
- Prevent a student from enrolling in a course before registering for an account.

FIFO queues also provide exactly-once processing but have a limited number of transactions per second (TPS):

- By default, FIFO queues support up to 3,000 messages per second with batching. To request a limit increase, file a support request.
- FIFO queues support up to 300 messages per second (300 send, receive, or delete operations per second) without batching.

Note
The name of a FIFO queue must end with the .fifo suffix. The suffix counts towards the 80-character queue name limit. To determine whether a queue is FIFO, you can check whether the queue name ends with the suffix.

For best practices of working with FIFO queues, see Additional Recommendations for Amazon SQS FIFO Queues and Recommendations for Amazon SQS Standard and FIFO (First-In-First-Out) Queues .

For information about compatibility of clients and services with FIFO queues, see Compatibility.

Topics
- Message Ordering
- Key Terms
- FIFO Delivery Logic
- Exactly-Once Processing
- Moving from a Standard Queue to a FIFO Queue
- Compatibility
- Working Java Example for FIFO Queues

Message Ordering

The FIFO queue improves upon and complements the standard queue. The most important features of this queue type are *FIFO (First-In-First-Out) delivery* and *exactly-once processing*:

- The order in which messages are sent and received is strictly preserved and a message is delivered once and remains available until a consumer processes and deletes it.
- Duplicates aren't introduced into the queue.

In addition, FIFO queues support *message groups* that allow multiple ordered message groups within a single queue.

Key Terms

The following key terms can help you better understand the functionality of FIFO queues. For more information, see the *Amazon Simple Queue Service API Reference*.

Message Deduplication ID
The token used for deduplication of sent messages. If a message with a particular message deduplication ID is sent successfully, any messages sent with the same message deduplication ID are accepted successfully but aren't delivered during the 5-minute deduplication interval.

Message deduplication applies to an entire queue, not to individual message groups.

Amazon SQS continues to keep track of the message deduplication ID even after the message is received and deleted.

Message Group ID
The tag that specifies that a message belongs to a specific message group. Messages that belong to the same message group are always processed one by one, in a strict order relative to the message group (however, messages that belong to different message groups might be processed out of order).

Receive Request Attempt ID
The token used for deduplication of `ReceiveMessage` calls.

Sequence Number
The large, non-consecutive number that Amazon SQS assigns to each message.

FIFO Delivery Logic

The following concepts can help you better understand the sending of messages to and receiving messages from FIFO.

Sending Messages
If multiple messages are sent in succession to a FIFO queue, each with a distinct message deduplication ID, Amazon SQS stores the messages and acknowledges the transmission. Then, each message can be received and processed in the exact order in which the messages were transmitted.

In FIFO queues, messages are ordered based on message group ID. If multiple hosts (or different threads on the same host) send messages with the same message group ID to a FIFO queue, Amazon SQS stores the messages in the order in which they arrive for processing. To ensure that Amazon SQS preserves the order in which messages are sent and received, ensure that each producer uses a unique message group ID to send all its messages.

FIFO queue logic applies only per message group ID. Each message group ID represents a distinct ordered message group within an Amazon SQS queue. For each message group ID, all messages are sent and received in strict order. However, messages with different message group ID values might be sent and received out of order. You must associate a message group ID with a message. If you don't provide a message group ID, the action fails. If you require a single group of ordered messages, provide the same message group ID for messages sent to the FIFO queue.

Receiving Messages
You can't request to receive messages with a specific message group ID.

When receiving messages from a FIFO queue with multiple message group IDs, Amazon SQS first attempts to return as many messages with the same message group ID as possible. This allows other consumers to process messages with a different message group ID.

It is possible to receive up to 10 messages in a single call using the `MaxNumberOfMessages` request parameter of the [ReceiveMessage](http://docs.aws.amazon.com/AWSSimpleQueueService/latest/APIReference/API_ReceiveMessage.html) action. These messages retain their FIFO order and can have the same message group ID. Thus, if there are fewer than 10 messages available with the same message group ID, you might receive messages from another message group ID, in the same batch of 10 messages, but still in FIFO order.

Retrying Multiple Times

FIFO queues allow the producer or consumer to attempt multiple retries:

- If the producer detects a failed `SendMessage` action, it can retry sending as many times as necessary, using the same message deduplication ID. Assuming that the producer receives at least one acknowledgement before the deduplication interval expires, multiple retries neither affect the ordering of messages nor introduce duplicates.
- If the consumer detects a failed `ReceiveMessage` action, it can retry as many times as necessary, using the same receive request attempt ID. Assuming that the consumer receives at least one acknowledgement before the visibility timeout expires, multiple retries don't affect the ordering of messages.
- When you receive a message with a message group ID, no more messages for the same message group ID are returned unless you delete the message or it becomes visible.

Exactly-Once Processing

Unlike standard queues, FIFO queues don't introduce duplicate messages. FIFO queues help you avoid sending duplicates to a queue. If you retry the `SendMessage` action within the 5-minute deduplication interval, Amazon SQS doesn't introduce any duplicates into the queue.

To configure deduplication, you must do one of the following:

- Enable content-based deduplication. This instructs Amazon SQS to use a SHA-256 hash to generate the message deduplication ID using the body of the message—but not the attributes of the message. For more information, see the documentation on the [CreateQueue](http://docs.aws.amazon.com/AWSSimpleQueueService/latest/APIReference/API_CreateQueue.html), [GetQueueAttributes](http://docs.aws.amazon.com/AWSSimpleQueueService/latest/APIReference/API_GetQueueAttributes.html), and [SetQueueAttributes](http://docs.aws.amazon.com/AWSSimpleQueueService/latest/APIReference/API_SetQueueAttributes.html) actions in the *Amazon Simple Queue Service API Reference*.
- Explicitly provide the message deduplication ID (or view the sequence number) for the message. For more information, see the documentation on the [SendMessage](http://docs.aws.amazon.com/AWSSimpleQueueService/latest/APIReference/API_SendMessage.html), [SendMessageBatch](http://docs.aws.amazon.com/AWSSimpleQueueService/latest/APIReference/API_SendMessageBatch.html), and [ReceiveMessage](http://docs.aws.amazon.com/AWSSimpleQueueService/latest/APIReference/API_ReceiveMessage.html) actions in the *Amazon Simple Queue Service API Reference*.

Moving from a Standard Queue to a FIFO Queue

If you have an existing application that uses standard queues and you want to take advantage of the ordering or exactly-once processing features of FIFO queues, you need to configure the queue and your application correctly.

Note

You can't convert an existing standard queue into a FIFO queue. To make the move, you must either create a new FIFO queue for your application or delete your existing standard queue and recreate it as a FIFO queue.

Use the following checklist to ensure that your application works correctly with a FIFO queue.

- By default, FIFO queues support up to 3,000 messages per second with batching. To request a limit increase, file a support request. FIFO queues support up to 300 messages per second (300 send, receive, or delete operations per second) without batching.

- FIFO queues don't support per-message delays, only per-queue delays. If your application sets the same value of the `DelaySeconds` parameter on each message, you must modify your application to remove the per-message delay and set `DelaySeconds` on the entire queue instead.
- Every message sent to a FIFO queue requires a message group ID. If you don't need multiple ordered message groups, specify the same message group ID for all your messages.
- Before sending messages to a FIFO queue, confirm the following:
    - If your application can send messages with identical message bodies, you can modify your application to provide a unique message deduplication ID for each sent message.
    - If your application sends messages with unique message bodies, you can enable content-based deduplication.
- You don't have to make any code changes to your consumer. However, if it takes a long time to process messages and your visibility timeout is set to a high value, consider adding a receive request attempt ID to each `ReceiveMessage` action. This allows you to retry receive attempts in case of networking failures and prevents queues from pausing due to failed receive attempts.

For more information, see the * Amazon Simple Queue Service API Reference*.

Compatibility

Clients
The Amazon SQS Buffered Asynchronous Client doesn't currently support FIFO queues.

Services
If your application uses multiple AWS services, or a mix of AWS and external services, it is important to understand which service functionality doesn't support FIFO queues.

Some AWS or external services that send notifications to Amazon SQS might not be compatible with FIFO queues, despite allowing you to set a FIFO queue as a target.

The following features of AWS services aren't currently compatible with FIFO queues:

- Auto Scaling Lifecycle Hooks
- AWS IoT Rule Actions
- AWS Lambda Dead-Letter Queues For information about compatibility of other services with FIFO queues, see your service documentation.

Working Java Example for FIFO Queues

Learn about Amazon SQS FIFO queue functionality using the provided Maven prerequisites and example Java code.

Prerequisites

Add the `aws-java-sdk-sqs.jar` package to your Java class path. The following example shows this dependency in a Maven project `pom.xml` file.

```
1 <dependencies>
2     <dependency>
3         <groupId>com.amazonaws</groupId>
4         <artifactId>aws-java-sdk-sqs</artifactId>
5         <version><replaceable>LATEST</replaceable></version>
6     </dependency>
7 </dependencies>
```

SQSFIFOJavaClientExample.java

The following example Java code creates a queue and sends, receives, and deletes a message.

```
1  /*
2   * Copyright 2010-2018 Amazon.com, Inc. or its affiliates. All Rights Reserved.
3   *
4   * Licensed under the Apache License, Version 2.0 (the "License").
5   * You may not use this file except in compliance with the License.
6   * A copy of the License is located at
7   *
8   *   https://aws.amazon.com/apache2.0
9   *
10  * or in the "license" file accompanying this file. This file is distributed
11  * on an "AS IS" BASIS, WITHOUT WARRANTIES OR CONDITIONS OF ANY KIND, either
12  * express or implied. See the License for the specific language governing
13  * permissions and limitations under the License.
14  *
15  */
16
17 import com.amazonaws.AmazonClientException;
18 import com.amazonaws.AmazonServiceException;
19 import com.amazonaws.services.sqs.AmazonSQS;
20 import com.amazonaws.services.sqs.AmazonSQSClientBuilder;
21 import com.amazonaws.services.sqs.model.*;
22
23 import java.util.HashMap;
24 import java.util.List;
25 import java.util.Map;
26 import java.util.Map.Entry;
27
28 public class SQSFIFOJavaClientExample {
29     public static void main(String[] args) {
30         /*
31          * Create a new instance of the builder with all defaults (credentials
```

```java
32      * and region) set automatically. For more information, see
33      * Creating Service Clients in the AWS SDK for Java Developer Guide.
34      */
35     final AmazonSQS sqs = AmazonSQSClientBuilder.defaultClient();
36
37     System.out.println("==========================================");
38     System.out.println("Getting Started with Amazon SQS FIFO Queues");
39     System.out.println("==========================================\n");
40
41     try {
42
43         // Create a FIFO queue.
44         System.out.println("Creating a new Amazon SQS FIFO queue called " +
45                 "MyFifoQueue.fifo.\n");
46         final Map<String, String> attributes = new HashMap<>();
47
48         // A FIFO queue must have the FifoQueue attribute set to true.
49         attributes.put("FifoQueue", "true");
50
51         /*
52          * If the user doesn't provide a MessageDeduplicationId, generate a
53          * MessageDeduplicationId based on the content.
54          */
55         attributes.put("ContentBasedDeduplication", "true");
56
57         // The FIFO queue name must end with the .fifo suffix.
58         final CreateQueueRequest createQueueRequest =
59                 new CreateQueueRequest("MyFifoQueue.fifo")
60                         .withAttributes(attributes);
61         final String myQueueUrl = sqs.createQueue(createQueueRequest).getQueueUrl();
62
63         // List all queues.
64         System.out.println("Listing all queues in your account.\n");
65         for (final String queueUrl : sqs.listQueues().getQueueUrls()) {
66             System.out.println("  QueueUrl: " + queueUrl);
67         }
68         System.out.println();
69
70         // Send a message.
71         System.out.println("Sending a message to MyFifoQueue.fifo.\n");
72         final SendMessageRequest sendMessageRequest =
73                 new SendMessageRequest(myQueueUrl,
74                         "This is my message text.");
75
76         /*
77          * When you send messages to a FIFO queue, you must provide a
78          * non-empty MessageGroupId.
79          */
80         sendMessageRequest.setMessageGroupId("messageGroup1");
81
82         // Uncomment the following to provide the MessageDeduplicationId
83         //sendMessageRequest.setMessageDeduplicationId("1");
84         final SendMessageResult sendMessageResult = sqs
85                 .sendMessage(sendMessageRequest);
```

```
86      final String sequenceNumber = sendMessageResult.getSequenceNumber();
87      final String messageId = sendMessageResult.getMessageId();
88      System.out.println("SendMessage succeed with messageId "
89              + messageId + ", sequence number " + sequenceNumber + "\n");
90
91      // Receive messages.
92      System.out.println("Receiving messages from MyFifoQueue.fifo.\n");
93      final ReceiveMessageRequest receiveMessageRequest =
94              new ReceiveMessageRequest(myQueueUrl);
95
96      // Uncomment the following to provide the ReceiveRequestDeduplicationId
97      //receiveMessageRequest.setReceiveRequestAttemptId("1");
98      final List<Message> messages = sqs.receiveMessage(receiveMessageRequest)
99              .getMessages();
100     for (final Message message : messages) {
101         System.out.println("Message");
102         System.out.println("  MessageId:      "
103                 + message.getMessageId());
104         System.out.println("  ReceiptHandle: "
105                 + message.getReceiptHandle());
106         System.out.println("  MD5OfBody:      "
107                 + message.getMD5OfBody());
108         System.out.println("  Body:           "
109                 + message.getBody());
110         for (final Entry<String, String> entry : message.getAttributes()
111                 .entrySet()) {
112             System.out.println("Attribute");
113             System.out.println("  Name:  " + entry.getKey());
114             System.out.println("  Value: " + entry.getValue());
115         }
116     }
117     System.out.println();
118
119     // Delete the message.
120     System.out.println("Deleting the message.\n");
121     final String messageReceiptHandle = messages.get(0).getReceiptHandle();
122     sqs.deleteMessage(new DeleteMessageRequest(myQueueUrl,
123             messageReceiptHandle));
124
125     // Delete the queue.
126     System.out.println("Deleting the queue.\n");
127     sqs.deleteQueue(new DeleteQueueRequest(myQueueUrl));
128 } catch (final AmazonServiceException ase) {
129     System.out.println("Caught an AmazonServiceException, which means " +
130             "your request made it to Amazon SQS, but was " +
131             "rejected with an error response for some reason.");
132     System.out.println("Error Message:    " + ase.getMessage());
133     System.out.println("HTTP Status Code: " + ase.getStatusCode());
134     System.out.println("AWS Error Code:   " + ase.getErrorCode());
135     System.out.println("Error Type:       " + ase.getErrorType());
136     System.out.println("Request ID:       " + ase.getRequestId());
137 } catch (final AmazonClientException ace) {
138     System.out.println("Caught an AmazonClientException, which means " +
139             "the client encountered a serious internal problem while " +
```

```
140                    "trying to communicate with Amazon SQS, such as not " +
141                    "being able to access the network.");
142           System.out.println("Error Message: " + ace.getMessage());
143       }
144   }
145 }
```

Amazon SQS Queue and Message Identifiers

This section describes the identifiers of standard and FIFO queues. These identifiers can help you find and manipulate specific queues and messages.

Topics

- Identifiers for Amazon SQS Standard and FIFO Queues
- Additional Identifiers for Amazon SQS FIFO Queues

Identifiers for Amazon SQS Standard and FIFO Queues

For more information about the following identifiers, see the *Amazon Simple Queue Service API Reference*.

Queue Name and URL

When you create a new queue, you must specify a queue name unique for your AWS account and region. Amazon SQS assigns each queue you create an identifier called a *queue URL* that includes the queue name and other Amazon SQS components. Whenever you want to perform an action on a queue, you provide its queue URL.

The name of a FIFO queue must end with the `.fifo` suffix. The suffix counts towards the 80-character queue name limit. To determine whether a queue is FIFO, you can check whether the queue name ends with the suffix.

The following is the queue URL for a queue named `MyQueue` owned by a user with the AWS account number 123456789012.

```
1 https://sqs.us-east-2.amazonaws.com/123456789012/MyQueue
```

Important
In your system, always store the entire queue URL exactly as Amazon SQS returns it to you when you create the queue (for example, `https://sqs.us-east-2.amazonaws.com/123456789012/MyQueue`). Don't build the queue URL from its separate components each time you need to specify the queue URL in a request because Amazon SQS can change the components that make up the queue URL.

You can also get the queue URL for a queue by listing your queues. For more information, see [ListQueues](http://docs.aws.amazon.com/AWSSimpleQueueService/latest/APIReference/API_ListQueues.html).

Message ID

Each message receives a system-assigned *message ID* that Amazon SQS returns to you in the [SendMessage](http://docs.aws.amazon.com/AWSSimpleQueueService/latest/APIReference/API_SendMessage.html) response. This identifier is useful for identifying messages. (However, to delete a message you need the message's *receipt handle*.) The maximum length of a message ID is 100 characters.

Receipt Handle

Every time you receive a message from a queue, you receive a *receipt handle* for that message. This handle is associated with the action of receiving the message, not with the message itself. To delete the message or to change the message visibility, you must provide the receipt handle (not the message ID). Thus, you must always receive a message before you can delete it (you can't put a message into the queue and then recall it). The maximum length of a receipt handle is 1,024 characters.

Important
If you receive a message more than once, each time you receive it, you get a different receipt handle. You must provide the most recently received receipt handle when you request to delete the message (otherwise, the message might not be deleted).

The following is an example of a receipt handle (broken across three lines).

```
1 MbZj6wDWli+JvwwJaBV+3dcjk2YW2vA3+STFFljTM8tJJg6HRG6PYSasuWXPJB+Cw
2 Lj1FjgXUv1uSj1gUPAWV66FU/WeR4mq2OKpEGYWbnLmpRCJVAyeMjeU5ZBdtcQ+QE
3 auMZc8ZRv37sIW2iJKq3M9MFx1YvV11A2x/KSbkJO=
```

Additional Identifiers for Amazon SQS FIFO Queues

For more information about the following identifiers, see Exactly-Once Processing and the *Amazon Simple Queue Service API Reference.*

Message Deduplication ID

The token used for deduplication of sent messages. If a message with a particular message deduplication ID is sent successfully, any messages sent with the same message deduplication ID are accepted successfully but aren't delivered during the 5-minute deduplication interval.

Message Group ID

The tag that specifies that a message belongs to a specific message group. Messages that belong to the same message group are always processed one by one, in a strict order relative to the message group (however, messages that belong to different message groups might be processed out of order).

Sequence Number

The large, non-consecutive number that Amazon SQS assigns to each message.

Amazon SQS Message Attributes

Amazon SQS lets you include structured metadata (such as timestamps, geospatial data, signatures, and identifiers) with messages using *message attributes*. Each message can have up to 10 attributes. Message attributes are optional and separate from the message body (however, they are sent alongside it). Your consumer can use message attributes to handle a message in a particular way without having to process the message body first. For information about sending messages with attributes using the AWS Management Console or the AWS SDK for Java, see Tutorial: Sending a Message with Attributes to an Amazon SQS Queue.

Topics

- Message Attribute Components
- Message Attribute Data Types
- Calculating the MD5 Message Digest for Message Attributes

Message Attribute Components

Important
All components of a message attribute are included in the 256 KB message size restriction.
The `Name`, `Type`, `Value`, and the message body must not be empty or null.

Each message attribute consists of the following components:

- **Name** – The message attribute name can contain the following characters: `A-Z`, `a-z`, `0-9`, underscore (`_`), hyphen (`-`), and period (`.`). The following restrictions apply:
  - Can be up to 256 characters long
  - Can't start with `AWS.` or `Amazon.` (or any casing variations)
  - Is case-sensitive
  - Must be unique among all attribute names for the message
  - Must not start or end with a period
  - Must not have periods in a sequence
- **Type** – The message attribute data type. Supported types include `String`, `Number`, and `Binary`. You can also add custom information for any data type. The data type has the same restrictions as the message body (for more information, see `[SendMessage](http://docs.aws.amazon.com/AWSSimpleQueueService/latest/APIReference/API_SendMessage.html)` in the *Amazon Simple Queue Service API Reference*). In addition, the following restrictions apply:
  - Can be up to 256 characters long
  - Is case-sensitive
- **Value** – The message attribute value. For `String` data types, the attribute values has the same restrictions as the message body.

Message Attribute Data Types

Message attribute data types instruct Amazon SQS how to handle the corresponding message attribute values. For example, if the type is `Number`, Amazon SQS validates numerical values.

Amazon SQS supports the logical data types `String`, `Number`, and `Binary` with optional custom data type labels with the format `.custom-data-type`

- **String** – `String` attributes can store Unicode text with UTF-8 binary encoding. For more information, see ASCII Printable Characters.
- **Number** – `Number` attributes can store positive or negative numerical values. A number can have up to 38 digits of precision, and it can be between 10^{-128} and 10^{+126}. **Note**
  Amazon SQS removes leading and trailing zeroes.
- **Binary** – Binary attributes can store any binary data such as compressed data, encrypted data, or images.

- **Custom** – To create a custom data type, append a custom-type label to any data type. For example:
  - `Number.byte`, `Number.short`, `Number.int`, and `Number.float` can help distinguish between number types.
  - `Binary.gif` and `Binary.png` can help distinguish between file types. **Note** Amazon SQS doesn't interpret, validate, or use the appended data.
    The custom-type label has the same restrictions as the message body.

Calculating the MD5 Message Digest for Message Attributes

If you use the AWS SDK for Java, you can skip this section. The `MessageMD5ChecksumHandler` class of the SDK for Java supports MD5 message digests for Amazon SQS message attributes.

If you use either the Query API or one of the AWS SDKs that doesn't support MD5 message digests for Amazon SQS message attributes, you must use the following guidelines to perform the MD5 message digest calculation.

Note
Always include custom data type suffixes in the MD5 message-digest calculation.

Overview

The following is an overview of the MD5 message digest calculation algorithm:

1. Sort all message attributes by name in ascending order.

2. Encode the individual parts of each attribute (`Name`, `Type`, and `Value`) into a buffer.

3. Compute the message digest of the entire buffer.

The following diagram shows the encoding of the MD5 message digest for a single message attribute:

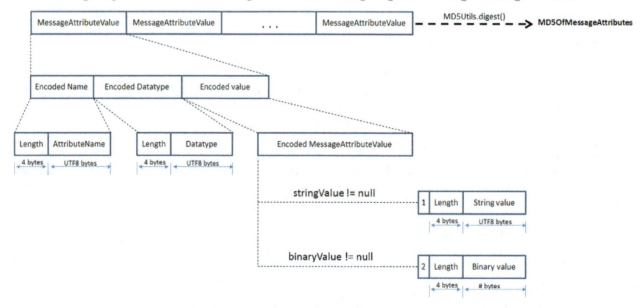

To encode a single Amazon SQS message attribute

1. Encode the name: the length (4 bytes) and the UTF-8 bytes of the name.

2. Encode the data type: the length (4 bytes) and the UTF-8 bytes of the data type.

3. Encode the transport type (`String` or `Binary`) of the value (1 byte). **Note**
   The logical data types `String` and `Number` use the `String` transport type.
   The logical data type `Binary` uses the `Binary` transport type.

   1. For the `String` transport type, encode 1.

   2. For the `Binary` transport type, encode 2.

4. Encode the attribute value.

   1. For the `String` transport type, encode the attribute value: the length (4 bytes) and the UTF-8 bytes of the value.

   2. For the `Binary` transport type, encode the attribute value: the length (4 bytes) and the raw bytes of the value..

Resources Required to Process Amazon SQS Messages

To help you estimate the resources you need to process queued messages, Amazon SQS can determine the approximate number of delayed, visible, and not visible messages in a queue. For more information about visibility, see Amazon SQS Visibility Timeout.

Note

For standard queues, the result is approximate because of the distributed architecture of Amazon SQS. In most cases, the count should be close to the actual number of messages in the queue.

For FIFO queues, the result is exact.

The following table lists the attribute name to use with the [GetQueueAttributes](http://docs.aws.amazon.com/AWSSimpleQueueService/latest/APIReference/API_GetQueueAttributes.html) action:

Task	Attribute Name
Get the approximate number of messages in a queue.	ApproximateNumberOfMessages
Get the approximate number of messages that are pending being added to a queue.	ApproximateNumberOfMessagesDelayed
Get the approximate number of in flight messages in a queue.	ApproximateNumberOfMessagesNotVisible

Amazon SQS Cost Allocation Tags

To organize and identify your Amazon SQS queues for cost allocation, you can add metadata *tags* that identify a queue's purpose, owner, or environment. —this is especially useful when you have many queues. For information about managing Amazon SQS queue tags using the AWS Management Console or the AWS SDK for Java (and the [TagQueue](http://docs.aws.amazon.com/AWSSimpleQueueService/latest/APIReference/API_TagQueue.html), [UntagQueue](http://docs.aws.amazon.com/AWSSimpleQueueService/latest/APIReference/API_UntagQueue.html), and [ListQueueTags](http://docs.aws.amazon.com/AWSSimpleQueueService/latest/APIReference/API_ListQueueTags.html) actions), see the Adding, Updating, and Removing Tags from an Amazon SQS Queue tutorial.

You can use cost allocation tags to organize your AWS bill to reflect your own cost structure. To do this, sign up to get your AWS account bill to include tag keys and values. For more information, see Setting Up a Monthly Cost Allocation Report in the *AWS Billing and Cost Management User Guide*.

Each tag consists of a key-value pair that you define. For example, you can easily identify your *production* and *testing* queues if you tag your queues as follows:

Queue	Key	Value
MyQueueA	QueueType	Production
MyQueueB	QueueType	Testing

Note
When you use queue tags, keep the following guidelines in mind:
We don't recommend adding more than 50 tags to a queue. Tags don't have any semantic meaning. Amazon SQS interprets tags as character strings. Tags are case-sensitive. A new tag with a key identical to that of an existing tag overwrites the existing tag. Tagging actions are limited to 5 TPS per AWS account. If your application requires a higher throughput, file a technical support request. For a full list of tag restrictions, see Limits Related to Queues.

You can't add tags to a new queue when you create it using the AWS Management Console (you *can* add tags after the queue is created). However, you can add, update, or remove queue tags at any time using the Amazon SQS actions.

Amazon SQS Long Polling

Long polling helps reduce the cost of using Amazon SQS by eliminating the number of empty responses (when there are no messages available for a [ReceiveMessage](http://docs.aws.amazon.com/AWSSimpleQueueService/latest/APIReference/API_ReceiveMessage.html) request) and false empty responses (when messages are available but aren't included in a response). For information about enabling long polling for a new or existing queue using the AWS Management Console or the AWS SDK for Java (and the [CreateQueue](http://docs.aws.amazon.com/AWSSimpleQueueService/latest/APIReference/API_CreateQueue.html), [SetQueueAttributes](http://docs.aws.amazon.com/AWSSimpleQueueService/latest/APIReference/API_SetQueueAttributes.html), and [ReceiveMessage](http://docs.aws.amazon.com/AWSSimpleQueueService/latest/APIReference/API_ReceiveMessage.html) actions), see the Tutorial: Configuring Long Polling for an Amazon SQS Queue tutorial. For best practices, see Setting Up Long Polling.

Long polling offers the following benefits:

- Eliminate empty responses by allowing Amazon SQS to wait until a message is available in a queue before sending a response. Unless the connection times out, the response to the ReceiveMessage request contains at least one of the available messages, up to the maximum number of messages specified in the ReceiveMessage action.
- Eliminate false empty responses by querying all—rather than a subset of—Amazon SQS servers.
- Return messages as soon as they become available.

Differences Between Long and Short Polling

By default, Amazon SQS uses *short polling*, querying only a subset of its servers (based on a weighted random distribution), to determine whether any messages are available for a response.

Short polling occurs when the WaitTimeSeconds parameter of a [ReceiveMessage](http://docs.aws.amazon.com/AWSSimpleQueueService/latest/APIReference/API_ReceiveMessage.html) request is set to 0 in one of two ways:

- The ReceiveMessage call sets WaitTimeSeconds to 0.
- The ReceiveMessage call doesn't set WaitTimeSeconds, but the queue attribute http://docs.aws.amazon.com/AWSSimpleQueueService/latest/APIReference/API_SetQueueAttributes.html is set to 0.

Note

For the WaitTimeSeconds parameter of the ReceiveMessage action, a value set between 1 and 20 has priority over any value set for the queue attribute ReceiveMessageWaitTimeSeconds.

110

Amazon SQS Dead-Letter Queues

Amazon SQS supports *dead-letter queues*, which other queues (*source queues*) can target for messages that can't be processed (consumed) successfully. Dead-letter queues are useful for debugging your application or messaging system because they let you isolate problematic messages to determine why their processing doesn't succeed. For information about creating a queue and configuring a dead-letter queue for it using the AWS Management Console or the AWS SDK for Java (and the [CreateQueue](http://docs.aws.amazon.com/AWSSimpleQueueService/latest/APIReference/API_CreateQueue.html), [SetQueueAttributes](http://docs.aws.amazon.com/AWSSimpleQueueService/latest/APIReference/API_SetQueueAttributes.html), and [GetQueueAttributes](http://docs.aws.amazon.com/AWSSimpleQueueService/latest/APIReference/API_GetQueueAttributes.html) actions), see Tutorial: Configuring an Amazon SQS Dead-Letter Queue.

Topics

- How Do Dead-Letter Queues Work?
- What are the Benefits of Dead-Letter Queues?
- How Do Different Queue Types Handle Message Failure?
- When Should I Use a Dead-Letter Queue?
- Troubleshooting Dead-Letter Queues

How Do Dead-Letter Queues Work?

Sometimes, messages can't be processed because of a variety of possible issues, such as erroneous conditions within the producer or consumer application or an unexpected state change that causes an issue with your application code. For example, if a user places a web order with a particular product ID, but the product ID is deleted, the web store's code fails and displays an error, and the message with the order request is sent to a dead-letter queue.

Occasionally, producers and consumers might fail to interpret aspects of the protocol that they use to communicate, causing message corruption or loss. Also, the consumer's hardware errors might corrupt message payload.

The *redrive policy* specifies the *source queue*, the *dead-letter queue*, and the conditions under which Amazon SQS moves messages from the former to the latter if the consumer of the source queue fails to process a message a specified number of times. For example, if the source queue has a redrive policy with `maxReceiveCount` set to 5, and the consumer of the source queue receives a message 5 times without ever deleting it, Amazon SQS moves the message to the dead-letter queue.

To specify a dead-letter queue, you can use the AWS Management Console or the AWS SDK for Java. You must do this for each queue that sends messages to a dead-letter queue. Multiple queues can target a single dead-letter queue. For more information, see Tutorial: Configuring an Amazon SQS Dead-Letter Queue and the `RedrivePolicy` attribute of the `CreateQueue` or `SetQueueAttributes` action.

Important

The dead-letter queue of a FIFO queue must also be a FIFO queue. Similarly, the dead-letter queue of a standard queue must also be a standard queue.

You must use the same AWS account to create the dead-letter queue and the other queues that send messages to the dead-letter queue. Also, dead-letter queues must reside in the same region as the other queues that use the dead-letter queue. For example, if you create a queue in the US East (Ohio) region and you want to use a dead-letter queue with that queue, the second queue must also be in the US East (Ohio) region.

The expiration of a message is always based on its original enqueue timestamp. When a message is moved to a dead-letter queue, the enqueue timestamp remains unchanged. For example, if a message spends 1 day in the original queue before being moved to a dead-letter queue, and the retention period of the dead-letter queue is set to 4 days, the message is deleted from the dead-letter queue after 3 days. Thus, it is a best practice to always set the retention period of a dead-letter queue to be longer than the retention period of the original queue.

What are the Benefits of Dead-Letter Queues?

The main task of a dead-letter queue is handling message failure. A dead-letter queue lets you set aside and isolate messages that can't be processed correctly to determine why their processing didn't succeed. Setting up a dead-letter queue allows you to do the following:

- Configure an alarm for any messages delivered to a dead-letter queue.
- Examine logs for exceptions that might have caused messages to be delivered to a dead-letter queue.
- Analyze the contents of messages delivered to a dead-letter queue to diagnose software or the producer's or consumer's hardware issues.
- Determine whether you have given your consumer sufficient time to process messages.

How Do Different Queue Types Handle Message Failure?

Standard Queues

Standard queues keep processing messages until the expiration of the retention period. This ensures continuous processing of messages, which minimizes the chances of your queue being blocked by messages that can't be processed. It also ensures fast recovery for your queue.

In a system that processes thousands of messages, having a large number of messages that the consumer repeatedly fails to acknowledge and delete might increase costs and place extra load on the hardware. Instead of trying to process failing messages until they expire, it is better to move them to a dead-letter queue after a few processing attempts.

Note
Standard queues allow a high number of in-flight messages. If the majority of your messages can't be consumed and aren't sent to a dead-letter queue, your rate of processing valid messages can slow down. Thus, to maintain the efficiency of your queue, you must ensure that your application handles message processing correctly.

FIFO Queues

FIFO queues ensure exactly-once processing by consuming messages in sequence from a message group. Thus, although the consumer can continue to retrieve ordered messages from another message group, the first message group remains unavailable until the message blocking the queue is processed successfully.

Note
FIFO queues allow a lower number of in-flight messages. Thus, to ensure that your FIFO queue doesn't get blocked by a message, you must ensure that your application handles message processing correctly.

When Should I Use a Dead-Letter Queue?

✔ Do use dead-letter queues with standard queues. You should always take advantage of dead-letter queues when your applications don't depend on ordering. Dead-letter queues can help you troubleshoot incorrect message transmission operations.

Note
Even when you use dead-letter queues, you should continue to monitor your queues and retry sending messages that fail for transient reasons.

✔ Do use dead-letter queues to decrease the number of messages and to reduce the possibility of exposing your system to *poison-pill messages* (messages that can be received but can't be processed).

✘ Don't use a dead-letter queue with standard queues when you want to be able to keep retrying the transmission of a message indefinitely. For example, don't use a dead-letter queue if your program must wait for a dependent process to become active or available.

✘ Don't use a dead-letter queue with a FIFO queue if you don't want to break the exact order of messages or operations. For example, don't use a dead-letter queue with instructions in an Edit Decision List (EDL) for a video editing suite, where changing the order of edits changes the context of subsequent edits.

Troubleshooting Dead-Letter Queues

In some cases, Amazon SQS dead-letter queues might not always behave as expected. This section gives an overview of common issues and shows how to resolve them.

Viewing Messages using the AWS Management Console Might Cause Messages to be Moved to a Dead-Letter Queue

Amazon SQS counts viewing a message in the AWS Management Console against the corresponding queue's redrive policy. Thus, if you view a message in the AWS Management Console the number of times specified in the corresponding queue's redrive policy, the message is moved to the corresponding queue's dead-letter queue.

To adjust this behavior, you can do one of the following:

- Increase the **Maximum Receives** setting for the corresponding queue's redrive policy.
- Avoid viewing the corresponding queue's messages in the AWS Management Console.

The `NumberOfMessagesSent` and `NumberOfMessagesReceived` for a Dead-Letter Queue Don't Match

If you send a message to a dead-letter queue manually, it is captured by the `NumberOfMessagesSent` metric. However, a message is sent to a dead-letter queue as a result of a failed processing attempt, it isn't captured by this metric. Thus, it is possible for the values of `NumberOfMessagesSent` and `NumberOfMessagesReceived` to be different.

Amazon SQS Visibility Timeout

When a consumer receives and processes a message from a queue, the message remains in the queue. Amazon SQS doesn't automatically delete the message. Because Amazon SQS is a distributed system, there's no guarantee that the consumer actually receives the message (for example, due to a connectivity issue, or due to an issue in the consumer application). Thus, the consumer must delete the message from the queue after receiving and processing it.

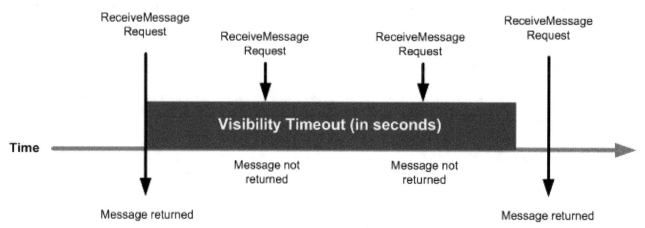

Immediately after a message is received, it remains in the queue. To prevent other consumers from processing the message again, Amazon SQS sets a *visibility timeout*, a period of time during which Amazon SQS prevents other consumers from receiving and processing the message. The default visibility timeout for a message is 30 seconds. The maximum is 12 hours. For information about configuring visibility timeout for a queue using the AWS Management Console and for single or multiple messages using the AWS SDK for Java (and the [SetQueueAttributes](http://docs.aws.amazon.com/AWSSimpleQueueService/latest/APIReference/API_SetQueueAttributes.html), [GetQueueAttributes](http://docs.aws.amazon.com/AWSSimpleQueueService/latest/APIReference/API_GetQueueAttributes.html), [ReceiveMessage](http://docs.aws.amazon.com/AWSSimpleQueueService/latest/APIReference/API_ReceiveMessage.html), [ChangeMessageVisibility](http://docs.aws.amazon.com/AWSSimpleQueueService/latest/APIReference/API_ChangeMessageVisibility.html), and [ChangeMessageVisibilityBatch](http://docs.aws.amazon.com/AWSSimpleQueueService/latest/APIReference/API_ChangeMessageVisibilityBatch.html) actions), see Tutorial: Configuring Visibility Timeout for an Amazon SQS Queue.

Note
For standard queues, the visibility timeout isn't a guarantee against receiving a message twice. For more information, see At-Least-Once Delivery.
FIFO queues allow the producer or consumer to attempt multiple retries:
If the producer detects a failed **SendMessage** action, it can retry sending as many times as necessary, using the same message deduplication ID. Assuming that the producer receives at least one acknowledgement before the deduplication interval expires, multiple retries neither affect the ordering of messages nor introduce duplicates. If the consumer detects a failed **ReceiveMessage** action, it can retry as many times as necessary, using the same receive request attempt ID. Assuming that the consumer receives at least one acknowledgement before the visibility timeout expires, multiple retries don't affect the ordering of messages. When you receive a message with a message group ID, no more messages for the same message group ID are returned unless you delete the message or it becomes visible.

Topics

- Inflight Messages
- Setting the Visibility Timeout
- Changing the Visibility Timeout for a Message
- Terminating the Visibility Timeout for a Message

Inflight Messages

An Amazon SQS message has three basic states: 1. Sent to a queue by a producer, 2. Received from the queue by a consumer, and 3. Deleted from the queue. A message is considered to be *in flight* after it is received from a queue by a consumer, but not yet deleted from the queue (that is, between states 2 and 3). There is no limit to the number of messages in a queue which are between states 1 and 2.

For standard queues, there can be a maximum of 120,000 inflight messages (received from a queue by a consumer, but not yet deleted from the queue). If you reach this limit, Amazon SQS returns the `OverLimit` error message. To avoid reaching the limit, you should delete messages from the queue after they're processed. You can also increase the number of queues you use to process your messages. To request a limit increase, file a support request.

For FIFO queues, there can be a maximum of 20,000 inflight messages (received from a queue by a consumer, but not yet deleted from the queue). If you reach this limit, Amazon SQS returns no error messages.

Setting the Visibility Timeout

The visibility timeout begins when Amazon SQS returns a message. During this time, the consumer processes and deletes the message. However, if the consumer fails before deleting the message and your system doesn't call the [DeleteMessage](http://docs.aws.amazon.com/AWSSimpleQueueService/latest/APIReference/API_DeleteMessage.html) action for that message before the visibility timeout expires, the message becomes visible to other consumers and the message is received again. If a message must be received only once, your consumer should delete it within the duration of the visibility timeout.

Every Amazon SQS queue has the default visibility timeout setting of 30 seconds. You can change this setting for the entire queue. Typically, you should set the visibility timeout to the maximum time that it takes your application to process and delete a message from the queue. When receiving messages, you can also set a special visibility timeout for the returned messages without changing the overall queue timeout. For more information, see the best practices in the Processing Messages in a Timely Manner section.

If you don't know how long it takes to process a message, create a *heartbeat* for your consumer process: Specify the initial visibility timeout (for example, 2 minutes) and then—as long as your consumer still works on the message—keep extending the visibility timeout by 2 minutes every minute.

Changing the Visibility Timeout for a Message

When you receive a message from a queue and begin to process it, the visibility timeout for the queue may be insufficient (for example, you might need to process and delete a message). You can shorten or extend a message's visibility by specifying a new timeout value using the [ChangeMessageVisibility](http://docs.aws.amazon.com/AWSSimpleQueueService/latest/APIReference/API_ChangeMessageVisibility.html) action.

For example, if the default timeout for a queue is 60 seconds, 15 seconds have elapsed since you received the message, and you send a `ChangeMessageVisibility` call with `VisibilityTimeout` set to 10 seconds, the 10 seconds begin to count from the time that you make the `ChangeMessageVisibility` call. Thus, any attempt to change the visibility timeout or to delete that message 10 seconds after you initially change the visibility timeout (a total of 25 seconds) might result in an error.

Note
The new timeout period takes effect from the time you call the `ChangeMessageVisibility` action. In addition, the new timeout period applies only to the particular receipt of the message. `ChangeMessageVisibility` doesn't affect the timeout of later receipts of the message or later queues.

Terminating the Visibility Timeout for a Message

When you receive a message from a queue, you might find that you actually don't want to process and delete that message. Amazon SQS allows you to terminate the visibility timeout for a specific message. This makes the message immediately visible to other components in the system and available for processing.

To terminate a message's visibility timeout after calling `ReceiveMessage`, call http://docs.aws.amazon.com/ AWSSimpleQueueService/latest/APIReference/API_ChangeMessageVisibility.html with `VisibilityTimeout` set to 0 seconds.

Amazon SQS Delay Queues

Delay queues let you postpone the delivery of new messages to a queue for a number of seconds. If you create a delay queue, any messages that you send to the queue remain invisible to consumers for the duration of the delay period. The minimum delay for a queue is 0 seconds. The maximum is 15 minutes. For information about configuring delay queues using the AWS Management Console or the AWS SDK for Java (and the [SetQueueAttributes](http://docs.aws.amazon.com/AWSSimpleQueueService/latest/APIReference/API_SetQueueAttributes.html) action), see Tutorial: Configuring an Amazon SQS Delay Queue.

Note

For standard queues, the per-queue delay setting is *not retroactive*—changing the setting doesn't affect the delay of messages already in the queue.

For FIFO queues, the per-queue delay setting is *retroactive*—changing the setting affects the delay of messages already in the queue.

Delay queues are similar to visibility timeouts because both features make messages unavailable to consumers for a specific period of time. The difference between the two is that, for delay queues, a message is hidden *when it is first added to queue*, whereas for visibility timeouts a message is hidden *only after it is consumed from the queue*. The following diagram illustrates the relationship between delay queues and visibility timeouts.

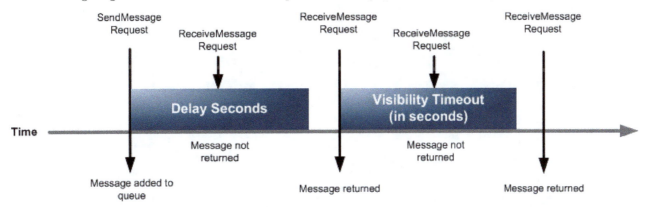

To set delay seconds on *individual messages*, rather than on an entire queue, use message timers to allow Amazon SQS to use the message timer's `DelaySeconds` value instead of the delay queue's `DelaySeconds` value.

117

Amazon SQS Message Timers

Message timers let you specify an initial invisibility period for a message added to a queue. For example, if you send a message with a 45-second timer, the message isn't visible to consumers for its first 45 seconds in the queue. The default is 0 seconds. For information about sending messages with timers using the AWS Management Console or the AWS SDK for Java (and the [SetQueueAttributes](http://docs.aws.amazon.com/AWSSimpleQueueService/latest/APIReference/API_SetQueueAttributes.html) action), see Tutorial: Sending a Message with a Timer to an Amazon SQS Queue.

Note
FIFO queues don't support timers on individual messages.

To set a delay period on *an entire queue*, rather than on individual messages, use delay queues. A message timer setting for an individual message overrides any `DelaySeconds` value on an Amazon SQS delay queue.

Managing Large Amazon SQS Messages Using Amazon S3

You can use Amazon S3 and the Amazon SQS Extended Client Library for Java to manage Amazon SQS messages. This is especially useful for storing and consuming messages up to 2 GB in size. Unless your application requires repeatedly creating queues and leaving them inactive or storing large amounts of data in your queue, consider using Amazon S3 for storing your data.

You can use the Amazon SQS Extended Client Library for Java library to do the following:

- Specify whether messages are always stored in Amazon S3 or only when the size of a message exceeds 256 KB.
- Send a message that references a single message object stored in an Amazon S3 bucket.
- Get the corresponding message object from an Amazon S3 bucket.
- Delete the corresponding message object from an Amazon S3 bucket.

Note
The SDK for Java and Amazon SQS Extended Client Library for Java require the J2SE Development Kit 8.0 or later.
You can use the Amazon SQS Extended Client Library for Java to manage Amazon SQS messages using Amazon S3. However, you can't do this using the AWS CLI, the Amazon SQS console, the Amazon SQS HTTP API, or any of the AWS SDKs—except for the SDK for Java.

Working Java Example for Using Amazon S3 for Large Amazon SQS Messages

Prerequisites

Add the `amazon-sqs-java-extended-client-lib.jar`, `aws-java-sdk-sqs.jar`, and `aws-java-sdk-s3.jar` packages to your Java class path. The following example shows these dependencies in a Maven project `pom.xml` file.

```xml
<dependencies>
    <dependency>
        <groupId>com.amazonaws</groupId>
        <artifactId>amazon-sqs-java-extended-client-lib</artifactId>
        <version>1.0.1</version>
    </dependency>
    <dependency>
        <groupId>com.amazonaws</groupId>
        <artifactId>aws-java-sdk-sqs</artifactId>
        <version>LATEST</version>
    </dependency>
    <dependency>
        <groupId>com.amazonaws</groupId>
        <artifactId>aws-java-sdk-s3</artifactId>
        <version>LATEST</version>
    </dependency>
</dependencies>
```

SQSExtendedClientExample.java

The following example code creates an Amazon S3 bucket with a random name and adds a lifecycle rule to permanently delete objects after 14 days. Next, the code creates a queue named `MyQueue` and sends a random message more than 256 KB in size to the queue; the message is stored in the Amazon S3 bucket. Finally, the code consumes the message, returns information about the message, and deletes the message, the queue, and the bucket.

```java
/*
 * Copyright 2010-2018 Amazon.com, Inc. or its affiliates. All Rights Reserved.
 *
 * Licensed under the Apache License, Version 2.0 (the "License").
 * You may not use this file except in compliance with the License.
 * A copy of the License is located at
 *
 *  https://aws.amazon.com/apache2.0
 *
 * or in the "license" file accompanying this file. This file is distributed
 * on an "AS IS" BASIS, WITHOUT WARRANTIES OR CONDITIONS OF ANY KIND, either
 * express or implied. See the License for the specific language governing
 * permissions and limitations under the License.
 *
 */

import com.amazon.sqs.javamessaging.AmazonSQSExtendedClient;
import com.amazon.sqs.javamessaging.ExtendedClientConfiguration;
```

```
19 import com.amazonaws.services.s3.AmazonS3;
20 import com.amazonaws.services.s3.AmazonS3ClientBuilder;
21 import com.amazonaws.services.s3.model.*;
22 import com.amazonaws.services.sqs.AmazonSQS;
23 import com.amazonaws.services.sqs.AmazonSQSClientBuilder;
24 import com.amazonaws.services.sqs.model.*;
25 import org.joda.time.DateTime;
26 import org.joda.time.format.DateTimeFormat;
27
28 import java.util.Arrays;
29 import java.util.List;
30 import java.util.UUID;
31
32 public class SQSExtendedClientExample {
33
34     // Create an Amazon S3 bucket with a random name.
35     private final static String S3_BUCKET_NAME = UUID.randomUUID() + "-"
36             + DateTimeFormat.forPattern("yyMMdd-hhmmss").print(new DateTime());
37
38     public static void main(String[] args) {
39
40         /*
41          * Create a new instance of the builder with all defaults (credentials
42          * and region) set automatically. For more information, see
43          * [Creating Service Clients](http://docs.aws.amazon.com/sdk-for-java/v1/developer-guide
44                /creating-clients.html) in the AWS SDK for Java Developer Guide.
44          */
45         final AmazonS3 s3 = AmazonS3ClientBuilder.defaultClient();
46
47         /*
48          * Set the Amazon S3 bucket name, and then set a lifecycle rule on the
49          * bucket to permanently delete objects 14 days after each object's
50          * creation date.
51          */
52         final BucketLifecycleConfiguration.Rule expirationRule =
53                 new BucketLifecycleConfiguration.Rule();
54         expirationRule.withExpirationInDays(14).withStatus("Enabled");
55         final BucketLifecycleConfiguration lifecycleConfig =
56                 new BucketLifecycleConfiguration().withRules(expirationRule);
57
58         // Create the bucket and allow message objects to be stored in the bucket.
59         s3.createBucket(S3_BUCKET_NAME);
60         s3.setBucketLifecycleConfiguration(S3_BUCKET_NAME, lifecycleConfig);
61         System.out.println("Bucket created and configured.");
62
63         /*
64          * Set the Amazon SQS extended client configuration with large payload
65          * support enabled.
66          */
67         final ExtendedClientConfiguration extendedClientConfig =
68                 new ExtendedClientConfiguration()
69                         .withLargePayloadSupportEnabled(s3, S3_BUCKET_NAME);
70
71         final AmazonSQS sqsExtended =
```

```
72          new AmazonSQSExtendedClient(AmazonSQSClientBuilder
73                  .defaultClient(), extendedClientConfig);
74
75      /*
76       * Create a long string of characters for the message object which will
77       * be stored in the bucket.
78       */
79      int stringLength = 300000;
80      char[] chars = new char[stringLength];
81      Arrays.fill(chars, 'x');
82      final String myLongString = new String(chars);
83
84      // Create a message queue for this example.
85      final String QueueName = "MyQueue" + UUID.randomUUID().toString();
86      final CreateQueueRequest createQueueRequest =
87              new CreateQueueRequest(QueueName);
88      final String myQueueUrl = sqsExtended
89              .createQueue(createQueueRequest).getQueueUrl();
90      System.out.println("Queue created.");
91
92      // Send the message.
93      final SendMessageRequest myMessageRequest =
94              new SendMessageRequest(myQueueUrl, myLongString);
95      sqsExtended.sendMessage(myMessageRequest);
96      System.out.println("Sent the message.");
97
98      // Receive the message.
99      final ReceiveMessageRequest receiveMessageRequest =
100             new ReceiveMessageRequest(myQueueUrl);
101     List<Message> messages = sqsExtended
102             .receiveMessage(receiveMessageRequest).getMessages();
103
104     // Print information about the message.
105     for (Message message : messages) {
106         System.out.println("\nMessage received.");
107         System.out.println("  ID: " + message.getMessageId());
108         System.out.println("  Receipt handle: " + message.getReceiptHandle());
109         System.out.println("  Message body (first 5 characters): "
110                 + message.getBody().substring(0, 5));
111     }
112
113     // Delete the message, the queue, and the bucket.
114     final String messageReceiptHandle = messages.get(0).getReceiptHandle();
115     sqsExtended.deleteMessage(new DeleteMessageRequest(myQueueUrl,
116             messageReceiptHandle));
117     System.out.println("Deleted the message.");
118
119     sqsExtended.deleteQueue(new DeleteQueueRequest(myQueueUrl));
120     System.out.println("Deleted the queue.");
121
122     deleteBucketAndAllContents(s3);
123     System.out.println("Deleted the bucket.");
124 }
125
```

```
126    private static void deleteBucketAndAllContents(AmazonS3 client) {
127
128        ObjectListing objectListing = client.listObjects(S3_BUCKET_NAME);
129
130        while (true) {
131            for (S3ObjectSummary objectSummary : objectListing
132                    .getObjectSummaries()) {
133                client.deleteObject(S3_BUCKET_NAME, objectSummary.getKey());
134            }
135
136            if (objectListing.isTruncated()) {
137                objectListing = client.listNextBatchOfObjects(objectListing);
138            } else {
139                break;
140            }
141        }
142
143        final VersionListing list = client.listVersions(
144                new ListVersionsRequest().withBucketName(S3_BUCKET_NAME));
145
146        for (S3VersionSummary s : list.getVersionSummaries()) {
147            client.deleteVersion(S3_BUCKET_NAME, s.getKey(), s.getVersionId());
148        }
149
150        client.deleteBucket(S3_BUCKET_NAME);
151    }
152 }
```

Working with JMS and Amazon SQS

The Amazon SQS Java Messaging Library is a JMS interface for Amazon SQS that lets you take advantage of Amazon SQS in applications that already use JMS. The interface lets you use Amazon SQS as the JMS provider with minimal code changes. Together with the AWS SDK for Java, the Amazon SQS Java Messaging Library lets you create JMS connections and sessions, as well as producers and consumers that send and receive messages to and from Amazon SQS queues.

The library supports sending and receiving messages to a queue (the JMS point-to-point model) according to the JMS 1.1 specification. The library supports sending text, byte, or object messages synchronously to Amazon SQS queues. The library also supports receiving objects synchronously or asynchronously.

For information about features of the Amazon SQS Java Messaging Library that support the JMS 1.1 specification, see Supported JMS 1.1 Implementations and the Amazon SQS FAQs.

Topics

- Prerequisites
- Getting Started with the Amazon SQS Java Messaging Library
- Using the JMS Client with Other Amazon SQS Clients
- Working Java Example for Using JMS with Amazon SQS Standard Queues
- Supported JMS 1.1 Implementations

Prerequisites

Before you begin, you must have the following prerequisites:

- **SDK for Java**

  There are two ways to include the SDK for Java in your project:

  - Download and install the SDK for Java.

  - Use Maven to get the Amazon SQS Java Messaging Library. **Note**
    The SDK for Java is included as a dependency.
    The SDK for Java and Amazon SQS Extended Client Library for Java require the J2SE Development Kit 8.0 or later.

  For information about downloading the SDK for Java, see SDK for Java.

- **Amazon SQS Java Messaging Library**

  If you don't use Maven, you must add the `amazon-sqs-java-messaging-lib.jar` package to the Java class path. For information about downloading the library, see Amazon SQS Java Messaging Library.
  Note
  The Amazon SQS Java Messaging Library includes support for Maven and the Spring Framework.
  For code samples that use Maven, the Spring Framework, and the Amazon SQS Java Messaging Library, see Working Java Example for Using JMS with Amazon SQS Standard Queues.

```
1 <dependency>
2   <groupId>com.amazonaws</groupId>
3   <artifactId>amazon-sqs-java-messaging-lib</artifactId>
4   <version>1.0.4</version>
5   <type>jar</type>
6 </dependency>
```

- **Amazon SQS Queue**

  Create a queue using the AWS Management Console for Amazon SQS, the `CreateQueue` API, or the wrapped Amazon SQS client included in the Amazon SQS Java Messaging Library.

  - For information about creating a queue with Amazon SQS using either the AWS Management Console or the `CreateQueue` API, see Creating a Queue.
  - For information about using the Amazon SQS Java Messaging Library, see Getting Started with the Amazon SQS Java Messaging Library.

Getting Started with the Amazon SQS Java Messaging Library

To get started using JMS with Amazon SQS, use the code examples in this section. The following sections show how to create a JMS connection and a session, and how to send and receive a message.

The wrapped Amazon SQS client object included in the Amazon SQS Java Messaging Library checks if an Amazon SQS queue exists. If the queue doesn't exist, the client creates it.

Creating a JMS Connection

1. Create a connection factory and call the `createConnection` method against the factory.

```
1 // Create a new connection factory with all defaults (credentials and region) set
     automatically
2 SQSConnectionFactory connectionFactory = new SQSConnectionFactory(
3         new ProviderConfiguration(),
4         AmazonSQSClientBuilder.defaultClient()
5         );
6
7 // Create the connection.
8 SQSConnection connection = connectionFactory.createConnection();
```

The `SQSConnection` class extends `javax.jms.Connection`. Together with the JMS standard connection methods, `SQSConnection` offers additional methods, such as `getAmazonSQSClient` and `getWrappedAmazonSQSClient`. Both methods let you perform administrative operations not included in the JMS specification, such as creating new queues. However, the `getWrappedAmazonSQSClient` method also provides a wrapped version of the Amazon SQS client used by the current connection. The wrapper transforms every exception from the client into an `JMSException`, allowing it to be more easily used by existing code that expects `JMSException` occurrences.

2. You can use the client objects returned from `getAmazonSQSClient` and `getWrappedAmazonSQSClient` to perform administrative operations not included in the JMS specification (for example, you can create an Amazon SQS queue).

   If you have existing code that expects JMS exceptions, then you should use `getWrappedAmazonSQSClient`:

   - If you use `getWrappedAmazonSQSClient`, the returned client object transforms all exceptions into JMS exceptions.
   - If you use `getAmazonSQSClient`, the exceptions are all Amazon SQS exceptions.

Creating an Amazon SQS Queue

The wrapped client object checks if an Amazon SQS queue exists.

If a queue doesn't exist, the client creates it. If the queue does exist, the function doesn't return anything. For more information, see the "Create the queue if needed" section in the TextMessageSender.java example.

To create a standard queue

```
1 // Get the wrapped client
2 AmazonSQSMessagingClientWrapper client = connection.getWrappedAmazonSQSClient();
3
4 // Create an SQS queue named MyQueue, if it doesn't already exist
5 if (!client.queueExists("MyQueue")) {
6     client.createQueue("MyQueue");
```

```
7 }
```

To create a FIFO queue

```
1 // Get the wrapped client
2 AmazonSQSMessagingClientWrapper client = connection.getWrappedAmazonSQSClient();
3
4 // Create an Amazon SQS FIFO queue named MyQueue.fifo, if it doesn't already exist
5 if (!client.queueExists("MyQueue.fifo")) {
6     Map<String, String> attributes = new HashMap<String, String>();
7     attributes.put("FifoQueue", "true");
8     attributes.put("ContentBasedDeduplication", "true");
9     client.createQueue(new CreateQueueRequest().withQueueName("MyQueue.fifo").withAttributes(
            attributes));
10 }
```

Note

The name of a FIFO queue must end with the `.fifo` suffix.

For more information about the `ContentBasedDeduplication` attribute, see Exactly-Once Processing.

Sending Messages Synchronously

1. When the connection and the underlying Amazon SQS queue are ready, create a nontransacted JMS session with `AUTO_ACKNOWLEDGE` mode.

```
1 // Create the nontransacted session with AUTO_ACKNOWLEDGE mode
2 Session session = connection.createSession(false, Session.AUTO_ACKNOWLEDGE);
```

2. To send a text message to the queue, create a JMS queue identity and a message producer.

```
1 // Create a queue identity and specify the queue name to the session
2 Queue queue = session.createQueue("MyQueue");
3
4 // Create a producer for the 'MyQueue'
5 MessageProducer producer = session.createProducer(queue);
```

3. Create a text message and send it to the queue.

   - To send a message to a standard queue, you don't need to set any additional parameters.

```
1 // Create the text message
2 TextMessage message = session.createTextMessage("Hello World!");
3
4 // Send the message
5 producer.send(message);
6 System.out.println("JMS Message " + message.getJMSMessageID());
```

   - To send a message to a FIFO queue, you must set the message group ID. You can also set a message deduplication ID. For more information, see Key Terms.

```
1 // Create the text message
2 TextMessage message = session.createTextMessage("Hello World!");
3
4 // Set the message group ID
5 message.setStringProperty("JMSXGroupID", "Default");
6
7 // You can also set a custom message deduplication ID
8 // message.setStringProperty("JMS_SQS_DeduplicationId", "hello");
```

```
 9 // Here, it's not needed because content-based deduplication is enabled for the queue
10
11 // Send the message
12 producer.send(message);
13 System.out.println("JMS Message " + message.getJMSMessageID());
14 System.out.println("JMS Message Sequence Number " + message.getStringProperty("
       JMS_SQS_SequenceNumber"));
```

Receiving Messages Synchronously

1. To receive messages, create a consumer for the same queue and invoke the **start** method.

   You can call the **start** method on the connection at any time. However, the consumer doesn't begin to receive messages until you call it.

```
1 // Create a consumer for the 'MyQueue'
2 MessageConsumer consumer = session.createConsumer(queue);
3 // Start receiving incoming messages
4 connection.start();
```

2. Call the **receive** method on the consumer with a timeout set to 1 second, and then print the contents of the received message.

   - After receiving a message from a standard queue, you can access the contents of the message.

```
1 // Receive a message from 'MyQueue' and wait up to 1 second
2 Message receivedMessage = consumer.receive(1000);
3
4 // Cast the received message as TextMessage and display the text
5 if (receivedMessage != null) {
6     System.out.println("Received: " + ((TextMessage) receivedMessage).getText());
7 }
```

   - After receiving a message from a FIFO queue, you can access the contents of the message and other, FIFO-specific message attributes, such as the message group ID, message deduplication ID, and sequence number. For more information, see Key Terms.

```
1 // Receive a message from 'MyQueue' and wait up to 1 second
2 Message receivedMessage = consumer.receive(1000);
3
4 // Cast the received message as TextMessage and display the text
5 if (receivedMessage != null) {
6     System.out.println("Received: " + ((TextMessage) receivedMessage).getText());
7     System.out.println("Group id: " + receivedMessage.getStringProperty("JMSXGroupID"))
           ;
8     System.out.println("Message deduplication id: " + receivedMessage.getStringProperty
           ("JMS_SQS_DeduplicationId"));
9     System.out.println("Message sequence number: " + receivedMessage.getStringProperty
           ("JMS_SQS_SequenceNumber"));
10 }
```

3. Close the connection and the session.

```
1 // Close the connection (and the session).
2 connection.close();
```

The output looks similar to the following:

```
1 JMS Message ID:8example-588b-44e5-bbcf-d816example2
2 Received: Hello World!
```

Note

You can use the Spring Framework to initialize these objects.

For additional information, see `SpringExampleConfiguration.xml`, `SpringExample.java`, and the other helper classes in `ExampleConfiguration.java` and `ExampleCommon.java` in the Working Java Example for Using JMS with Amazon SQS Standard Queues section.

For complete examples of sending and receiving objects, see TextMessageSender.java and SyncMessageReceiver.java.

Receiving Messages Asynchronously

In the example in Getting Started with the Amazon SQS Java Messaging Library, a message is sent to `MyQueue` and received synchronously.

The following example shows how to receive the messages asynchronously through a listener.

1. Implement the `MessageListener` interface.

```
1 class MyListener implements MessageListener {
2
3     @Override
4     public void onMessage(Message message) {
5         try {
6             // Cast the received message as TextMessage and print the text to screen.
7             System.out.println("Received: " + ((TextMessage) message).getText());
8         } catch (JMSException e) {
9             e.printStackTrace();
10         }
11     }
12 }
```

The `onMessage` method of the `MessageListener` interface is called when you receive a message. In this listener implementation, the text stored in the message is printed.

2. Instead of explicitly calling the `receive` method on the consumer, set the message listener of the consumer to an instance of the `MyListener` implementation. The main thread waits for one second.

```
1 // Create a consumer for the 'MyQueue'.
2 MessageConsumer consumer = session.createConsumer(queue);
3
4 // Instantiate and set the message listener for the consumer.
5 consumer.setMessageListener(new MyListener());
6
7 // Start receiving incoming messages.
8 connection.start();
9
10 // Wait for 1 second. The listener onMessage() method is invoked when a message is received
11 Thread.sleep(1000);
```

The rest of the steps are identical to the ones in the Getting Started with the Amazon SQS Java Messaging Library example. For a complete example of an asynchronous consumer, see `AsyncMessageReceiver.java` in Working Java Example for Using JMS with Amazon SQS Standard Queues.

The output for this example looks similar to the following:

```
1 JMS Message ID:8example-588b-44e5-bbcf-d816example2
2 Received: Hello World!
```

Using Client Acknowledge Mode

The example in Getting Started with the Amazon SQS Java Messaging Library uses `AUTO_ACKNOWLEDGE` mode where every received message is acknowledged automatically (and therefore deleted from the underlying Amazon SQS queue).

1. To explicitly acknowledge the messages after they're processed, you must create the session with `CLIENT_ACKNOWLEDGE` mode.

```
1 // Create the non-transacted session with CLIENT_ACKNOWLEDGE mode.
2 Session session = connection.createSession(false, Session.CLIENT_ACKNOWLEDGE);
```

2. When the message is received, display it and then explicitly acknowledge it.

```
1 // Cast the received message as TextMessage and print the text to screen. Also acknowledge
      the message.
2 if (receivedMessage != null) {
3     System.out.println("Received: " + ((TextMessage) receivedMessage).getText());
4     receivedMessage.acknowledge();
5     System.out.println("Acknowledged: " + message.getJMSMessageID());
6 }
```

Note

In this mode, when a message is acknowledged, all messages received before this message are implicitly acknowledged as well. For example, if 10 messages are received, and only the 10th message is acknowledged (in the order the messages are received), then all of the previous nine messages are also acknowledged.

The rest of the steps are identical to the ones in the Getting Started with the Amazon SQS Java Messaging Library example. For a complete example of a synchronous consumer with client acknowledge mode, see `SyncMessageReceiverClientAcknowledge.java` in Working Java Example for Using JMS with Amazon SQS Standard Queues.

The output for this example looks similar to the following:

```
1 JMS Message ID:4example-aa0e-403f-b6df-5e02example5
2 Received: Hello World!
3 Acknowledged: ID:4example-aa0e-403f-b6df-5e02example5
```

Using Unordered Acknowledge Mode

When using `CLIENT_ACKNOWLEDGE` mode, all messages received before an explicitly-acknowledged message are acknowledged automatically. For more information, see Using Client Acknowledge Mode.

The Amazon SQS Java Messaging Library provides another acknowledgement mode. When using `UNORDERED_ACKNOWLEDGE` mode, all received messages must be individually and explicitly acknowledged by the client, regardless of their reception order. To do this, create a session with `UNORDERED_ACKNOWLEDGE` mode.

```
1 // Create the non-transacted session with UNORDERED_ACKNOWLEDGE mode.
2 Session session = connection.createSession(false, SQSSession.UNORDERED_ACKNOWLEDGE);
```

The remaining steps are identical to the ones in the Using Client Acknowledge Mode example. For a complete example of a synchronous consumer with UNORDERED_ACKNOWLEDGE mode, see SyncMessageReceiverUnorderedAcknowledge.java.

In this example, the output looks similar to the following:

```
1 JMS Message ID:dexample-73ad-4adb-bc6c-4357example7
2 Received: Hello World!
3 Acknowledged: ID:dexample-73ad-4adb-bc6c-4357example7
```

Using the Amazon SQS Java Message Service (JMS) Client with Other Amazon SQS Clients

Using the Amazon SQS Java Message Service (JMS) Client with the AWS SDK limits Amazon SQS message size to 256 KB. However, you can create a JMS provider using any Amazon SQS client. For example, you can use the JMS Client with the Amazon SQS Extended Client Library for Java to send an Amazon SQS message that contains a reference to a message payload (up to 2 GB) in Amazon S3. For more information, see Managing Large Amazon SQS Messages Using Amazon S3.

The following Java code example creates the JMS provider for the Extended Client Library:

```
1  AmazonS3 s3 = new AmazonS3Client(credentials);
2  Region s3Region = Region.getRegion(Regions.US_WEST_2);
3  s3.setRegion(s3Region);
4
5  // Set the Amazon S3 bucket name, and set a lifecycle rule on the bucket to
6  // permanently delete objects a certain number of days after each object's creation date.
7  // Next, create the bucket, and enable message objects to be stored in the bucket.
8  BucketLifecycleConfiguration.Rule expirationRule = new BucketLifecycleConfiguration.Rule();
9  expirationRule.withExpirationInDays(14).withStatus("Enabled");
10 BucketLifecycleConfiguration lifecycleConfig = new BucketLifecycleConfiguration().withRules(
       expirationRule);
11
12 s3.createBucket(s3BucketName);
13 s3.setBucketLifecycleConfiguration(s3BucketName, lifecycleConfig);
14 System.out.println("Bucket created and configured.");
15
16 // Set the SQS extended client configuration with large payload support enabled.
17 ExtendedClientConfiguration extendedClientConfig = new ExtendedClientConfiguration()
18     .withLargePayloadSupportEnabled(s3, s3BucketName);
19
20 AmazonSQS sqsExtended = new AmazonSQSExtendedClient(new AmazonSQSClient(credentials),
       extendedClientConfig);
21 Region sqsRegion = Region.getRegion(Regions.US_WEST_2);
22 sqsExtended.setRegion(sqsRegion);
```

The following Java code example creates the connection factory:

```
1  // Create the connection factory using the environment variable credential provider.
2  // Pass the configured Amazon SQS Extended Client to the JMS connection factory.
3  SQSConnectionFactory connectionFactory = new SQSConnectionFactory(
4        new ProviderConfiguration(),
5        sqsExtended
6        );
7
8  // Create the connection.
9  SQSConnection connection = connectionFactory.createConnection();
```

Working Java Example for Using JMS with Amazon SQS Standard Queues

The following code examples show how to use JMS with Amazon SQS standard queues. For more information about working with FIFO queues, see To create a FIFO queue, Sending Messages Synchronously, and Receiving Messages Synchronously. (Receiving messages synchronously is the same for standard and FIFO queues. However, messages in FIFO queues contain more attributes.)

ExampleConfiguration.java

The following Java code example sets the default queue name, the region, and the credentials to be used with the other Java examples.

```java
/*
 * Copyright 2010-2018 Amazon.com, Inc. or its affiliates. All Rights Reserved.
 *
 * Licensed under the Apache License, Version 2.0 (the "License").
 * You may not use this file except in compliance with the License.
 * A copy of the License is located at
 *
 *  https://aws.amazon.com/apache2.0
 *
 * or in the "license" file accompanying this file. This file is distributed
 * on an "AS IS" BASIS, WITHOUT WARRANTIES OR CONDITIONS OF ANY KIND, either
 * express or implied. See the License for the specific language governing
 * permissions and limitations under the License.
 *
 */

public class ExampleConfiguration {
    public static final String DEFAULT_QUEUE_NAME = "SQSJMSClientExampleQueue";

    public static final Region DEFAULT_REGION = Region.getRegion(Regions.US_EAST_2);

    private static String getParameter( String args[], int i ) {
        if( i + 1 >= args.length ) {
            throw new IllegalArgumentException( "Missing parameter for " + args[i] );
        }
        return args[i+1];
    }

    /**
     * Parse the command line and return the resulting config. If the config parsing fails
     * print the error and the usage message and then call System.exit
     *
     * @param app the app to use when printing the usage string
     * @param args the command line arguments
     * @return the parsed config
     */
    public static ExampleConfiguration parseConfig(String app, String args[]) {
        try {
            return new ExampleConfiguration(args);
        } catch (IllegalArgumentException e) {
```

```
41      System.err.println( "ERROR: " + e.getMessage() );
42      System.err.println();
43      System.err.println( "Usage: " + app + " [--queue <queue>] [--region <region>] [--
            credentials <credentials>] ");
44      System.err.println( "  or" );
45      System.err.println( "      " + app + " <spring.xml>" );
46      System.exit(-1);
47      return null;
48    }
49  }
50
51  private ExampleConfiguration(String args[]) {
52    for( int i = 0; i < args.length; ++i ) {
53      String arg = args[i];
54      if( arg.equals( "--queue" ) ) {
55        setQueueName(getParameter(args, i));
56        i++;
57      } else if( arg.equals( "--region" ) ) {
58        String regionName = getParameter(args, i);
59        try {
60          setRegion(Region.getRegion(Regions.fromName(regionName)));
61        } catch( IllegalArgumentException e ) {
62          throw new IllegalArgumentException( "Unrecognized region " + regionName );
63        }
64        i++;
65      } else if( arg.equals( "--credentials" ) ) {
66        String credsFile = getParameter(args, i);
67        try {
68          setCredentialsProvider( new PropertiesFileCredentialsProvider(credsFile) );
69        } catch (AmazonClientException e) {
70          throw new IllegalArgumentException("Error reading credentials from " +
              credsFile, e );
71        }
72        i++;
73      } else {
74        throw new IllegalArgumentException("Unrecognized option " + arg);
75      }
76    }
77  }
78
79  private String queueName = DEFAULT_QUEUE_NAME;
80  private Region region = DEFAULT_REGION;
81  private AWSCredentialsProvider credentialsProvider = new DefaultAWSCredentialsProviderChain
        ();
82
83  public String getQueueName() {
84    return queueName;
85  }
86
87  public void setQueueName(String queueName) {
88    this.queueName = queueName;
89  }
90
91  public Region getRegion() {
```

```
92        return region;
93    }
94
95    public void setRegion(Region region) {
96        this.region = region;
97    }
98
99    public AWSCredentialsProvider getCredentialsProvider() {
100       return credentialsProvider;
101   }
102
103   public void setCredentialsProvider(AWSCredentialsProvider credentialsProvider) {
104       // Make sure they're usable first
105       credentialsProvider.getCredentials();
106       this.credentialsProvider = credentialsProvider;
107   }
108 }
```

TextMessageSender.java

The following Java code example creates a text message producer.

```
1  /*
2   * Copyright 2010-2018 Amazon.com, Inc. or its affiliates. All Rights Reserved.
3   *
4   * Licensed under the Apache License, Version 2.0 (the "License").
5   * You may not use this file except in compliance with the License.
6   * A copy of the License is located at
7   *
8   *  https://aws.amazon.com/apache2.0
9   *
10  * or in the "license" file accompanying this file. This file is distributed
11  * on an "AS IS" BASIS, WITHOUT WARRANTIES OR CONDITIONS OF ANY KIND, either
12  * express or implied. See the License for the specific language governing
13  * permissions and limitations under the License.
14  *
15  */
16
17 public class TextMessageSender {
18     public static void main(String args[]) throws JMSException {
19         ExampleConfiguration config = ExampleConfiguration.parseConfig("TextMessageSender", args
               );
20
21         ExampleCommon.setupLogging();
22
23         // Create the connection factory based on the config
24         SQSConnectionFactory connectionFactory = new SQSConnectionFactory(
25                 new ProviderConfiguration(),
26                 AmazonSQSClientBuilder.standard()
27                         .withRegion(config.getRegion().getName())
28                         .withCredentials(config.getCredentialsProvider())
29                 );
30
31         // Create the connection
```

```
32        SQSConnection connection = connectionFactory.createConnection();
33
34        // Create the queue if needed
35        ExampleCommon.ensureQueueExists(connection, config.getQueueName());
36
37        // Create the session
38        Session session = connection.createSession(false, Session.AUTO_ACKNOWLEDGE);
39        MessageProducer producer = session.createProducer( session.createQueue( config.
              getQueueName() ) );
40
41        sendMessages(session, producer);
42
43        // Close the connection. This closes the session automatically
44        connection.close();
45        System.out.println( "Connection closed" );
46    }
47
48    private static void sendMessages( Session session, MessageProducer producer ) {
49        BufferedReader inputReader = new BufferedReader(
50            new InputStreamReader( System.in, Charset.defaultCharset() ) );
51
52        try {
53            String input;
54            while( true ) {
55                System.out.print( "Enter message to send (leave empty to exit): " );
56                input = inputReader.readLine();
57                if( input == null || input.equals("") ) break;
58
59                TextMessage message = session.createTextMessage(input);
60                producer.send(message);
61                System.out.println( "Send message " + message.getJMSMessageID() );
62            }
63        } catch (EOFException e) {
64            // Just return on EOF
65        } catch (IOException e) {
66            System.err.println( "Failed reading input: " + e.getMessage() );
67        } catch (JMSException e) {
68            System.err.println( "Failed sending message: " + e.getMessage() );
69            e.printStackTrace();
70        }
71    }
72 }
```

SyncMessageReceiver.java

The following Java code example creates a synchronous message consumer.

```
1 /*
2  * Copyright 2010-2018 Amazon.com, Inc. or its affiliates. All Rights Reserved.
3  *
4  * Licensed under the Apache License, Version 2.0 (the "License").
5  * You may not use this file except in compliance with the License.
6  * A copy of the License is located at
7  *
```

```
 8  *  https://aws.amazon.com/apache2.0
 9  *
10  * or in the "license" file accompanying this file. This file is distributed
11  * on an "AS IS" BASIS, WITHOUT WARRANTIES OR CONDITIONS OF ANY KIND, either
12  * express or implied. See the License for the specific language governing
13  * permissions and limitations under the License.
14  *
15  */
16
17  public class SyncMessageReceiver {
18  public static void main(String args[]) throws JMSException {
19      ExampleConfiguration config = ExampleConfiguration.parseConfig("SyncMessageReceiver", args);
20
21      ExampleCommon.setupLogging();
22
23      // Create the connection factory based on the config
24      SQSConnectionFactory connectionFactory = new SQSConnectionFactory(
25              new ProviderConfiguration(),
26              AmazonSQSClientBuilder.standard()
27                      .withRegion(config.getRegion().getName())
28                      .withCredentials(config.getCredentialsProvider())
29              );
30
31      // Create the connection
32      SQSConnection connection = connectionFactory.createConnection();
33
34      // Create the queue if needed
35      ExampleCommon.ensureQueueExists(connection, config.getQueueName());
36
37      // Create the session
38      Session session = connection.createSession(false, Session.CLIENT_ACKNOWLEDGE);
39      MessageConsumer consumer = session.createConsumer( session.createQueue( config.getQueueName
              () ) );
40
41      connection.start();
42
43      receiveMessages(session, consumer);
44
45      // Close the connection. This closes the session automatically
46      connection.close();
47      System.out.println( "Connection closed" );
48  }
49
50  private static void receiveMessages( Session session, MessageConsumer consumer ) {
51      try {
52          while( true ) {
53              System.out.println( "Waiting for messages");
54              // Wait 1 minute for a message
55              Message message = consumer.receive(TimeUnit.MINUTES.toMillis(1));
56              if( message == null ) {
57                  System.out.println( "Shutting down after 1 minute of silence" );
58                  break;
59              }
60              ExampleCommon.handleMessage(message);
```

```
61              message.acknowledge();
62              System.out.println( "Acknowledged message " + message.getJMSMessageID() );
63          }
64      } catch (JMSException e) {
65          System.err.println( "Error receiving from SQS: " + e.getMessage() );
66          e.printStackTrace();
67      }
68  }
69  }
```

AsyncMessageReceiver.java

The following Java code example creates an asynchronous message consumer.

```
1  /*
2   * Copyright 2010-2018 Amazon.com, Inc. or its affiliates. All Rights Reserved.
3   *
4   * Licensed under the Apache License, Version 2.0 (the "License").
5   * You may not use this file except in compliance with the License.
6   * A copy of the License is located at
7   *
8   *  https://aws.amazon.com/apache2.0
9   *
10  * or in the "license" file accompanying this file. This file is distributed
11  * on an "AS IS" BASIS, WITHOUT WARRANTIES OR CONDITIONS OF ANY KIND, either
12  * express or implied. See the License for the specific language governing
13  * permissions and limitations under the License.
14  *
15  */
16
17 public class AsyncMessageReceiver {
18     public static void main(String args[]) throws JMSException, InterruptedException {
19         ExampleConfiguration config = ExampleConfiguration.parseConfig("AsyncMessageReceiver",
20             args);
21
22         ExampleCommon.setupLogging();
23
24         // Create the connection factory based on the config
25         SQSConnectionFactory connectionFactory = new SQSConnectionFactory(
26             new ProviderConfiguration(),
27             AmazonSQSClientBuilder.standard()
28                     .withRegion(config.getRegion().getName())
29                     .withCredentials(config.getCredentialsProvider())
30             );
31
32         // Create the connection
33         SQSConnection connection = connectionFactory.createConnection();
34
35         // Create the queue if needed
36         ExampleCommon.ensureQueueExists(connection, config.getQueueName());
37
38         // Create the session
39         Session session = connection.createSession(false, Session.CLIENT_ACKNOWLEDGE);
```

```java
39      MessageConsumer consumer = session.createConsumer( session.createQueue( config.
            getQueueName() ) );
40
41      ReceiverCallback callback = new ReceiverCallback();
42      consumer.setMessageListener( callback );
43
44      // No messages are processed until this is called
45      connection.start();
46
47      callback.waitForOneMinuteOfSilence();
48      System.out.println( "Returning after one minute of silence" );
49
50      // Close the connection. This closes the session automatically
51      connection.close();
52      System.out.println( "Connection closed" );
53    }
54
55
56    private static class ReceiverCallback implements MessageListener {
57      // Used to listen for message silence
58      private volatile long timeOfLastMessage = System.nanoTime();
59
60      public void waitForOneMinuteOfSilence() throws InterruptedException {
61        for(;;) {
62          long timeSinceLastMessage = System.nanoTime() - timeOfLastMessage;
63          long remainingTillOneMinuteOfSilence =
64              TimeUnit.MINUTES.toNanos(1) - timeSinceLastMessage;
65          if( remainingTillOneMinuteOfSilence < 0 ) {
66            break;
67          }
68          TimeUnit.NANOSECONDS.sleep(remainingTillOneMinuteOfSilence);
69        }
70      }
71
72
73      @Override
74      public void onMessage(Message message) {
75        try {
76          ExampleCommon.handleMessage(message);
77          message.acknowledge();
78          System.out.println( "Acknowledged message " + message.getJMSMessageID() );
79          timeOfLastMessage = System.nanoTime();
80        } catch (JMSException e) {
81          System.err.println( "Error processing message: " + e.getMessage() );
82          e.printStackTrace();
83        }
84      }
85    }
86 }
```

SyncMessageReceiverClientAcknowledge.java

The following Java code example creates a synchronous consumer with client acknowledge mode.

```java
1  /*
2   * Copyright 2010-2018 Amazon.com, Inc. or its affiliates. All Rights Reserved.
3   *
4   * Licensed under the Apache License, Version 2.0 (the "License").
5   * You may not use this file except in compliance with the License.
6   * A copy of the License is located at
7   *
8   *  https://aws.amazon.com/apache2.0
9   *
10  * or in the "license" file accompanying this file. This file is distributed
11  * on an "AS IS" BASIS, WITHOUT WARRANTIES OR CONDITIONS OF ANY KIND, either
12  * express or implied. See the License for the specific language governing
13  * permissions and limitations under the License.
14  *
15  */
16
17  /**
18   * An example class to demonstrate the behavior of CLIENT_ACKNOWLEDGE mode for received messages
         . This example
19   * complements the example given in {@link SyncMessageReceiverUnorderedAcknowledge} for
         UNORDERED_ACKNOWLEDGE mode.
20   *
21   * First, a session, a message producer, and a message consumer are created. Then, two messages
         are sent. Next, two messages
22   * are received but only the second one is acknowledged. After waiting for the visibility time
         out period, an attempt to
23   * receive another message is made. It's shown that no message is returned for this attempt
         since in CLIENT_ACKNOWLEDGE mode,
24   * as expected, all the messages prior to the acknowledged messages are also acknowledged.
25   *
26   * This ISN'T the behavior for UNORDERED_ACKNOWLEDGE mode. Please see {@link
         SyncMessageReceiverUnorderedAcknowledge}
27   * for an example.
28   */
29  public class SyncMessageReceiverClientAcknowledge {
30
31      // Visibility time-out for the queue. It must match to the one set for the queue for this
             example to work.
32      private static final long TIME_OUT_SECONDS = 1;
33
34      public static void main(String args[]) throws JMSException, InterruptedException {
35          // Create the configuration for the example
36          ExampleConfiguration config = ExampleConfiguration.parseConfig("
                 SyncMessageReceiverClientAcknowledge", args);
37
38          // Setup logging for the example
39          ExampleCommon.setupLogging();
40
41          // Create the connection factory based on the config
42          SQSConnectionFactory connectionFactory = new SQSConnectionFactory(
43                  new ProviderConfiguration(),
44                  AmazonSQSClientBuilder.standard()
45                          .withRegion(config.getRegion().getName())
46                          .withCredentials(config.getCredentialsProvider())
```

```
47                 );
48
49        // Create the connection
50        SQSConnection connection = connectionFactory.createConnection();
51
52        // Create the queue if needed
53        ExampleCommon.ensureQueueExists(connection, config.getQueueName());
54
55        // Create the session  with client acknowledge mode
56        Session session = connection.createSession(false, Session.CLIENT_ACKNOWLEDGE);
57
58        // Create the producer and consume
59        MessageProducer producer = session.createProducer(session.createQueue(config.
                getQueueName()));
60        MessageConsumer consumer = session.createConsumer(session.createQueue(config.
                getQueueName()));
61
62        // Open the connection
63        connection.start();
64
65        // Send two text messages
66        sendMessage(producer, session, "Message 1");
67        sendMessage(producer, session, "Message 2");
68
69        // Receive a message and don't acknowledge it
70        receiveMessage(consumer, false);
71
72        // Receive another message and acknowledge it
73        receiveMessage(consumer, true);
74
75        // Wait for the visibility time out, so that unacknowledged messages reappear in the
                queue
76        System.out.println("Waiting for visibility timeout...");
77        Thread.sleep(TimeUnit.SECONDS.toMillis(TIME_OUT_SECONDS));
78
79        // Attempt to receive another message and acknowledge it. This results in receiving no
                messages since
80        // we have acknowledged the second message. Although we didn't explicitly acknowledge
                the first message,
81        // in the CLIENT_ACKNOWLEDGE mode, all the messages received prior to the explicitly
                acknowledged message
82        // are also acknowledged. Therefore, we have implicitly acknowledged the first message.
83        receiveMessage(consumer, true);
84
85        // Close the connection. This closes the session automatically
86        connection.close();
87        System.out.println("Connection closed.");
88    }
89
90    /**
91     * Sends a message through the producer.
92     *
93     * @param producer Message producer
94     * @param session Session
```

```
 95      * @param messageText Text for the message to be sent
 96      * @throws JMSException
 97      */
 98     private static void sendMessage(MessageProducer producer, Session session, String
           messageText) throws JMSException {
 99         // Create a text message and send it
100         producer.send(session.createTextMessage(messageText));
101     }
102
103     /**
104      * Receives a message through the consumer synchronously with the default timeout (
           TIME_OUT_SECONDS).
105      * If a message is received, the message is printed. If no message is received, "Queue is
           empty!" is
106      * printed.
107      *
108      * @param consumer Message consumer
109      * @param acknowledge If true and a message is received, the received message is
           acknowledged.
110      * @throws JMSException
111      */
112     private static void receiveMessage(MessageConsumer consumer, boolean acknowledge) throws
           JMSException {
113         // Receive a message
114         Message message = consumer.receive(TimeUnit.SECONDS.toMillis(TIME_OUT_SECONDS));
115
116         if (message == null) {
117             System.out.println("Queue is empty!");
118         } else {
119             // Since this queue has only text messages, cast the message object and print the
                   text
120             System.out.println("Received: " + ((TextMessage) message).getText());
121
122             // Acknowledge the message if asked
123             if (acknowledge) message.acknowledge();
124         }
125     }
126 }
```

SyncMessageReceiverUnorderedAcknowledge.java

The following Java code example creates a synchronous consumer with unordered acknowledge mode.

```
 1 /*
 2  * Copyright 2010-2018 Amazon.com, Inc. or its affiliates. All Rights Reserved.
 3  *
 4  * Licensed under the Apache License, Version 2.0 (the "License").
 5  * You may not use this file except in compliance with the License.
 6  * A copy of the License is located at
 7  *
 8  *  https://aws.amazon.com/apache2.0
 9  *
10  * or in the "license" file accompanying this file. This file is distributed
11  * on an "AS IS" BASIS, WITHOUT WARRANTIES OR CONDITIONS OF ANY KIND, either
```

```
12  * express or implied. See the License for the specific language governing
13  * permissions and limitations under the License.
14  *
15  */
16
17  /**
18   * An example class to demonstrate the behavior of UNORDERED_ACKNOWLEDGE mode for received
          messages. This example
19   * complements the example given in {@link SyncMessageReceiverClientAcknowledge} for
          CLIENT_ACKNOWLEDGE mode.
20   *
21   * First, a session, a message producer, and a message consumer are created. Then, two messages
          are sent. Next, two messages
22   * are received but only the second one is acknowledged. After waiting for the visibility time
          out period, an attempt to
23   * receive another message is made. It's shown that the first message received in the prior
          attempt is returned again
24   * for the second attempt. In UNORDERED_ACKNOWLEDGE mode, all the messages must be explicitly
          acknowledged no matter what
25   * the order they're received.
26   *
27   * This ISN'T the behavior for CLIENT_ACKNOWLEDGE mode. Please see {@link
          SyncMessageReceiverClientAcknowledge}
28   * for an example.
29   */
30  public class SyncMessageReceiverUnorderedAcknowledge {
31
32      // Visibility time-out for the queue. It must match to the one set for the queue for this
             example to work.
33      private static final long TIME_OUT_SECONDS = 1;
34
35      public static void main(String args[]) throws JMSException, InterruptedException {
36          // Create the configuration for the example
37          ExampleConfiguration config = ExampleConfiguration.parseConfig("
                 SyncMessageReceiverUnorderedAcknowledge", args);
38
39          // Setup logging for the example
40          ExampleCommon.setupLogging();
41
42          // Create the connection factory based on the config
43          SQSConnectionFactory connectionFactory = new SQSConnectionFactory(
44                  new ProviderConfiguration(),
45                  AmazonSQSClientBuilder.standard()
46                          .withRegion(config.getRegion().getName())
47                          .withCredentials(config.getCredentialsProvider())
48          );
49
50          // Create the connection
51          SQSConnection connection = connectionFactory.createConnection();
52
53          // Create the queue if needed
54          ExampleCommon.ensureQueueExists(connection, config.getQueueName());
55
56          // Create the session  with unordered acknowledge mode
```

```java
57        Session session = connection.createSession(false, SQSSession.UNORDERED_ACKNOWLEDGE);
58
59        // Create the producer and consume
60        MessageProducer producer = session.createProducer(session.createQueue(config.
              getQueueName()));
61        MessageConsumer consumer = session.createConsumer(session.createQueue(config.
              getQueueName()));
62
63        // Open the connection
64        connection.start();
65
66        // Send two text messages
67        sendMessage(producer, session, "Message 1");
68        sendMessage(producer, session, "Message 2");
69
70        // Receive a message and don't acknowledge it
71        receiveMessage(consumer, false);
72
73        // Receive another message and acknowledge it
74        receiveMessage(consumer, true);
75
76        // Wait for the visibility time out, so that unacknowledged messages reappear in the
              queue
77        System.out.println("Waiting for visibility timeout...");
78        Thread.sleep(TimeUnit.SECONDS.toMillis(TIME_OUT_SECONDS));
79
80        // Attempt to receive another message and acknowledge it. This results in receiving the
              first message since
81        // we have acknowledged only the second message. In the UNORDERED_ACKNOWLEDGE mode, all
              the messages must
82        // be explicitly acknowledged.
83        receiveMessage(consumer, true);
84
85        // Close the connection. This closes the session automatically
86        connection.close();
87        System.out.println("Connection closed.");
88    }
89
90    /**
91     * Sends a message through the producer.
92     *
93     * @param producer Message producer
94     * @param session Session
95     * @param messageText Text for the message to be sent
96     * @throws JMSException
97     */
98    private static void sendMessage(MessageProducer producer, Session session, String
          messageText) throws JMSException {
99        // Create a text message and send it
100       producer.send(session.createTextMessage(messageText));
101    }
102
103    /**
```

```
104    * Receives a message through the consumer synchronously with the default timeout (
           TIME_OUT_SECONDS).
105    * If a message is received, the message is printed. If no message is received, "Queue is
           empty!" is
106    * printed.
107    *
108    * @param consumer Message consumer
109    * @param acknowledge If true and a message is received, the received message is
           acknowledged.
110    * @throws JMSException
111    */
112   private static void receiveMessage(MessageConsumer consumer, boolean acknowledge) throws
          JMSException {
113       // Receive a message
114       Message message = consumer.receive(TimeUnit.SECONDS.toMillis(TIME_OUT_SECONDS));
115
116       if (message == null) {
117           System.out.println("Queue is empty!");
118       } else {
119           // Since this queue has only text messages, cast the message object and print the
                  text
120           System.out.println("Received: " + ((TextMessage) message).getText());
121
122           // Acknowledge the message if asked
123           if (acknowledge) message.acknowledge();
124       }
125   }
126 }
```

SpringExampleConfiguration.xml

The following XML code example is a bean configuration file for SpringExample.java.

```
1  <!--
2      Copyright 2010-2018 Amazon.com, Inc. or its affiliates. All Rights Reserved.
3
4      Licensed under the Apache License, Version 2.0 (the "License").
5      You may not use this file except in compliance with the License.
6      A copy of the License is located at
7
8      https://aws.amazon.com/apache2.0
9
10     or in the "license" file accompanying this file. This file is distributed
11     on an "AS IS" BASIS, WITHOUT WARRANTIES OR CONDITIONS OF ANY KIND, either
12     express or implied. See the License for the specific language governing
13     permissions and limitations under the License.
14 -->
15
16 <?xml version="1.0" encoding="UTF-8"?>
17 <beans
18     xmlns="http://www.springframework.org/schema/beans"
19     xmlns:xsi="http://www.w3.org/2001/XMLSchema-instance"
20     xmlns:util="http://www.springframework.org/schema/util"
21     xmlns:p="http://www.springframework.org/schema/p"
```

```
22    xsi:schemaLocation="
23        http://www.springframework.org/schema/beans http://www.springframework.org/schema/beans/
              spring-beans-3.0.xsd
24        http://www.springframework.org/schema/util http://www.springframework.org/schema/util/
              spring-util-3.0.xsd
25    ">
26
27    <bean id="CredentialsProviderBean" class="com.amazonaws.auth.
      DefaultAWSCredentialsProviderChain"/>
28
29    <bean id="ClientBuilder" class="com.amazonaws.services.sqs.AmazonSQSClientBuilder" factory-
          method="standard">
30        <property name="region" value="us-east-2"/>
31        <property name="credentials" ref="CredentialsProviderBean"/>
32    </bean>
33
34    <bean id="ProviderConfiguration" class="com.amazon.sqs.javamessaging.ProviderConfiguration">
35        <property name="numberOfMessagesToPrefetch" value="5"/>
36    </bean>
37
38    <bean id="ConnectionFactory" class="com.amazon.sqs.javamessaging.SQSConnectionFactory">
39        <constructor-arg ref="ProviderConfiguration" />
40        <constructor-arg ref="ClientBuilder" />
41    </bean>
42
43    <bean id="Connection" class="javax.jms.Connection"
44        factory-bean="ConnectionFactory"
45        factory-method="createConnection"
46        init-method="start"
47        destroy-method="close" />
48
49    <bean id="QueueName" class="java.lang.String">
50        <constructor-arg value="SQSJMSClientExampleQueue"/>
51    </bean>
52 </beans>
```

SpringExample.java

The following Java code example uses the bean configuration file to initialize your objects.

```
1  /*
2   * Copyright 2010-2018 Amazon.com, Inc. or its affiliates. All Rights Reserved.
3   *
4   * Licensed under the Apache License, Version 2.0 (the "License").
5   * You may not use this file except in compliance with the License.
6   * A copy of the License is located at
7   *
8   *  https://aws.amazon.com/apache2.0
9   *
10  * or in the "license" file accompanying this file. This file is distributed
11  * on an "AS IS" BASIS, WITHOUT WARRANTIES OR CONDITIONS OF ANY KIND, either
12  * express or implied. See the License for the specific language governing
13  * permissions and limitations under the License.
14  *
```

```java
15  */
16
17  public class SpringExample {
18      public static void main(String args[]) throws JMSException {
19          if( args.length != 1 || !args[0].endsWith(".xml")) {
20              System.err.println( "Usage: " + SpringExample.class.getName() + " <spring config.xml
                      >" );
21              System.exit(1);
22          }
23
24          File springFile = new File( args[0] );
25          if( !springFile.exists() || !springFile.canRead() ) {
26              System.err.println( "File " + args[0] + " doesn't exist or isn't readable.");
27              System.exit(2);
28          }
29
30          ExampleCommon.setupLogging();
31
32          FileSystemXmlApplicationContext context =
33              new FileSystemXmlApplicationContext( "file://" + springFile.getAbsolutePath() );
34
35          Connection connection;
36          try {
37              connection = context.getBean(Connection.class);
38          } catch( NoSuchBeanDefinitionException e ) {
39              System.err.println( "Can't find the JMS connection to use: " + e.getMessage() );
40              System.exit(3);
41              return;
42          }
43
44          String queueName;
45          try {
46              queueName = context.getBean("QueueName", String.class);
47          } catch( NoSuchBeanDefinitionException e ) {
48              System.err.println( "Can't find the name of the queue to use: " + e.getMessage() );
49              System.exit(3);
50              return;
51          }
52
53          if( connection instanceof SQSConnection ) {
54              ExampleCommon.ensureQueueExists( (SQSConnection) connection, queueName );
55          }
56
57          // Create the session
58          Session session = connection.createSession(false, Session.CLIENT_ACKNOWLEDGE);
59          MessageConsumer consumer = session.createConsumer( session.createQueue( queueName) );
60
61          receiveMessages(session, consumer);
62
63          // The context can be setup to close the connection for us
64          context.close();
65          System.out.println( "Context closed" );
66      }
67
```

```
68    private static void receiveMessages( Session session, MessageConsumer consumer ) {
69        try {
70            while( true ) {
71                System.out.println( "Waiting for messages");
72                // Wait 1 minute for a message
73                Message message = consumer.receive(TimeUnit.MINUTES.toMillis(1));
74                if( message == null ) {
75                    System.out.println( "Shutting down after 1 minute of silence" );
76                    break;
77                }
78                ExampleCommon.handleMessage(message);
79                message.acknowledge();
80                System.out.println( "Acknowledged message" );
81            }
82        } catch (JMSException e) {
83            System.err.println( "Error receiving from SQS: " + e.getMessage() );
84            e.printStackTrace();
85        }
86    }
87 }
```

ExampleCommon.java

The following Java code example checks if an Amazon SQS queue exists and then creates one if it doesn't. It also includes example logging code.

```
1  /*
2   * Copyright 2010-2018 Amazon.com, Inc. or its affiliates. All Rights Reserved.
3   *
4   * Licensed under the Apache License, Version 2.0 (the "License").
5   * You may not use this file except in compliance with the License.
6   * A copy of the License is located at
7   *
8   *  https://aws.amazon.com/apache2.0
9   *
10  * or in the "license" file accompanying this file. This file is distributed
11  * on an "AS IS" BASIS, WITHOUT WARRANTIES OR CONDITIONS OF ANY KIND, either
12  * express or implied. See the License for the specific language governing
13  * permissions and limitations under the License.
14  *
15  */
16
17 public class ExampleCommon {
18     /**
19      * A utility function to check the queue exists and create it if needed. For most
20      * use cases this is usually done by an administrator before the application is run.
21      */
22     public static void ensureQueueExists(SQSConnection connection, String queueName) throws
           JMSException {
23         AmazonSQSMessagingClientWrapper client = connection.getWrappedAmazonSQSClient();
24
25         /**
26          * In most cases, you can do this with just a createQueue call, but GetQueueUrl
27          * (called by queueExists) is a faster operation for the common case where the queue
```

```
28       * already exists. Also many users and roles have permission to call GetQueueUrl
29       * but don't have permission to call CreateQueue.
30       */
31      if( !client.queueExists(queueName) ) {
32          client.createQueue( queueName );
33      }
34  }
35
36  public static void setupLogging() {
37      // Setup logging
38      BasicConfigurator.configure();
39      Logger.getRootLogger().setLevel(Level.WARN);
40  }
41
42  public static void handleMessage(Message message) throws JMSException {
43      System.out.println( "Got message " + message.getJMSMessageID() );
44      System.out.println( "Content: ");
45      if( message instanceof TextMessage ) {
46          TextMessage txtMessage = ( TextMessage ) message;
47          System.out.println( "\t" + txtMessage.getText() );
48      } else if( message instanceof BytesMessage ){
49          BytesMessage byteMessage = ( BytesMessage ) message;
50          // Assume the length fits in an int - SQS only supports sizes up to 256k so that
51          // should be true
52          byte[] bytes = new byte[(int)byteMessage.getBodyLength()];
53          byteMessage.readBytes(bytes);
54          System.out.println( "\t" +  Base64.encodeAsString( bytes ) );
55      } else if( message instanceof ObjectMessage ) {
56          ObjectMessage objMessage = (ObjectMessage) message;
57          System.out.println( "\t" + objMessage.getObject() );
58      }
59  }
60 }
```

Supported JMS 1.1 Implementations

The Amazon SQS Java Messaging Library supports the following JMS 1.1 implementations. For more information about the supported features and capabilities of the Amazon SQS Java Messaging Library, see the Amazon SQS FAQ.

Supported Common Interfaces

- `Connection`
- `ConnectionFactory`
- `Destination`
- `Session`
- `MessageConsumer`
- `MessageProducer`

Supported Message Types

- `ByteMessage`
- `ObjectMessage`
- `TextMessage`

Supported Message Acknowledgment Modes

- `AUTO_ACKNOWLEDGE`
- `CLIENT_ACKNOWLEDGE`
- `DUPS_OK_ACKNOWLEDGE`
- `UNORDERED_ACKNOWLEDGE`

Note
The `UNORDERED_ACKNOWLEDGE` mode isn't part of the JMS 1.1 specification. This mode helps Amazon SQS allow a JMS client to explicitly acknowledge a message.

JMS-Defined Headers and Reserved Properties

For Sending Messages

When you send messages, you can set the following headers and properties for each message:

- `JMSXGroupID` (required for FIFO queues, not allowed for standard queues)
- `JMS_SQS_DeduplicationId` (optional for FIFO queues, not allowed for standard queues)

After you send messages, Amazon SQS sets the following headers and properties for each message:

- `JMSMessageID`
- `JMS_SQS_SequenceNumber` (only for FIFO queues)

For Receiving Messages

When you receive messages, Amazon SQS sets the following headers and properties for each message:

- `JMSDestination`
- `JMSMessageID`

- JMSRedelivered
- JMSXDeliveryCount
- JMSXGroupID (only for FIFO queues)
- JMS_SQS_DeduplicationId (only for FIFO queues)
- JMS_SQS_SequenceNumber (only for FIFO queues)

Best Practices for Amazon SQS

These best practices can help you make the most of Amazon SQS.

Topics

- Recommendations for Amazon SQS Standard and FIFO (First-In-First-Out) Queues
- Additional Recommendations for Amazon SQS FIFO Queues

Recommendations for Amazon SQS Standard and FIFO (First-In-First-Out) Queues

The following best practices can help you reduce costs and process messages efficiently using Amazon SQS.

Topics

- Working with Amazon SQS Messages
- Reducing Amazon SQS Costs
- Moving from an Amazon SQS Standard Queue to a FIFO Queue

Working with Amazon SQS Messages

The following guidelines can help you process messages efficiently using Amazon SQS.

Topics

- Processing Messages in a Timely Manner
- Handling Request Errors
- Setting Up Long Polling
- Capturing Problematic Messages
- Setting Up Dead-Letter Queue Retention
- Avoiding Inconsistent Message Processing
- Implementing Request-Response Systems

Processing Messages in a Timely Manner

Setting the visibility timeout depends on how long it takes your application to process and delete a message. For example, if your application requires 10 seconds to process a message and you set the visibility timeout to 15 minutes, you must wait for a relatively long time to attempt to process the message again if the previous processing attempt fails. Alternatively, if your application requires 10 seconds to process a message but you set the visibility timeout to only 2 seconds, a duplicate message is received by another consumer while the original consumer is still working on the message.

To ensure that there is sufficient time to process messages, use one of the following strategies:

- If you know (or can reasonably estimate) how long it takes to process a message, extend the message's *visibility timeout* to the maximum time it takes to process and delete the message. For more information, see Configuring the Visibility Timeout and Changing a Message's Visibility Timeout.
- If you don't know how long it takes to process a message, create a *heartbeat* for your consumer process: Specify the initial visibility timeout (for example, 2 minutes) and then—as long as your consumer still works on the message—keep extending the visibility timeout by 2 minutes every minute.

Note
If you need to extend the visibility timeout for longer than 12 hours, consider using AWS Step Functions.

Handling Request Errors

To handle request errors, use one of the following strategies:

- If you use an AWS SDK, you already have automatic *retry and backoff* logic at your disposal. For more information, see Error Retries and Exponential Backoff in AWS in the *Amazon Web Services General Reference.*
- If you don't use the AWS SDK features for retry and backoff, allow a pause (for example, 200 ms) before retrying the ReceiveMessage action after receiving no messages, a timeout, or an error message from Amazon SQS. For subsequent use of `ReceiveMessage` that gives the same results, allow a longer pause (for example, 400 ms).

Setting Up Long Polling

Long polling helps reduce the cost of using Amazon SQS by eliminating the number of empty responses (when there are no messages available for a [ReceiveMessage](http://docs.aws.amazon.com/AWSSimpleQueueService/latest/APIReference/API_ReceiveMessage.html) request) and false empty responses (when messages are available but aren't included in a response). For more information, see Amazon SQS Long Polling.

To ensure optimal message processing, use the following strategies:

- In most cases, you can set the `ReceiveMessage` wait time to 20 seconds. If 20 seconds is too long for your application, set a shorter `ReceiveMessage` wait time (1 second minimum). If you don't use an AWS SDK to access Amazon SQS, or if you configure an AWS SDK to have a shorter wait time, you might have to modify your Amazon SQS client to either allow longer requests or use a shorter wait time for long polling.
- If you implement long polling for multiple queues, use one thread for each queue instead of a single thread for all queues. Using a single thread for each queue allows your application to process the messages in each of the queues as they become available, while using a single thread for polling multiple queues might cause your application to become unable to process messages available in other queues while the application waits (up to 20 seconds) for the queue which doesn't have any available messages.

Capturing Problematic Messages

To capture all messages that can't be processed, and to ensure the correctness of CloudWatch metrics, configure a dead-letter queue.

- The redrive policy redirects messages to a dead-letter queue after the source queue fails to process a message a specified number of times.
- Using a dead-letter queue decreases the number of messages and reduces the possibility of exposing you to *poison pill* messages (messages that are received but can't be processed).
- Including a poison pill message in a queue can distort the `ApproximateAgeOfOldestMessage` CloudWatch metric by giving an incorrect age of the poison pill message. Configuring a dead-letter queue helps avoid false alarms when using this metric.

Setting Up Dead-Letter Queue Retention

The expiration of a message is always based on its original enqueue timestamp. When a message is moved to a dead-letter queue, the enqueue timestamp remains unchanged. For example, if a message spends 1 day in the original queue before being moved to a dead-letter queue, and the retention period of the dead-letter queue is set to 4 days, the message is deleted from the dead-letter queue after 3 days. Thus, it is a best practice to always set the retention period of a dead-letter queue to be longer than the retention period of the original queue.

Avoiding Inconsistent Message Processing

To avoid inconsistent message processing by standard queues, avoid setting the number of maximum receives to 1 when you configure a dead-letter queue.

Important
In some unlikely scenarios, if you set the number of maximum receives to 1, any time a `ReceiveMessage` call fails, a message might be moved to a dead-letter queue without being received.

Implementing Request-Response Systems

When implementing a request-response or remote procedure call (RPC) system, keep the following best practices in mind:

- Don't create reply queues *per message*. Instead, create reply queues on startup, *per producer*, and use a correlation ID message attribute to map replies to requests.
- Don't let your producers share reply queues. This can cause a producer to receive response messages intended for another producer.

Reducing Amazon SQS Costs

The following best practices can help you reduce costs and take advantage of additional potential cost reduction and near-instantaneous response.

Batching Message Actions

To reduce costs, batch your message actions:

- To send, receive, and delete messages, and to change the message visibility timeout for multiple messages with a single action, use the Amazon SQS batch API actions.
- To combine client-side buffering with request batching, use long polling together with the buffered asynchronous client included with the AWS SDK for Java. **Note**
  The Amazon SQS Buffered Asynchronous Client doesn't currently support FIFO queues.

Using the Appropriate Polling Mode

- Long polling lets you consume messages from your Amazon SQS queue as soon as they become available.
  - To reduce the cost of using Amazon SQS and to decrease the number of empty receives to an empty queue (responses to the `ReceiveMessage` action which return no messages), enable long polling. For more information, see Amazon SQS Long Polling.
  - To increase efficiency when polling for multiple threads with multiple receives, decrease the number of threads.
  - Long polling is preferable over short polling in most cases.
- Short polling returns responses immediately, even if the polled Amazon SQS queue is empty.
  - To satisfy the requirements of an application that expects immediate responses to the `ReceiveMessage` request, use short polling.
  - Short polling is billed the same as long polling.

Moving from an Amazon SQS Standard Queue to a FIFO Queue

If you're not setting the `DelaySeconds` parameter on each message, you can move to a FIFO queue by providing a message group ID for every sent message.

For more information, see Moving from a Standard Queue to a FIFO Queue.

Additional Recommendations for Amazon SQS FIFO Queues

The following best practices can help you use the message deduplication ID and message group ID optimally. For more information, see the http://docs.aws.amazon.com/AWSSimpleQueueService/latest/APIReference/API_SendMessage.html and http://docs.aws.amazon.com/AWSSimpleQueueService/latest/APIReference/API_SendMessageBatch.html actions in the *Amazon Simple Queue Service API Reference*.

Topics

- Using the Amazon SQS Message Deduplication ID
- Using the Amazon SQS Message Group ID
- Using the Amazon SQS Receive Request Attempt ID

Using the Amazon SQS Message Deduplication ID

The message deduplication ID is the token used for deduplication of sent messages. If a message with a particular message deduplication ID is sent successfully, any messages sent with the same message deduplication ID are accepted successfully but aren't delivered during the 5-minute deduplication interval.

Note
Message deduplication applies to an entire queue, not to individual message groups.
Amazon SQS continues to keep track of the message deduplication ID even after the message is received and deleted.

Providing the Message Deduplication ID

The producer should provide message deduplication ID values for each message send in the following scenarios:

- Messages sent with identical message bodies that Amazon SQS must treat as unique.
- Messages sent with identical content but different message attributes that Amazon SQS must treat as unique.
- Messages sent with different content (for example, retry counts included in the message body) that Amazon SQS must treat as duplicates.

Enabling Deduplication for a Single-Producer/Consumer System

If you have a single producer and a single consumer and the messages are unique because an application-specific message ID is included in the body of the message, follow these best practices:

- Enable content-based deduplication for the queue (each of your messages has a unique body). The producer can omit the message deduplication ID.
- Although the consumer isn't required to provide a receive request attempt ID for each request, it's a best practice because it allows fail-retry sequences to execute faster.
- You can retry send or receive requests because they don't interfere with the ordering of messages in FIFO queues.

Designing for Outage Recovery Scenarios

The deduplication process in FIFO queues is time-sensitive. When designing your application, ensure that both the producer and the consumer can recover in case of a client or network outage.

- The producer must be aware of the deduplication interval of the queue. Amazon SQS has a *minimum* deduplication interval of 5 minutes. Retrying `SendMessage` requests after the deduplication interval expires can introduce duplicate messages into the queue. For example, a mobile device in a car sends messages whose order is important. If the car loses cellular connectivity for a period of time before receiving an acknowledgement, retrying the request after regaining cellular connectivity can create a duplicate.
- The consumer must have a visibility timeout that minimizes the risk of being unable to process messages before the visibility timeout expires. You can extend the visibility timeout while the messages are being processed by calling the `ChangeMessageVisibility` action. However, if the visibility timeout expires, another consumer can immediately begin to process the messages, causing a message to be processed multiple times. To avoid this scenario, configure a dead-letter queue.

Using the Amazon SQS Message Group ID

The message group ID is the tag that specifies that a message belongs to a specific message group. Messages that belong to the same message group are always processed one by one, in a strict order relative to the message group (however, messages that belong to different message groups might be processed out of order).

Interleaving Multiple Ordered Message Groups

To interleave multiple ordered message groups within a single FIFO queue, use message group ID values (for example, session data for multiple users). In this scenario, multiple consumers can process the queue, but the session data of each user is processed in a FIFO manner.

Note
When messages that belong to a particular message group ID are invisible, no other consumer can process messages with the same message group ID.

Avoiding Processing Duplicates in a Multiple-Producer/Consumer System

To avoid processing duplicate messages in a system with multiple producers and consumers where throughput and latency are more important than ordering, the producer should generate a unique message group ID for each message.

Note
In this scenario, duplicates are eliminated. However, the ordering of message can't be guaranteed.
Any scenario with multiple producers and consumers increases the risk of inadvertently delivering a duplicate message if a worker doesn't process the message within the visibility timeout and the message becomes available to another worker.

Using the Amazon SQS Receive Request Attempt ID

The receive request attempt ID is the token used for deduplication of `ReceiveMessage` calls.

During a long-lasting network outage that causes connectivity issues between your SDK and Amazon SQS, it's a best practice to provide the receive request attempt ID and to retry with the same receive request attempt ID if the SDK operation fails.

Amazon SQS Limits

This topic lists limits within Amazon Simple Queue Service (Amazon SQS).

Topics

- Limits Related to Queues
- Limits Related to Messages
- Limits Related to Policies

Limits Related to Queues

The following table lists limits related to queues.

[See the AWS documentation website for more details]

Limits Related to Messages

The following table lists limits related to messages.

[See the AWS documentation website for more details]

Limits Related to Policies

The following table lists limits related to policies.

Name	Maximum
Actions	7
Bytes	8,192
Conditions	10
Principals	50
Statements	20

Monitoring, Logging, and Automating Amazon SQS Queues

This section provides information about monitoring, logging, and automating Amazon SQS queues.

Topics

- Monitoring Amazon SQS Queues Using CloudWatch
- Logging Amazon SQS Actions Using AWS CloudTrail
- Automating Notifications from AWS Services to Amazon SQS using CloudWatch Events

Monitoring Amazon SQS Queues Using CloudWatch

Amazon SQS and Amazon CloudWatch are integrated so you can use CloudWatch to view and analyze metrics for your Amazon SQS queues. You can view and analyze your queues' metrics from the Amazon SQS console, the CloudWatch console, using the AWS CLI, or using the CloudWatch API. You can also set CloudWatch alarms for Amazon SQS metrics.

CloudWatch metrics for your Amazon SQS queues are automatically collected and pushed to CloudWatch every five minutes. These metrics are gathered on all queues that meet the CloudWatch guidelines for being *active*. CloudWatch considers a queue to be active for up to six hours if it contains any messages or if any action accesses it.

Note
There is no charge for the Amazon SQS metrics reported in CloudWatch. They're provided as part of the Amazon SQS service.
Detailed monitoring (or one-minute metrics) is currently unavailable for Amazon SQS. Making requests to CloudWatch at this resolution might return no data.
CloudWatch metrics are supported for both standard and FIFO queues.

Topics

- Access CloudWatch Metrics for Amazon SQS
- Setting CloudWatch Alarms for Amazon SQS Metrics
- Available CloudWatch Metrics for Amazon SQS

Access CloudWatch Metrics for Amazon SQS

Amazon SQS and Amazon CloudWatch are integrated so you can use CloudWatch to view and analyze metrics for your Amazon SQS queues. You can view and analyze your queues' metrics from the Amazon SQS console, the CloudWatch console, using the AWS CLI, or using the CloudWatch API. You can also set CloudWatch alarms for Amazon SQS metrics.

Amazon SQS Console

1. Sign in to the Amazon SQS console.

2. In the list of queues, choose (check) the boxes for the queues that you want to access metrics for. You can show metrics for up to 10 queues.

3. Choose the **Monitoring** tab.

   Various graphs are displayed in the **SQS metrics** section.

4. To understand what a particular graph represents, hover over  next to the desired graph, or see Available CloudWatch Metrics for Amazon SQS.

5. To change the time range for all of the graphs at the same time, for **Time Range**, choose the desired time range (for example, **Last Hour**).

6. To view additional statistics for an individual graph, choose the graph.

7. In the **CloudWatch Monitoring Details** dialog box, select a **Statistic**, (for example, **Sum**). For a list of supported statistics, see Available CloudWatch Metrics for Amazon SQS.

8. To change the time range and time interval that an individual graph displays (for example, to show a time range of the last 24 hours instead of the last 5 minutes, or to show a time period of every hour instead of every 5 minutes), with the graph's dialog box still displayed, for **Time Range**, choose the desired time range (for example, **Last 24 Hours**). For **Period**, choose the desired time period within the specified time range (for example, **1 Hour**). When you're finished looking at the graph, choose **Close**.

9. (Optional) To work with additional CloudWatch features, on the **Monitoring** tab, choose **View all CloudWatch metrics**, and then follow the instructions in the Amazon CloudWatch Console procedure.

Amazon CloudWatch Console

1. Sign in to the CloudWatch console.

2. On the navigation panel, choose **Metrics**.

3. Select the **SQS** metric namespace.

4. Select the **Queue Metrics** metric dimension.

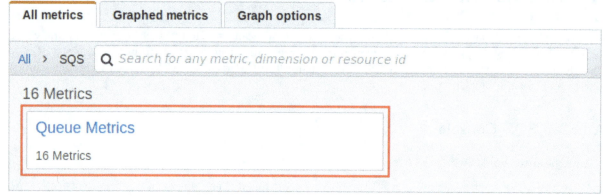

5. You can now examine your Amazon SQS metrics:

  - To sort the metrics, use the column heading.
  - To graph a metric, select the check box next to the metric.
  - To filter by metric, choose the metric name and then choose **Add to search**.

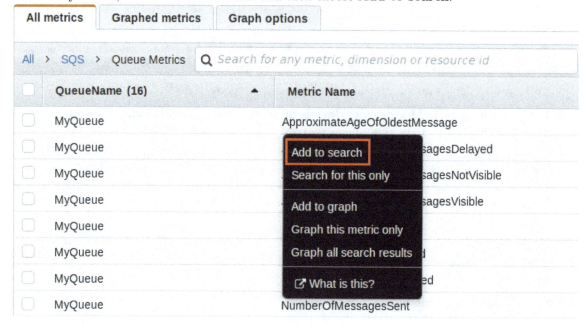

For more information and additional options, see Graph Metrics and Using Amazon CloudWatch Dashboards in the *Amazon CloudWatch User Guide*.

AWS Command Line Interface

To access Amazon SQS metrics using the AWS CLI, run the [get\-metric\-statistics](http://docs.aws.amazon.com/cli/latest/reference/cloudwatch/get-metric-statistics.html) command.

For more information, see Get Statistics for a Metric in the *Amazon CloudWatch User Guide*.

CloudWatch API

To access Amazon SQS metrics using the CloudWatch API, use the [GetMetricStatistics](http://docs.aws.amazon.com/AmazonCloudWatch/latest/APIReference/API_GetMetricStatistics.html) action.

For more information, see Get Statistics for a Metric in the *Amazon CloudWatch User Guide*.

Setting CloudWatch Alarms for Amazon SQS Metrics

CloudWatch allows you to trigger alarms when a threshold is met for a metric. For example, you can set an alarm for the `NumberOfMessagesSent` metric so that when the number of messages exceeds a specified limit over a specified time period, then an email notification can be sent to inform you of the event.

Amazon CloudWatch Console

1. Sign in to the AWS Management Console and open the CloudWatch console at https://console.aws.amazon.com/cloudwatch/.

2. In the navigation pane, choose **Alarms**, and then choose **Create Alarm**. The **Create Alarm** dialog box displays.

3. On the **Select Metric** page, choose **Browse Metrics**, **SQS**:

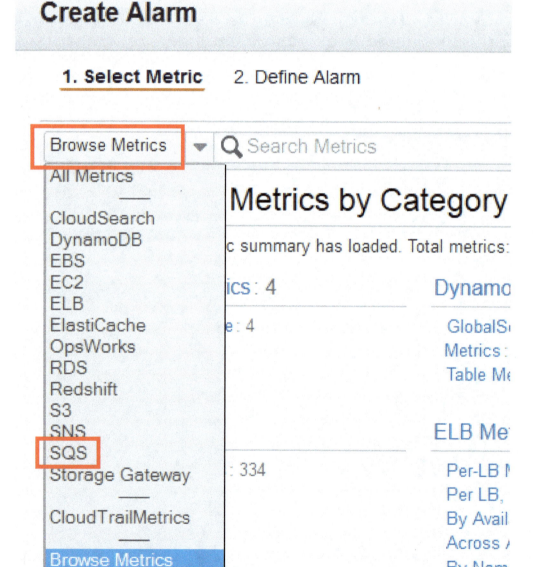

4. For **SQS > Queue Metrics**, choose (check) the box that you want to set an alarm for the combination of **QueueName** and **Metric Name**. (For a list of available metrics, see Available CloudWatch Metrics for Amazon SQS). For example, choosing (checking) the box for **MyQueue**, **NumberOfMessagesSent**

sets an alarm based on the number of messages sent to the `MyQueue` queue.

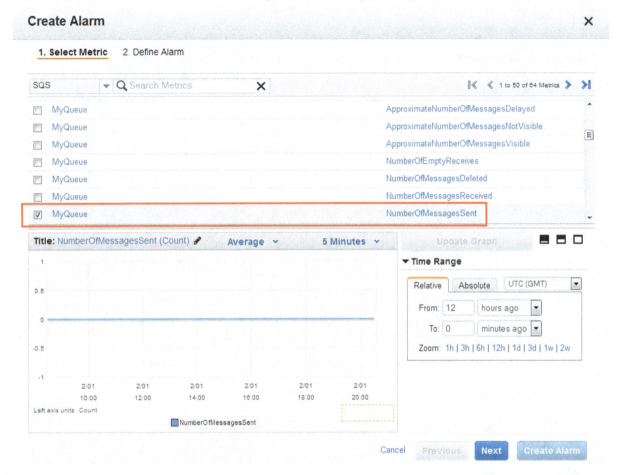

5. Choose **Next**. The **Define Alarm** page displays.

6. For **Alarm Threshold**, fill in the **Name** and **Description** boxes. For **is**, **for**, **Period**, and **Statistic**, specify the conditions for the alarm. For example, let's say you chose (checked) the box for **MyQueue**, **NumberOfMessagesSent** on the **Select Metric** page, and you want to alarm when more than 100 messages are sent in any hour to the `MyQueue` queue. You'd then set the following:

- Set **is** to > **100**.
- Set **for** to **1**.
- Set **Period** to **1 Hour**.
- Set **Statistic** to **Sum**.

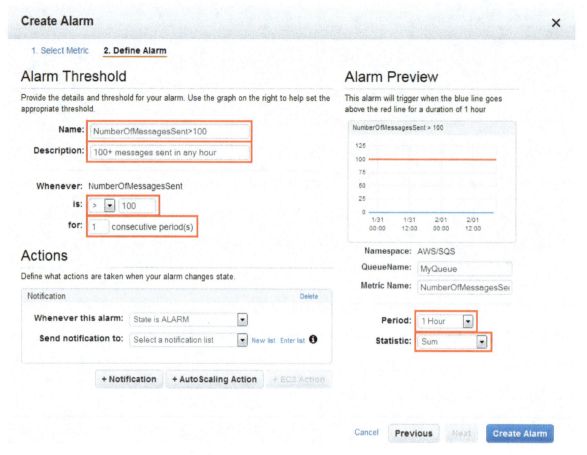

7. For **Actions** and **Whenever this alarm**, choose **State is ALARM**. For **Send notification to**, if you want CloudWatch to send you an email when the alarm state is reached, either select an existing Amazon SNS topic or choose **New list**. If you choose **New list**, you can set the name and list comma-separated email addresses for a new topic. This list is saved; it appears for future alarms. **Note**

If you choose **New list** to create a new Amazon SNS topic, the email addresses must be verified before they receive any notifications. Emails are sent only when the alarm enters an alarm state. If this alarm state change happens before the email addresses are verified, they won't receive a notification.

8. Choose **Create Alarm**. CloudWatch creates the alarm and then displays the alarms list.

For more information, see Creating Amazon CloudWatch Alarms.

Available CloudWatch Metrics for Amazon SQS

Amazon SQS sends the following metrics to CloudWatch.

Note
For standard queues, the result is approximate because of the distributed architecture of Amazon SQS. In most cases, the count should be close to the actual number of messages in the queue.
For FIFO queues, the result is exact.

Amazon SQS Metrics

The `AWS/SQS` namespace includes the following metrics.

Metric	Description
ApproximateAgeOfOldestMessage	The approximate age of the oldest non-deleted message in the queue. Units: *Seconds* Valid Statistics: Average, Minimum, Maximum, Sum, Data Samples (displays as Sample Count in the Amazon SQS console)
ApproximateNumberOfMessagesDelayed	The number of messages in the queue that are delayed and not available for reading immediately. This can happen when the queue is configured as a delay queue or when a message has been sent with a delay parameter. Units: *Count* Valid Statistics: Average, Minimum, Maximum, Sum, Data Samples (displays as Sample Count in the Amazon SQS console)
ApproximateNumberOfMessagesNotVisible	The number of messages that are "in flight." Messages are considered in flight if they have been sent to a client but have not yet been deleted or have not yet reached the end of their visibility window. Units: *Count* Valid Statistics: Average, Minimum, Maximum, Sum, Data Samples (displays as Sample Count in the Amazon SQS console)
ApproximateNumberOfMessagesVisible	The number of messages available for retrieval from the queue. Units: *Count* Valid Statistics: Average, Minimum, Maximum, Sum, Data Samples (displays as Sample Count in the Amazon SQS console)
NumberOfEmptyReceives	The number of `ReceiveMessage` API calls that did not return a message. Units: *Count* Valid Statistics: Average, Minimum, Maximum, Sum, Data Samples (displays as Sample Count in the Amazon SQS console)

Metric	Description
NumberOfMessagesDeleted	The number of messages deleted from the queue. Units: *Count* Valid Statistics: Average, Minimum, Maximum, Sum, Data Samples (displays as Sample Count in the Amazon SQS console) Amazon SQS emits the `NumberOfMessagesDeleted` metric for every successful deletion operation that uses a valid receipt handle, including duplicate deletions. The following scenarios might cause the value of the `NumberOfMessagesDeleted` metric to be higher than expected: [See the AWS documentation website for more details]
NumberOfMessagesReceived	The number of messages returned by calls to the `ReceiveMessage` action. Units: *Count* Valid Statistics: Average, Minimum, Maximum, Sum, Data Samples (displays as Sample Count in the Amazon SQS console)
NumberOfMessagesSent	The number of messages added to a queue. Units: *Count* Valid Statistics: Average, Minimum, Maximum, Sum, Data Samples (displays as Sample Count in the Amazon SQS console)
SentMessageSize	The size of messages added to a queue. Units: *Bytes* Valid Statistics: Average, Minimum, Maximum, Sum, Data Samples (displays as Sample Count in the Amazon SQS console) Note that `SentMessageSize` does not display as an available metric in the CloudWatch console until at least one message is sent to the corresponding queue.

Dimensions for Amazon SQS Metrics

The only dimension that Amazon SQS sends to CloudWatch is `QueueName`. This means that all available statistics are filtered by `QueueName`.

Logging Amazon SQS Actions Using AWS CloudTrail

Amazon SQS is integrated with CloudTrail, a service that captures API calls made by or on behalf of Amazon SQS in your AWS account and delivers the log files to the specified Amazon S3 bucket. CloudTrail captures API calls made from the Amazon SQS console or from the Amazon SQS API. You can use the information collected by CloudTrail to determine which requests are made to Amazon SQS, the source IP address from which the request is made, who made the request, when it is made, and so on. To learn more about CloudTrail, including how to configure and enable it, see the http://docs.aws.amazon.com/awscloudtrail/latest/userguide/.

Note
CloudTrail logging is supported for both standard and FIFO queues.

Amazon SQS Information in CloudTrail

When CloudTrail logging is enabled in your AWS account, API calls made to Amazon SQS actions are tracked in log files. Amazon SQS records are written together with other AWS service records in a log file. CloudTrail determines when to create and write to a new file based on a time period and file size.

The following actions are supported:

- [AddPermission](http://docs.aws.amazon.com/AWSSimpleQueueService/latest/APIReference/API_AddPermission.html)
- [CreateQueue](http://docs.aws.amazon.com/AWSSimpleQueueService/latest/APIReference/API_CreateQueue.html)
- [DeleteQueue](http://docs.aws.amazon.com/AWSSimpleQueueService/latest/APIReference/API_DeleteQueue.html)
- [PurgeQueue](http://docs.aws.amazon.com/AWSSimpleQueueService/latest/APIReference/API_PurgeQueue.html)
- [RemovePermission](http://docs.aws.amazon.com/AWSSimpleQueueService/latest/APIReference/API_RemovePermission.html)
- [SetQueueAttributes](http://docs.aws.amazon.com/AWSSimpleQueueService/latest/APIReference/API_SetQueueAttributes.html)

Every log entry contains information about who generated the request. The user identity information in the log helps you determine whether the request was made with root or IAM user credentials, with temporary security credentials for a role or federated user, or by another AWS service. For more information, see the **userIdentity** field in the CloudTrail Event Reference.

You can store your log files in your bucket for as long as you want, but you can also define Amazon S3 lifecycle rules to archive or delete log files automatically. By default, your log files are encrypted using Amazon S3 server-side encryption (SSE).

You can choose to have CloudTrail publish Amazon SNS notifications when new log files are delivered if you want to take quick action upon log file delivery. For more information, see Configuring Amazon SNS Notifications for CloudTrail.

You can also aggregate Amazon SQS log files from multiple AWS regions and multiple AWS accounts into a single Amazon S3 bucket. For more information, see Receiving CloudTrail Log Files from Multiple Regions.

Understanding Amazon SQS Log File Entries

CloudTrail log files contain one or more log entries where each entry is made up of multiple JSON-formatted events. A log entry represents a single request from any source and includes information about the requested action, any parameters, the date and time of the action, and so on. The log entries aren't guaranteed to be in any particular order. That is, they're not an ordered stack trace of the public API calls.

AddPermission

The following example shows a CloudTrail log entry for AddPermission:

```
1  {
2    "Records": [
3      {
4        "eventVersion": "1.01",
5        "userIdentity": {
6          "type": "IAMUser",
7          "principalId": "EX_PRINCIPAL_ID",
8          "arn": "arn:aws:iam::123456789012:user/Alice",
9          "accountId": "123456789012",
10         "accessKeyId": "EXAMPLE_KEY_ID",
11         "userName": "Alice"
12       },
13       "eventTime": "2014-07-16T00:44:19Z",
14       "eventSource": "sqs.amazonaws.com",
15       "eventName": "AddPermission",
16       "awsRegion": "us-east-2",
17       "sourceIPAddress": "192.0.2.0",
18       "userAgent": "Mozilla/5.0 (X11; Linux x86_64; rv:24.0) Gecko/20100101 Firefox/24.0",
19       "requestParameters": {
20         "actions": [
21           "SendMessage"
22         ],
23         "aWSAccountIds": [
24           "123456789012"
25         ],
26         "label": "label",
27         "queueUrl": "https://test-sqs.amazon.com/123456789012/hello1"
28       },
29       "responseElements": null,
30       "requestID": "334ccccd-b9bb-50fa-abdb-80f274981d60",
31       "eventID": "0552b000-09a3-47d6-a810-c5f9fd2534fe"
32     }
33   ]
34 }
```

CreateQueue

The following example shows a CloudTrail log entry for CreateQueue:

```
1  {
2    "Records": [
3      {
4        "eventVersion": "1.01",
5        "userIdentity": {
6          "type": "IAMUser",
7          "principalId": "EX_PRINCIPAL_ID",
8          "arn": "arn:aws:iam::123456789012:user/Alice",
9          "accountId": "123456789012",
10         "accessKeyId": "EXAMPLE_KEY_ID",
11         "userName": "Alice"
12       },
```

```
13      "eventTime": "2014-07-16T00:42:42Z",
14      "eventSource": "sqs.amazonaws.com",
15      "eventName": "CreateQueue",
16      "awsRegion": "us-east-2",
17      "sourceIPAddress": "192.0.2.0",
18      "userAgent": "Mozilla/5.0 (X11; Linux x86_64; rv:24.0) Gecko/20100101 Firefox/24.0",
19      "requestParameters": {
20        "queueName": "hello1"
21      },
22      "responseElements": {
23        "queueUrl": "https://test-sqs.amazon.com/123456789012/hello1"
24      },
25      "requestID": "49ebbdb7-5cd3-5323-8a00-f1889011fee9",
26      "eventID": "68f4e71c-4f2f-4625-8378-130ac89660b1"
27    }
28  ]
29 }
```

DeleteQueue

The following example shows a CloudTrail log entry for DeleteQueue:

```
1  {
2    "Records": [
3      {
4        "eventVersion": "1.01",
5        "userIdentity": {
6          "type": "IAMUser",
7          "principalId": "EX_PRINCIPAL_ID",
8          "arn": "arn:aws:iam::123456789012:user/Alice",
9          "accountId": "123456789012",
10         "accessKeyId": "EXAMPLE_KEY_ID",
11         "userName": "Alice"
12       },
13       "eventTime": "2014-07-16T00:44:47Z",
14       "eventSource": "sqs.amazonaws.com",
15       "eventName": "DeleteQueue",
16       "awsRegion": "us-east-2",
17       "sourceIPAddress": "192.0.2.0",
18       "userAgent": "Mozilla/5.0 (X11; Linux x86_64; rv:24.0) Gecko/20100101 Firefox/24.0",
19       "requestParameters": {
20         "queueUrl": "https://test-sqs.amazon.com/123456789012/hello1"
21       },
22       "responseElements": null,
23       "requestID": "e4c0cc05-4faa-51d5-aab2-803a8294388d",
24       "eventID": "af1bb158-6443-4b4d-abfd-1b867280d964"
25     }
26   ]
27 }
```

RemovePermission

The following example shows a CloudTrail log entry for RemovePermission:

```
 1  {
 2    "Records": [
 3      {
 4        "eventVersion": "1.01",
 5        "userIdentity": {
 6         "type": "IAMUser",
 7         "principalId": "EX_PRINCIPAL_ID",
 8         "arn": "arn:aws:iam::123456789012:user/Alice",
 9         "accountId": "123456789012",
10         "accessKeyId": "EXAMPLE_KEY_ID",
11         "userName": "Alice"
12        },
13        "eventTime": "2014-07-16T00:44:36Z",
14        "eventSource": "sqs.amazonaws.com",
15        "eventName": "RemovePermission",
16        "awsRegion": "us-east-2",
17        "sourceIPAddress": "192.0.2.0",
18        "userAgent": "Mozilla/5.0 (X11; Linux x86_64; rv:24.0) Gecko/20100101 Firefox/24.0",
19        "requestParameters": {
20         "label": "label",
21         "queueUrl": "https://test-sqs.amazon.com/123456789012/hello1"
22        },
23        "responseElements": null,
24        "requestID": "48178821-9c2b-5be0-88bf-c41e5118162a",
25        "eventID": "fed8a623-3fe9-4e64-9543-586d9e500159"
26      }
27    ]
28  }
```

SetQueueAttributes

The following example shows a CloudTrail log entry for SetQueueAttributes:

```
 1  {
 2    "Records": [
 3      {
 4        "eventVersion": "1.01",
 5        "userIdentity": {
 6         "type": "IAMUser",
 7         "principalId": "EX_PRINCIPAL_ID",
 8         "arn": "arn:aws:iam::123456789012:user/Alice",
 9         "accountId": "123456789012",
10         "accessKeyId": "EXAMPLE_KEY_ID",
11         "userName": "Alice"
12        },
13        "eventTime": "2014-07-16T00:43:15Z",
14        "eventSource": "sqs.amazonaws.com",
15        "eventName": "SetQueueAttributes",
16        "awsRegion": "us-east-2",
17        "sourceIPAddress": "192.0.2.0",
18        "userAgent": "Mozilla/5.0 (X11; Linux x86_64; rv:24.0) Gecko/20100101 Firefox/24.0",
19        "requestParameters": {
20         "attributes": {
21           "VisibilityTimeout": "100"
```

```
22          },
23          "queueUrl": "https://test-sqs.amazon.com/123456789012/hello1"
24        },
25        "responseElements": null,
26        "requestID": "7f15d706-f3d7-5221-b9ca-9b393f349b79",
27        "eventID": "8b6fb2dc-2661-49b1-b328-94317815088b"
28      }
29    ]
30  }
```

Automating Notifications from AWS Services to Amazon SQS using CloudWatch Events

Amazon CloudWatch Events lets you automate AWS services and respond to system events such as application availability issues or resource changes. Events from AWS services are delivered to CloudWatch Events nearly in real time. You can write simple rules to indicate which events are of interest to you and what automated actions to take when an event matches a rule.

CloudWatch Events lets you set a variety of *targets*—such as Amazon SQS standard and FIFO queues—which receive events in JSON format. For more information, see the *Amazon CloudWatch Events User Guide*.

Amazon SQS Security

This section provides information about Amazon SQS security, authentication and access control, and the Amazon SQS Access Policy Language.

Topics

- Controlling User Access to Your AWS Account
- Protecting Data Using Server-Side Encryption (SSE) and AWS KMS

Authentication and Access Control for Amazon SQS

Access to Amazon SQS requires credentials that AWS can use to authenticate your requests. These credentials must have permissions to access AWS resources, such an Amazon SQS queues and messages. The following sections provide details on how you can use AWS Identity and Access Management (IAM) and Amazon SQS to help secure your resources by controlling access to them.

Topics

- Authentication
- Access Control

Authentication

You can access AWS as any of the following types of identities:

- **AWS account root user** – When you first create an AWS account, you begin with a single sign-in identity that has complete access to all AWS services and resources in the account. This identity is called the AWS account *root user* and is accessed by signing in with the email address and password that you used to create the account. We strongly recommend that you do not use the root user for your everyday tasks, even the administrative ones. Instead, adhere to the best practice of using the root user only to create your first IAM user. Then securely lock away the root user credentials and use them to perform only a few account and service management tasks.

- **IAM user** – An IAM user is an identity within your AWS account that has specific custom permissions (for example, permissions to create a queue in Amazon SQS). You can use an IAM user name and password to sign in to secure AWS webpages like the AWS Management Console, AWS Discussion Forums, or the AWS Support Center.

  In addition to a user name and password, you can also generate access keys for each user. You can use these keys when you access AWS services programmatically, either through one of the several SDKs or by using the AWS Command Line Interface (CLI). The SDK and CLI tools use the access keys to cryptographically sign your request. If you don't use AWS tools, you must sign the request yourself. Amazon SQS supports *Signature Version 4*, a protocol for authenticating inbound API requests. For more information about authenticating requests, see Signature Version 4 Signing Process in the *AWS General Reference*.

- **IAM role** – An IAM role is an IAM identity that you can create in your account that has specific permissions. It is similar to an *IAM user*, but it is not associated with a specific person. An IAM role enables you to obtain temporary access keys that can be used to access AWS services and resources. IAM roles with temporary credentials are useful in the following situations:

  - **Federated user access** – Instead of creating an IAM user, you can use existing user identities from AWS Directory Service, your enterprise user directory, or a web identity provider. These are known as *federated users*. AWS assigns a role to a federated user when access is requested through an identity provider. For more information about federated users, see Federated Users and Roles in the *IAM User Guide*.

  - **AWS service access** – You can use an IAM role in your account to grant an AWS service permissions to access your account's resources. For example, you can create a role that allows Amazon Redshift to access an Amazon S3 bucket on your behalf and then load data from that bucket into an Amazon

180

Redshift cluster. For more information, see Creating a Role to Delegate Permissions to an AWS Service in the *IAM User Guide.*

- **Applications running on Amazon EC2** – You can use an IAM role to manage temporary credentials for applications that are running on an EC2 instance and making AWS API requests. This is preferable to storing access keys within the EC2 instance. To assign an AWS role to an EC2 instance and make it available to all of its applications, you create an instance profile that is attached to the instance. An instance profile contains the role and enables programs that are running on the EC2 instance to get temporary credentials. For more information, see Using an IAM Role to Grant Permissions to Applications Running on Amazon EC2 Instances in the *IAM User Guide.*

Access Control

Amazon SQS has its own resource-based permissions system that uses policies written in the same language used for AWS Identity and Access Management (IAM) policies. This means that you can achieve similar things with Amazon SQS policies and IAM policies.

Note
It is important to understand that all AWS accounts can delegate their permissions to users under their accounts. Cross-account access allows you to share access to your AWS resources without having to manage additional users. For information about using cross-account access, see Enabling Cross-Account Access in the *IAM User Guide.*
Cross-account permissions don't apply to the following actions:
[AddPermission](http://docs.aws.amazon.com/AWSSimpleQueueService/latest/APIReference/ API_AddPermission.html)   [CreateQueue](http://docs.aws.amazon.com/AWSSimpleQueueService /latest/APIReference/API_CreateQueue.html)   [DeleteQueue](http://docs.aws.amazon.com/ AWSSimpleQueueService/latest/APIReference/API_DeleteQueue.html)   [ListQueues](http://docs. aws.amazon.com/AWSSimpleQueueService/latest/APIReference/API_ListQueues.html) [ListQueueTags](http://docs.aws.amazon.com/AWSSimpleQueueService/latest/APIReference/API_ListQueueTags .html)   [RemovePermission](http://docs.aws.amazon.com/AWSSimpleQueueService/latest/ APIReference/API_RemovePermission.html)   [SetQueueAttributes](http://docs.aws.amazon.com/ AWSSimpleQueueService/latest/APIReference/API_SetQueueAttributes.html)   [TagQueue](http:// docs.aws.amazon.com/AWSSimpleQueueService/latest/APIReference/API_TagQueue.html) [UntagQueue](http://docs.aws.amazon.com/AWSSimpleQueueService/latest/APIReference/API_UntagQueue.html)
Currently, Amazon SQS supports only a limited subset of the condition keys available in IAM. For more information, see Amazon SQS API Permissions: Actions and Resource Reference.

The following sections describe how to manage permissions for Amazon SQS. We recommend that you read the overview first.

- Overview of Managing Access Permissions to Your Amazon Simple Queue Service Resource
- Using Identity-Based (IAM) Policies for Amazon SQS
- Using Custom Policies with the Amazon SQS Access Policy Language
- Using Temporary Security Credentials
- Amazon SQS API Permissions: Actions and Resource Reference

Overview of Managing Access Permissions to Your Amazon Simple Queue Service Resource

Every AWS resource is owned by an AWS account, and permissions to create or access a resource are governed by permissions policies. An account administrator can attach permissions policies to IAM identities (users, groups, and roles), and some services (such as Amazon SQS) also support attaching permissions policies to resources.

Note
An *account administrator* (or administrator user) is a user with administrative privileges. For more information, see IAM Best Practices in the *IAM User Guide*.

When granting permissions, you specify what users get permissions, the resource they get permissions for, and the specific actions that you want to allow on the resource.

Topics
- Amazon Simple Queue Service Resource and Operations
- Understanding Resource Ownership
- Managing Access to Resources
- Specifying Policy Elements: Actions, Effects, Resources, and Principals
- Specifying Conditions in a Policy

Amazon Simple Queue Service Resource and Operations

In Amazon SQS, the only resource is the *queue*. In a policy, use an Amazon Resource Name (ARN) to identify the resource that the policy applies to. The following resource has a unique ARN associated with it:

Resource Type	ARN Format
Queue	arn:aws:sqs:region:account_id:queue_name

The following are examples of the ARN format for queues:

- An ARN for a queue named `my_queue` in the US East (Ohio) region, belonging to AWS Account 123456789012:

```
1 arn:aws:sqs:us-east-2:123456789012:my_queue
```

- An ARN for a queue named `my_queue` in each of the different regions that Amazon SQS supports:

```
1 arn:aws:sqs:*:123456789012:my_queue
```

- An ARN that uses * or ? as a wildcard for the queue name. In the following examples, the ARN matches all queues prefixed with `my_prefix_`:

```
1 arn:aws:sqs:*:123456789012:my_prefix_*
```

You can get the ARN value for an existing queue by calling the http://docs.aws.amazon.com/ AWSSimpleQueueService/latest/APIReference/API_GetQueueAttributes.html action. The value of the `QueueArn` attribute is the ARN of the queue. For more information about ARNs, see IAM ARNs in the *IAM User Guide*.

Amazon SQS provides a set of actions that work with the queue resource. For more information, see Amazon SQS API Permissions: Actions and Resource Reference.

Understanding Resource Ownership

The AWS account owns the resources that are created in the account, regardless of who created the resources. Specifically, the resource owner is the AWS account of the *principal entity* (that is, the root account, an IAM user, or an IAM role) that authenticates the resource creation request. The following examples illustrate how this works:

- If you use the root account credentials of your AWS account to create an Amazon SQS queue, your AWS account is the owner of the resource (in Amazon SQS, the resource is the Amazon SQS queue).
- If you create an IAM user in your AWS account and grant permissions to create a queue to the user, the user can create the queue. However, your AWS account (to which the user belongs) owns the queue resource.
- If you create an IAM role in your AWS account with permissions to create an Amazon SQS queue, anyone who can assume the role can create a queue. Your AWS account (to which the role belongs) owns the queue resource.

Managing Access to Resources

A *permissions policy* describes the permissions granted to accounts. The following section explains the available options for creating permissions policies.

Note
This section discusses using IAM in the context of Amazon SQS. It doesn't provide detailed information about the IAM service. For complete IAM documentation, see What is IAM? in the *IAM User Guide*. For information about IAM policy syntax and descriptions, see AWS IAM Policy Reference in the *IAM User Guide*.

Policies attached to an IAM identity are referred to as *identity-based* policies (IAM polices) and policies attached to a resource are referred to as *resource-based* policies.

Identity-Based Policies (IAM Policies and Amazon SQS Policies)

There are two ways to give your users permissions to your Amazon SQS queues: using the Amazon SQS policy system and using the IAM policy system. You can use either system, or both, to attach policies to users or roles. In most cases, you can achieve the same result using either system. For example, you can do the following:

- **Attach a permission policy to a user or a group in your account** – To grant user permissions to create an Amazon SQS queue, attach a permissions policy to a user or group that the user belongs to.
- **Attach a permission policy to a user in another AWS account** – To grant user permissions to create an Amazon SQS queue, attach an Amazon SQS permissions policy to a user in another AWS account.
- **Attach a permission policy to a role (grant cross-account permissions)** – To grant cross-account permissions, attach an identity-based permissions policy to an IAM role. For example, the AWS account A administrator can create a role to grant cross-account permissions to AWS account B (or an AWS service) as follows:
  - The account A administrator creates an IAM role and attaches a permissions policy—that grants permissions on resources in account A—to the role.
  - The account A administrator attaches a trust policy to the role that identifies account B as the principal who can assume the role.
  - The account B administrator delegates the permission to assume the role to any users in account B. This allows users in account B to create or access queues in account A. **Note**
    If you want to grant the permission to assume the role to an AWS service, the principal in the trust policy can also be an AWS service principal.

For more information about using IAM to delegate permissions, see Access Management in the *IAM User Guide*.

While Amazon SQS works with IAM policies, it has its own policy infrastructure. You can use an Amazon SQS policy with a queue to specify which AWS Accounts have access to the queue. You can specify the type of access and conditions (for example, a condition that grants permissions to use `SendMessage`, `ReceiveMessage` if the request is made before December 31, 2010). The specific actions you can grant permissions for are a subset of the overall list of Amazon SQS actions. When you write an Amazon SQS policy and specify * to "allow all Amazon SQS actions," it means that a user can perform all actions in this subset.

The following diagram illustrates the concept of one of these basic Amazon SQS policies that covers the subset of actions. The policy is for `queue_xyz`, and it gives AWS Account 1 and AWS Account 2 permissions to use any of the allowed actions with the specified queue.

Note
The resource in the policy is specified as `123456789012/queue_xyz`, where `123456789012` is the AWS Account ID of the account that owns the queue.

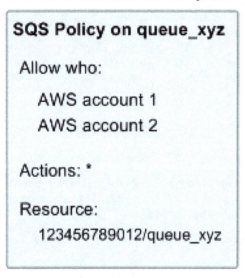

With the introduction of IAM and the concepts of *Users* and *Amazon Resource Names (ARNs)*, a few things have changed about SQS policies. The following diagram and table describe the changes.

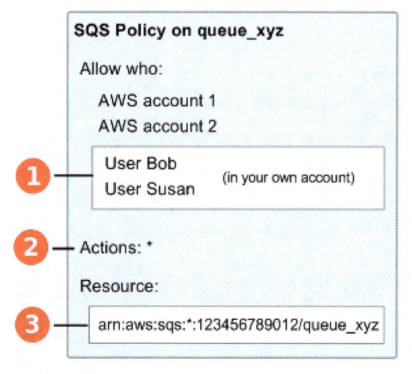

184

① In addition to specifying which AWS Accounts have access to a queue, you can specify which users *in your own AWS account* have access to the queue. If the users are in different accounts, see Tutorial: Delegate Access Across AWS Accounts Using IAM Roles in the *IAM User Guide*.

② The subset of actions included in * has expanded. For a list of allowed actions, see Amazon SQS API Permissions: Actions and Resource Reference.

③ You can specify the resource using the Amazon Resource Name (ARN), the standard means of specifying resources in IAM policies. For information about the ARN format for Amazon SQS queues, see Amazon Simple Queue Service Resource and Operations.

For example, according to the Amazon SQS policy in the preceding diagram, anyone who possesses the security credentials for AWS Account 1 or AWS Account 2 can access `queue_xyz`. In addition, Users Bob and Susan in your own AWS Account (with ID `123456789012`) can access the queue.

Before the introduction of IAM, Amazon SQS automatically gave the creator of a queue full control over the queue (that is, access to all of the possible Amazon SQS actions on that queue). This is no longer true, unless the creator uses AWS security credentials. Any user who has permissions to create a queue must also have permissions to use other Amazon SQS actions in order to do anything with the created queues.

The following is an example policy that allows a user to use all Amazon SQS actions, but only with queues whose names are prefixed with the literal string `bob_queue_`.

```
1 {
2     "Version": "2012-10-17",
3     "Statement": [{
4         "Effect": "Allow",
5         "Action": "sqs:*",
6         "Resource": "arn:aws:sqs:*:123456789012:bob_queue_*"
7     }]
8 }
```

For more information, see Using Identity-Based (IAM) Policies for Amazon SQS, and Identities (Users, Groups, and Roles) in the *IAM User Guide*.

Resource-Based Policies

Other AWS services, such as Amazon S3, support resource-based permissions policies. For example, to manage access permissions for an S3 bucket, you can attach a policy the S3 bucket.

Amazon SQS doesn't support resource-level permissions in identity-based policies (attached to a user or role), in which you can specify resources on which users are allowed to perform specified actions. For more information, see Overview of AWS IAM Permissions in the *IAM User Guide*.

Specifying Policy Elements: Actions, Effects, Resources, and Principals

For each Amazon Simple Queue Service resource, the service defines a set of actions. To grant permissions for these actions, Amazon SQS defines a set of actions that you can specify in a policy.

Note
Performing an action can require permissions for more than one action. When granting permissions for specific actions, you also identify the resource for which the actions are allowed or denied.

The following are the most basic policy elements:

- **Resource** – In a policy, you use an Amazon Resource Name (ARN) to identify the resource to which the policy applies.

- **Action** – You use action keywords to identify resource actions that you want to allow or deny. For example, the `sqs:CreateQueue` permission allows the user to perform the Amazon Simple Queue Service `CreateQueue` action.
- **Effect** – You specify the effect when the user requests the specific action—this can be either allow or deny. If you don't explicitly grant access to a resource, access is implicitly denied. You can also explicitly deny access to a resource, which you might do to make sure that a user can't access it, even if a different policy grants access.
- **Principal** – In identity-based policies (IAM policies), the user that the policy is attached to is the implicit principal. For resource-based policies, you specify the user, account, service, or other entity that you want to receive permissions (applies to resource-based policies only).

To learn more about Amazon SQS policy syntax and descriptions, see AWS IAM Policy Reference in the *IAM User Guide*.

For a table of all Amazon Simple Queue Service actions and the resources that they apply to, see Amazon SQS API Permissions: Actions and Resource Reference.

Specifying Conditions in a Policy

When you grant permissions, you can use the Amazon SQS Access Policy Language to specify the conditions for when a policy should take effect. For example, you might want a policy to be applied only after a specific date. For more information about specifying conditions in a policy language, see Condition in the *IAM User Guide*.

To express conditions, you use predefined condition keys. There are no condition keys specific to Amazon SQS. However, there are AWS-wide condition keys that you can use with Amazon SQS. Currently, Amazon SQS supports only a limited subset of the condition keys available in IAM:

- `aws:CurrentTime`
- `aws:EpochTime`
- `aws:SecureTransport`
- `aws:SourceArn`
- `aws:SourceIP`
- `aws:UserAgent`
- `aws:MultiFactorAuthAge`
- `aws:MultiFactorAuthPresent`
- `aws:TokenAge`

Using Identity-Based (IAM) Policies for Amazon SQS

This topic provides examples of identity-based policies in which an account administrator can attach permissions policies to IAM identities (users, groups, and roles).

Important

We recommend that you first review the introductory topics that explain the basic concepts and options available for you to manage access to your Amazon Simple Queue Service resources. For more information, see Overview of Managing Access Permissions to Your Amazon Simple Queue Service Resource.

With the exception of `ListQueues`, all Amazon SQS actions support resource-level permissions. For more information, see Amazon SQS API Permissions: Actions and Resource Reference.

Topics

- Using Amazon SQS and IAM Policies
- Permissions Required to Use the Amazon SQS Console
- AWS-Managed (Predefined) Policies for Amazon SQS
- Basic Amazon SQS Policy Examples
- Advanced Amazon SQS Policy Examples

Using Amazon SQS and IAM Policies

There are two ways to give your users permissions to your Amazon SQS resources: using the Amazon SQS policy system and using the IAM policy system. You can use one or the other, or both. For the most part, you can achieve the same result with either one.

For example, the following diagram shows an IAM policy and an Amazon SQS policy equivalent to it. The IAM policy grants the rights to the Amazon SQS `ReceiveMessage` and `SendMessage` actions for the queue called `queue_xyz` in your AWS Account, and the policy is attached to users named Bob and Susan (Bob and Susan have the permissions stated in the policy). This Amazon SQS policy also gives Bob and Susan rights to the `ReceiveMessage` and `SendMessage` actions for the same queue.

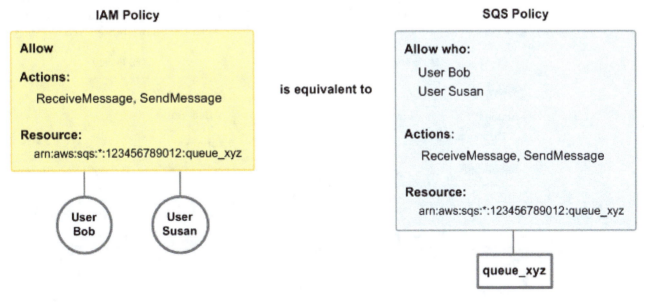

Note

This example shows simple policies without conditions. You can specify a particular condition in either policy and get the same result.

There is one major difference between IAM and Amazon SQS policies: the Amazon SQS policy system lets you grant permission to other AWS Accounts, whereas IAM doesn't.

It is up to you how you use both of the systems together to manage your permissions. The following examples show how the two policy systems work together.

- In the first example, Bob has both an IAM policy and an Amazon SQS policy that apply to his account. The IAM policy grants his account permission for the `ReceiveMessage` action on `queue_xyz`, whereas the Amazon SQS policy gives his account permission for the `SendMessage` action on the same queue. The following diagram illustrates the concept.

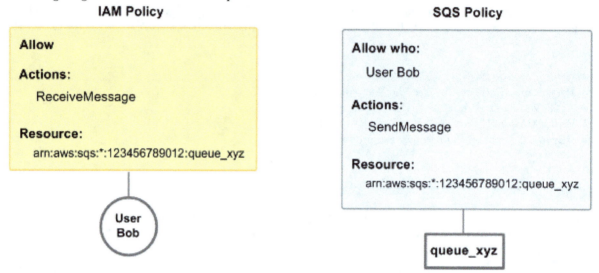

If Bob sends a `ReceiveMessage` request to `queue_xyz`, the IAM policy allows the action. If Bob sends a `SendMessage` request to `queue_xyz`, the Amazon SQS policy allows the action.

- In the second example, Bob abuses his access to `queue_xyz`, so it becomes necessary to remove his entire access to the queue. The easiest thing to do is to add a policy that denies him access to all actions for the queue. This policy overrides the other two because an explicit `deny` always overrides an `allow`. For more information about policy evaluation logic, see Using Custom Policies with the Amazon SQS Access Policy Language. The following diagram illustrates the concept.

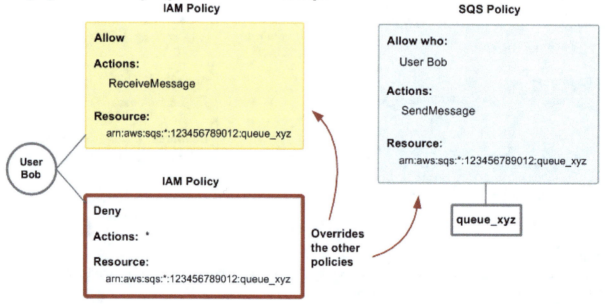

You can also add an additional statement to the Amazon SQS policy that denies Bob any type of access to the queue. It has the same effect as adding an IAM policy that denies Bob access to the queue. For examples of policies that cover Amazon SQS actions and resources, see Advanced Amazon SQS Policy Examples. For more information about writing Amazon SQS policies, see Using Custom Policies with the Amazon SQS Access Policy Language.

Permissions Required to Use the Amazon SQS Console

A user who wants to work with the Amazon SQS console must have the minimum set of permissions to work with the Amazon SQS queues in the user's AWS account. For example, the user must have the permission to call the `ListQueues` action to be able to list queues, or the permission to call the `CreateQueue` action to be able to create queues. In addition to Amazon SQS permissions, to subscribe an Amazon SQS queue to an Amazon SNS topic, the console also requires permissions for Amazon SNS actions.

If you create an IAM policy that is more restrictive than the minimum required permissions, the console might not function as intended for users with that IAM policy.

You don't need to allow minimum console permissions for users that make calls only to the AWS CLI or Amazon SQS actions.

AWS-Managed (Predefined) Policies for Amazon SQS

AWS addresses many common use cases by providing standalone AWS managed IAM policies. These AWS managed policies simplify working with permissions by granting the permissions necessary for common use cases. For more information, see AWS Managed Policies in the *IAM User Guide*.

The following AWS managed policies (that you can attach to users in your account) are specific to Amazon SQS:

- **AmazonSQSReadOnlyAccess** – Grants read-only access to Amazon SQS queues using the AWS Management Console.
- **AmazonSQSFullAccess** – Grants full access to Amazon SQS queues using the AWS Management Console.

You can search and review available policies on the IAM console. You can also create your own custom IAM policies to allow permissions for Amazon SQS actions and queues. You can attach these custom policies to the IAM users or groups that require permissions.

Basic Amazon SQS Policy Examples

The following examples provide an introduction to Amazon SQS permission policies.

Example 1: Allow a User to Create Queues

In the following example, we create a policy for Bob that lets him access all Amazon SQS actions, but only with queues whose names are prefixed with the literal string `bob_queue_`.

Amazon SQS doesn't automatically grant the creator of a queue permissions to use the queue. Therefore, we must explicitly grant Bob permissions to use all Amazon SQS actions in addition to `CreateQueue` action in the IAM policy.

```
1  {
2      "Version": "2012-10-17",
3      "Statement": [{
4          "Effect": "Allow",
5          "Action": "sqs:*",
6          "Resource": "arn:aws:sqs:*:123456789012:bob_queue_*"
7      }]
8  }
```

Example 2: Allow Developers to Write Messages to a Shared Queue

In the following example, we create a group for developers and attach a policy that lets the group use the Amazon SQS `SendMessage` action, but only with the queue that belongs to the specified AWS account and is named `MyCompanyQueue`.

```
1  {
2      "Version": "2012-10-17",
3      "Statement": [{
4          "Effect": "Allow",
5          "Action": "sqs:SendMessage",
6          "Resource": "arn:aws:sqs:*:123456789012:MyCompanyQueue"
7      }]
8  }
```

You can use * instead of `SendMessage` to grant the following actions to a principal on a shared queue: `ChangeMessageVisibility`, `DeleteMessage`, `GetQueueAttributes`, `GetQueueUrl`, `ReceiveMessage`, and `SendMessage`.

Note
Although * includes access provided by other permission types, Amazon SQS considers permissions separately. For example, it is possible to grant both * and `SendMessage` permissions to a user, even though a * includes the access provided by `SendMessage`.
This concept also applies when you remove a permission. If a principal has only a * permission, requesting to remove a `SendMessage` permission *doesn't* leave the principal with an *everything-but* permission. Instead, the request has no effect, because the principal doesn't possess an explicit `SendMessage` permission. To leave the principal with onlt the `ReceiveMessage` permission, first add the `ReceiveMessage` permission and then remove the * permission.

Example 3: Allow Managers to Get the General Size of Queues

In the following example, we create a group for managers and attach a policy that lets the group use the Amazon SQS `GetQueueAttributes` action with all of the queues that belong to the specified AWS account.

```
1 {
2     "Version": "2012-10-17",
3     "Statement": [{
4         "Effect": "Allow",
5         "Action": "sqs:GetQueueAttributes",
6         "Resource": "*"
7     }]
8 }
```

Example 4: Allow a Partner to Send Messages to a Specific Queue

You can accomplish this task using an Amazon SQS policy or an IAM policy. If your partner has an AWS account, it might be easier to use an Amazon SQS policy. However, any user in the partner's company who possesses the AWS security credentials can send messages to the queue. If you want to limit access to a particular user or application, you must treat the partner like a user in your own company and use an IAM policy instead of an Amazon SQS policy.

This example performs the following actions:

1. Create a group called WidgetCo to represent the partner company.

2. Create a user for the specific user or application at the partner's company who needs access.

3. Add the user to the group.

4. Attach a policy that gives the group access only to the **SendMessage** action for only the queue named `WidgetPartnerQueue`.

```
1 {
2     "Version": "2012-10-17",
3     "Statement": [{
4         "Effect": "Allow",
5         "Action": "sqs:SendMessage",
6         "Resource": "arn:aws:sqs:*:123456789012:WidgetPartnerQueue"
7     }]
8 }
```

Advanced Amazon SQS Policy Examples

This section shows example policies for common Amazon SQS use cases.

You can use the console to verify the effects of each policy as you attach the policy to the user. Initially, the user doesn't have permissions and won't be able to do anything in the console. As you attach policies to the user, you can verify that the user can perform various actions in the console.

Note
We recommend that you use two browser windows: one to grant permissions and the other to sign into the AWS Management Console using the user's credentials to verify permissions as you grant them to the user.

Example 1: Grant One Permission to One AWS Account

The following example policy grants AWS account number 111122223333 the `SendMessage` permission for the queue named 444455556666/queue1 in the US East (Ohio) region.

```
1  {
2      "Version": "2012-10-17",
3      "Id": "Queue1_Policy_UUID",
4      "Statement": [{
5          "Sid":"Queue1_SendMessage",
6          "Effect": "Allow",
7          "Principal": {
8              "AWS": [
9                  "111122223333"
10             ]
11         },
12         "Action": "sqs:SendMessage",
13         "Resource": "arn:aws:sqs:us-east-2:444455556666:queue1"
14     }]
15 }
```

Example 2: Grant Two Permissions to One AWS Account

The following example policy grants AWS account number 111122223333 both the `SendMessage` and `ReceiveMessage` permission for the queue named 444455556666/queue1.

```
1  {
2      "Version": "2012-10-17",
3      "Id": "Queue1_Policy_UUID",
4      "Statement": [{
5          "Sid":"Queue1_Send_Receive",
6          "Effect": "Allow",
7          "Principal": {
8              "AWS": [
9                  "111122223333"
10             ]
11         },
12         "Action": [
13             "sqs:SendMessage",
14             "sqs:ReceiveMessage"
15         ],
16         "Resource": "arn:aws:sqs:*:444455556666:queue1"
```

```
17    }]
18 }
```

Example 3: Grant All Permissions to Two AWS Accounts

The following example policy grants two different AWS accounts numbers (111122223333 and 444455556666) permission to use all actions to which Amazon SQS allows shared access for the queue named 123456789012/queue1 in the US East (Ohio) region.

```
1  {
2      "Version": "2012-10-17",
3      "Id": "Queue1_Policy_UUID",
4      "Statement": [{
5          "Sid":"Queue1_AllActions",
6          "Effect": "Allow",
7          "Principal": {
8              "AWS": [
9                  "111122223333",
10                 "444455556666"
11             ]
12         },
13         "Action": "sqs:*",
14         "Resource": "arn:aws:sqs:us-east-2:123456789012:queue1"
15     }]
16 }
```

Example 4: Grant Cross-Account Permissions to a Role and a User Name

The following example policy grants role1 and username1 under AWS account number 111122223333 cross-account permission to use all actions to which Amazon SQS allows shared access for the queue named 123456789012/queue1 in the US East (Ohio) region.

Cross-account permissions don't apply to the following actions:

- [AddPermission](http://docs.aws.amazon.com/AWSSimpleQueueService/latest/APIReference/API_AddPermission.html)
- [CreateQueue](http://docs.aws.amazon.com/AWSSimpleQueueService/latest/APIReference/API_CreateQueue.html)
- [DeleteQueue](http://docs.aws.amazon.com/AWSSimpleQueueService/latest/APIReference/API_DeleteQueue.html)
- [ListQueues](http://docs.aws.amazon.com/AWSSimpleQueueService/latest/APIReference/API_ListQueues.html)
- [ListQueueTags](http://docs.aws.amazon.com/AWSSimpleQueueService/latest/APIReference/API_ListQueueTags.html)
- [RemovePermission](http://docs.aws.amazon.com/AWSSimpleQueueService/latest/APIReference/API_RemovePermission.html)
- [SetQueueAttributes](http://docs.aws.amazon.com/AWSSimpleQueueService/latest/APIReference/API_SetQueueAttributes.html)
- [TagQueue](http://docs.aws.amazon.com/AWSSimpleQueueService/latest/APIReference/API_TagQueue.html)
- [UntagQueue](http://docs.aws.amazon.com/AWSSimpleQueueService/latest/APIReference/API_UntagQueue.html)

```
1  {
2      "Version": "2012-10-17",
3      "Id": "Queue1_Policy_UUID",
4      "Statement": [{
5          "Sid":"Queue1_AllActions",
6          "Effect": "Allow",
7          "Principal": {
8              "AWS": [
9                  "arn:aws:iam::111122223333:role/role1",
10                 "arn:aws:iam::111122223333:user/username1"
11             ]
12         },
13         "Action": "sqs:*",
14         "Resource": "arn:aws:sqs:us-east-2:123456789012:queue1"
15     }]
16 }
```

Example 5: Grant a Permission to All Users

The following example policy grants all users (anonymous users) `ReceiveMessage` permission for the queue named 111122223333/queue1.

```
1  {
2      "Version": "2012-10-17",
3      "Id": "Queue1_Policy_UUID",
4      "Statement": [{
5          "Sid":"Queue1_AnonymousAccess_ReceiveMessage",
6          "Effect": "Allow",
7          "Principal": "*",
8          "Action": "sqs:ReceiveMessage",
9          "Resource": "arn:aws:sqs:*:111122223333:queue1"
10     }]
11 }
```

Example 6: Grant a Time-Limited Permission to All Users

The following example policy grants all users (anonymous users) `ReceiveMessage` permission for the queue named 111122223333/queue1, but only between 12:00 p.m. (noon) and 3:00 p.m. on January 31, 2009.

```
1  {
2      "Version": "2012-10-17",
3      "Id": "Queue1_Policy_UUID",
4      "Statement": [{
5          "Sid":"Queue1_AnonymousAccess_ReceiveMessage_TimeLimit",
6          "Effect": "Allow",
7          "Principal": "*",
8          "Action": "sqs:ReceiveMessage",
9          "Resource": "arn:aws:sqs:*:111122223333:queue1",
10         "Condition" : {
11             "DateGreaterThan" : {
12                 "aws:CurrentTime":"2009-01-31T12:00Z"
13             },
14             "DateLessThan" : {
```

```
15            "aws:CurrentTime":"2009-01-31T15:00Z"
16        }
17      }
18    }]
19 }
```

Example 7: Grant All Permissions to All Users in a CIDR Range

The following example policy grants all users (anonymous users) permission to use all possible Amazon SQS actions that can be shared for the queue named 111122223333/queue1, but only if the request comes from the 192.168.143.0/24 CIDR range.

```
1 {
2    "Version": "2012-10-17",
3    "Id": "Queue1_Policy_UUID",
4    "Statement": [{
5      "Sid":"Queue1_AnonymousAccess_AllActions_WhitelistIP",
6      "Effect": "Allow",
7      "Principal": "*",
8      "Action": "sqs:*",
9      "Resource": "arn:aws:sqs:*:111122223333:queue1",
10      "Condition" : {
11        "IpAddress" : {
12          "aws:SourceIp":"192.168.143.0/24"
13        }
14      }
15    }]
16 }
```

Example 8: Whitelist and Blacklist Permissions for Users in Different CIDR Ranges

The following example policy has two statements:

- The first statement grants all users (anonymous users) in the 192.168.143.0/24 CIDR range (except for 192.168.143.188) permission to use the **SendMessage** action for the queue named 111122223333/queue1.
- The second statement blacklists all users (anonymous users) in the 10.1.2.0/24 CIDR range from using the queue.

```
1 {
2    "Version": "2012-10-17",
3    "Id": "Queue1_Policy_UUID",
4    "Statement": [{
5      "Sid":"Queue1_AnonymousAccess_SendMessage_IPLimit",
6      "Effect": "Allow",
7      "Principal": "*",
8      "Action": "sqs:SendMessage",
9      "Resource": "arn:aws:sqs:*:111122223333:queue1",
10      "Condition" : {
11        "IpAddress" : {
12          "aws:SourceIp":"192.168.143.0/24"
13        },
14        "NotIpAddress" : {
15          "aws:SourceIp":"192.168.143.188/32"
```

```
16            }
17          }
18      }, {
19          "Sid":"Queue1_AnonymousAccess_AllActions_IPLimit_Deny",
20          "Effect": "Deny",
21          "Principal": "*",
22          "Action": "sqs:*",
23          "Resource": "arn:aws:sqs:*:111122223333:queue1",
24          "Condition" : {
25            "IpAddress" : {
26              "aws:SourceIp":"10.1.2.0/24"
27            }
28          }
29      }]
30  }
```

Using Custom Policies with the Amazon SQS Access Policy Language

If you want to allow Amazon SQS access based only on an AWS account ID and basic permissions (such as for http://docs.aws.amazon.com/AWSSimpleQueueService/latest/APIReference/API_SendMessage.html or http://docs.aws.amazon.com/AWSSimpleQueueService/latest/APIReference/API_ReceiveMessage.html), you don't need to write your own policies. You can just use the Amazon SQS http://docs.aws.amazon.com/AWSSimpleQueueService/latest/APIReference/API_AddPermission.html action.

If you want to explicitly deny or allow access based on more specific conditions (such as the time the request comes in or the IP address of the requester), you need to write your own Amazon SQS policies and upload them to the AWS system using the Amazon SQS `SetQueueAttributes` action.

Topics

- Amazon SQS Access Control Architecture
- Amazon SQS Access Control Process Workflow
- Amazon SQS Access Policy Language Key Concepts
- Amazon SQS Access Policy Language Evaluation Logic
- Relationships Between Explicit and Default Denials in the Amazon SQS Access Policy Language
- Custom Amazon SQS Access Policy Language Examples

Amazon SQS Access Control Architecture

The following diagram describes the access control for your Amazon SQS resources.

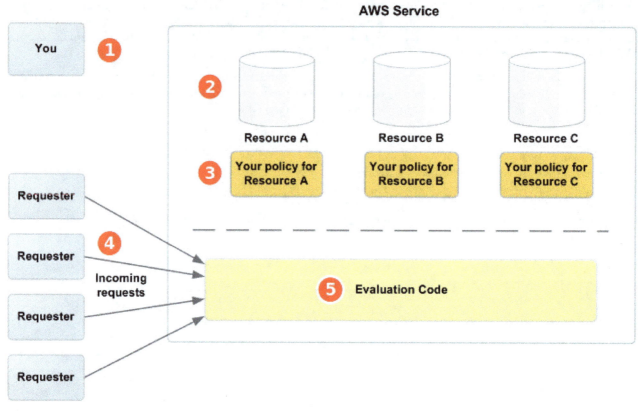

① You, the resource owner.

② Your resources contained within the AWS service (for example, Amazon SQS queues).

③ Your policies. It is a good practice to have one policy per resource The AWS service itself provides an API you use to upload and manage your policies.

④ Requesters and their incoming requests to the AWS service.

⑤ The access policy language evaluation code. This is the set of code within the AWS service that evaluates incoming requests against the applicable policies and determines whether the requester is allowed access to the resource.

Amazon SQS Access Control Process Workflow

The following diagram describes the general workflow of access control with the Amazon SQS access policy language.

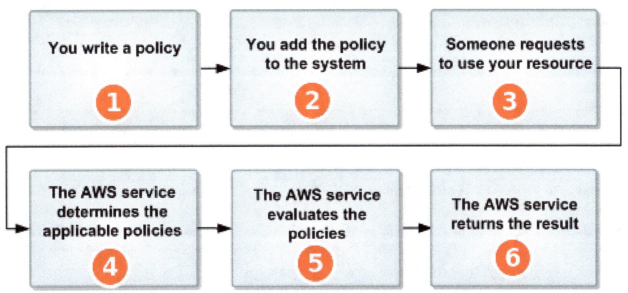

① You write an Amazon SQS policy for your queue.

② You upload your policy to AWS. The AWS service provides an API that you use to upload your policies. For example, you use the Amazon SQS `SetQueueAttributes` action to upload a policy for a particular Amazon SQS queue.

③ Someone sends a request to use your Amazon SQS queue.

④ Amazon SQS examines all available Amazon SQS policies and determines which ones are applicable.

⑤ Amazon SQS evaluates the policies and determines whether the requester is allowed to use your queue.

⑥ Based on the policy evaluation result, Amazon SQS either returns an `Access denied` error to the requester or continues to process the request.

Amazon SQS Access Policy Language Key Concepts

To write your own policies, you must be familiar with JSON and a number of key concepts.

allow The result of a statement that has effect set to `allow`.

action The activity that the principal has permission to perform, typically a request to AWS.

default-deny The result of a statement that that has no allow or explicit-deny settings.

condition Any restriction or detail about a permission. Typical conditions are related to date and time and IP addresses.

effect The result that you want the statement of a policy to return at evaluation time. You specify the `deny` or `allow` value when you write the policy statement. There can be three possible results at policy evaluation time: default-deny, allow, and explicit-deny.

explicit-deny The result of a statement that has effect set to `deny`.

evaluation The process that Amazon SQS uses to determine whether an incoming request should be denied or allowed based on a policy.

issuer The user who writes a policy to grant permissions to a resource. The issuer, by definition is always the resource owner. AWS doesn't permit Amazon SQS users to create policies for resources they don't own.

key The specific characteristic that is the basis for access restriction.

permission The concept of allowing or disallowing access to a resource using a condition and a key.

policy The document that acts as a container for one or more **statements**.

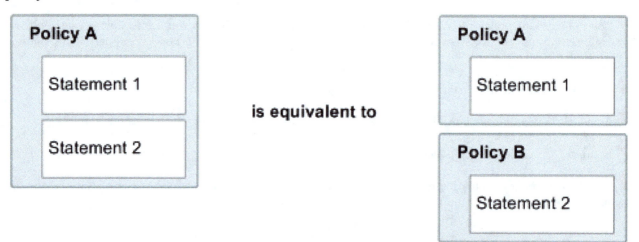

Amazon SQS uses the policy to determine whether to grant access to a user for a resource.

principal The user who receives permission in the policy.

resource The object that the principal requests access to.

statement The formal description of a single permission, written in the access policy language as part of a broader policy document.

requester The user who sends a request for access to a resource.

Amazon SQS Access Policy Language Evaluation Logic

At evaluation time, Amazon SQS determines whether a request from someone other than the resource owner should be allowed or denied. The evaluation logic follows several basic rules:

- By default, all requests to use your resource coming from anyone but you are denied.
- An *allow* overrides any *default-deny*.
- An *explicit-deny* overrides any **allow**.
- The order in which the policies are evaluated isn't important.

The following diagram describes in detail how Amazon SQS evaluates decisions about access permissions.

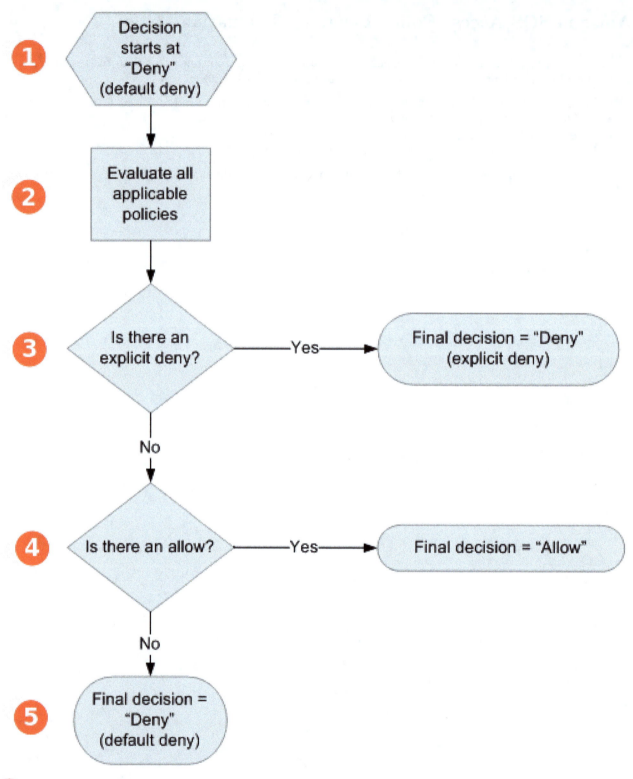

① The decision starts with a **default-deny**.

② The enforcement code evaluates all the policies that are applicable to the request (based on the resource, principal, action, and conditions). The order in which the enforcement code evaluates the policies isn't important.

③ The enforcement code looks for an **explicit-deny** instruction that can apply to the request. If it finds even one, the enforcement code returns a decision of **deny** and the process finishes.

4 If no **explicit-deny** instruction is found, the enforcement code looks for any **allow** instructions that can apply to the request. If it finds even one, the enforcement code returns a decision of **allow** and the process finishes (the service continues to process the request).

5 If no **allow** instruction is found, then the final decision is **deny** (because there is no **explicit-deny** or **allow**, this is considered a **default-deny**).

Relationships Between Explicit and Default Denials in the Amazon SQS Access Policy Language

If an Amazon SQS policy doesn't directly apply to a request, the request results in a *default-deny*. For example, if a user requests permission to use Amazon SQS but the only policy that applies to the user can use DynamoDB, the requests results in a **default-deny**.

If a condition in a statement isn't met, the request results in a **default-deny**. If all conditions in a statement are met, the request results in either an *allow* or an *explicit-deny* based on the value of the *effect* element of the policy. Policies don't specify what to do if a condition isn't met, so the default result in this case is a **default-deny**. For example, you want to prevent requests that come from Antarctica. You write Policy A1 that allows a request only if it doesn't come from Antarctica. The following diagram illustrates the Amazon SQS policy.

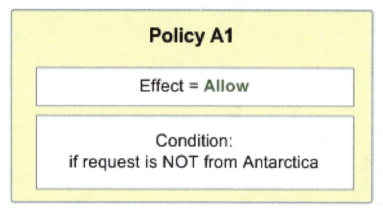

If a user sends a request from the U.S., the condition is met (the request isn't from Antarctica), and the request results in an **allow**. However, if a user sends a request from Antarctica, the condition isn't met and the request defaults to a **default-deny**. You can change the result to an **explicit-deny** by writing Policy A2 that explicitly denies a request if it comes from Antarctica. The following diagram illustrates the policy.

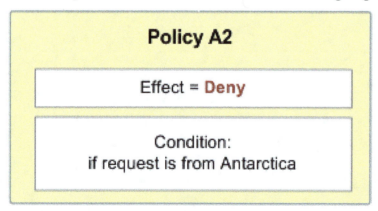

If a user sends a request from Antarctica, the condition is met and the request results in an **explicit-deny**.

The distinction between a **default-deny** and an **explicit-deny** is important because an **allow** can overwrite the former but not the latter. For example, Policy B allows requests if they arrive on June 1, 2010. The following diagram compares combining this policy with Policy A1 and Policy A2.

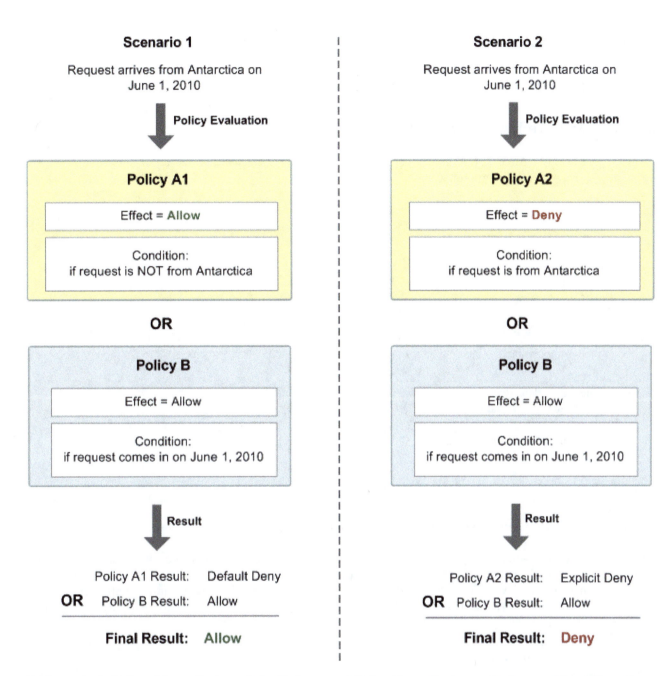

In Scenario 1, Policy A1 results in a **default-deny** and Policy B results in an allo because the policy allows requests that come in on June 1, 2010. The **allow** from Policy B overrides the **default-deny** from Policy A1, and the request is allowed.

In Scenario 2, Policy B2 results in an **explicit-deny** and Policy B results in an **allow**. The **explicit-deny** from Policy A2 overrides the **allow** from Policy B, and the request is denied.

Custom Amazon SQS Access Policy Language Examples

The following are examples of typical Amazon SQS access policies.

Example 1: Give Permission to One Account

The following example Amazon SQS policy gives AWS account 111122223333 permission to send to and receive from **queue2** owned by AWS account 444455556666.

```
1  {
2      "Version": "2012-10-17",
3      "Id": "UseCase1",
4      "Statement" : [{
5        "Sid": "1",
6        "Effect": "Allow",
7        "Principal": {
8          "AWS": [
9            "111122223333"
10         ]
11       },
12       "Action": [
13         "sqs:SendMessage",
14         "sqs:ReceiveMessage"
15       ],
16       "Resource": "arn:aws:sqs:us-east-2:444455556666:queue2"
17     }]
18  }
```

Example 2: Give Permission to One or More Accounts

The following example Amazon SQS policy gives one or more AWS accounts access to queues owned by your account for a specific time period. It is necessary to write this policy and to upload it to Amazon SQS using the http://docs.aws.amazon.com/AWSSimpleQueueService/latest/APIReference/API_SetQueueAttributes.html action because the http://docs.aws.amazon.com/AWSSimpleQueueService/latest/APIReference/API_AddPermission.html action doesn't permit specifying a time restriction when granting access to a queue.

```
1  {
2      "Version": "2012-10-17",
3      "Id": "UseCase2",
4      "Statement" : [{
5        "Sid": "1",
6        "Effect": "Allow",
7        "Principal": {
8          "AWS": [
9            "111122223333",
10           "444455556666"
11         ]
12       },
13       "Action": [
14         "sqs:SendMessage",
15         "sqs:ReceiveMessage"
16       ],
17       "Resource": "arn:aws:sqs:us-east-2:444455556666:queue2",
```

```
18      "Condition": {
19        "DateLessThan": {
20          "AWS:CurrentTime": "2009-06-30T12:00Z"
21        }
22      }
23    }]
24  }
```

Example 3: Give Permission to Requests from Amazon EC2 Instances

The following example Amazon SQS policy gives access to requests that come from Amazon EC2 instances. This example builds on the "Example 2: Give Permission to One or More Accounts" example: it restricts access to before June 30, 2009 at 12 noon (UTC), it restricts access to the IP range 10.52.176.0/24. It is necessary to write this policy and to upload it to Amazon SQS using the http://docs.aws.amazon.com/AWSSimpleQueueService/latest/APIReference/API_SetQueueAttributes.html action because the http://docs.aws.amazon.com/AWSSimpleQueueService/latest/APIReference/API_AddPermission.html action doesn't permit specifying an IP address restriction when granting access to a queue.

```
1  {
2    "Version": "2012-10-17",
3    "Id": "UseCase3",
4    "Statement" : [{
5      "Sid": "1",
6      "Effect": "Allow",
7      "Principal": {
8        "AWS": [
9          "111122223333"
10       ]
11     },
12     "Action": [
13       "sqs:SendMessage",
14       "sqs:ReceiveMessage"
15     ],
16     "Resource": "arn:aws:sqs:us-east-2:444455556666:queue2",
17     "Condition": {
18       "DateLessThan": {
19         "AWS:CurrentTime": "2009-06-30T12:00Z"
20       },
21       "IpAddress": {
22         "AWS:SourceIp": "10.52.176.0/24"
23       }
24     }
25   }]
26 }
```

Example 4: Deny Access to a Specific Account

The following example Amazon SQS policy denies a specific AWS account access to your queue. This example builds on the "Example 1: Give Permission to One Account" example: it denies access to the specified AWS account. It is necessary to write this policy and to upload it to Amazon SQS using the http://docs.aws.amazon.com/AWSSimpleQueueService/latest/APIReference/API_SetQueueAttributes.html action because the http://docs.aws.amazon.com/AWSSimpleQueueService/latest/APIReference/API_AddPermission.html action doesn't permit deny access to a queue (it allows only granting access to a queue).

```
1  {
2     "Version": "2012-10-17",
3     "Id": "UseCase4",
4     "Statement" : [{
5        "Sid": "1",
6        "Effect": "Deny",
7        "Principal": {
8           "AWS": [
9              "111122223333"
10          ]
11       },
12       "Action": [
13          "sqs:SendMessage",
14          "sqs:ReceiveMessage"
15       ],
16       "Resource": "arn:aws:sqs:us-east-2:444455556666:queue2"
17    }]
18 }
```

Using Temporary Security Credentials

In addition to creating IAM users with their own security credentials, IAM also allows you to grant temporary security credentials to any user, allowing the user to access your AWS services and resources. You can manage users who have AWS accounts (IAM users). You can also manage users for your system who don't have AWS accounts (federated users). In addition, applications that you create to access your AWS resources can also be considered to be "users."

You can use these temporary security credentials to make requests to Amazon SQS. The API libraries compute the necessary signature value using those credentials to authenticate your request. If you send requests using expired credentials, Amazon SQS denies the request.

Note
You can't set a policy based on temporary credentials.

Prerequisites

1. Use IAM to create temporary security credentials:

   - Security token
   - Access Key ID
   - Secret Access Key

2. Prepare your string to sign with the temporary Access Key ID and the security token.

3. Use the temporary Secret Access Key instead of your own Secret Access Key to sign your Query API request.

Note
When you submit the signed Query API request, use the temporary Access Key ID instead of your own Access Key ID and to include the security token. For more information about IAM support for temporary security credentials, see Granting Temporary Access to Your AWS Resources in the *IAM User Guide*.

To call an Amazon SQS Query API action using temporary security credentials

1. Request a temporary security token using AWS Identity and Access Management. For more information, see Creating Temporary Security Credentials to Enable Access for IAM Users in the *IAM User Guide*.

   IAM returns a security token, an Access Key ID, and a Secret Access Key.

2. Prepare your query using the temporary Access Key ID instead of your own Access Key ID and include the security token. Sign your request using the temporary Secret Access Key instead of your own.

3. Submit your signed query string with the temporary Access Key ID and the security token.

   The following example demonstrates how to use temporary security credentials to authenticate an Amazon SQS request. The structure of *AUTHPARAMS* depends on the signature of the API request. For more information, see Signing AWS API Requests in the *Amazon Web Services General Reference*.

```
1 https://sqs.us-east-2.amazonaws.com/
2 ?Action=CreateQueue
3 &DefaultVisibilityTimeout=40
4 &QueueName=MyQueue
5 &Attribute.1.Name=VisibilityTimeout
6 &Attribute.1.Value=40
7 &Expires=2020-12-18T22%3A52%3A43PST
8 &SecurityToken=wJalrXUtnFEMI/K7MDENG/bPxRfiCYEXAMPLEKEY
9 &AWSAccessKeyId=AKIAIOSFODNN7EXAMPLE
```

```
10 &Version=2012-11-05
11 &AUTHPARAMS
```

The following example uses temporary security credentials to send two messages using the SendMessageBatch action.

```
1  https://sqs.us-east-2.amazonaws.com/
2  ?Action=SendMessageBatch
3  &SendMessageBatchRequestEntry.1.Id=test_msg_001
4  &SendMessageBatchRequestEntry.1.MessageBody=test%20message%20body%201
5  &SendMessageBatchRequestEntry.2.Id=test_msg_002
6  &SendMessageBatchRequestEntry.2.MessageBody=test%20message%20body%202
7  &SendMessageBatchRequestEntry.2.DelaySeconds=60
8  &Expires=2020-12-18T22%3A52%3A43PST
9  &SecurityToken=je7MtGbClwBF/2Zp9Utk/h3yCo8nvbEXAMPLEKEY
10 &AWSAccessKeyId=AKIAI44QH8DHBEXAMPLE
11 &Version=2012-11-05
12 &AUTHPARAMS
```

Amazon SQS API Permissions: Actions and Resource Reference

When you set up Access Control and write permissions policies that you can attach to an IAM identity, you can use the following table as a reference. The table lists each Amazon Simple Queue Service action, the corresponding actions for which you can grant permissions to perform the action, and the AWS resource for which you can grant the permissions.

Specify the actions in the policy's `Action` field, and the resource value in the policy's `Resource` field. To specify an action, use the `sqs:` prefix followed by the action name (for example, `sqs:CreateQueue`).

Currently, Amazon SQS supports only a limited subset of the condition keys available in IAM:

- `aws:CurrentTime`
- `aws:EpochTime`
- `aws:SecureTransport`
- `aws:SourceArn`
- `aws:SourceIP`
- `aws:UserAgent`
- `aws:MultiFactorAuthAge`
- `aws:MultiFactorAuthPresent`
- `aws:TokenAge`

If you see an expand arrow () in the upper-right corner of the table, you can open the table in a new window. To close the window, choose the close button (**X**) in the lower-right corner.

Amazon Simple Queue Service API and Required Permissions for Actions
[See the AWS documentation website for more details]

Protecting Data Using Server-Side Encryption (SSE) and AWS KMS

Server-side encryption (SSE) for Amazon SQS is available in all commercial regions where Amazon SQS is available, except for the China Regions. SSE lets you transmit sensitive data in encrypted queues. SSE protects the contents of messages in Amazon SQS queues using keys managed in AWS Key Management Service (AWS KMS). For information about managing SSE using the AWS Management Console or the AWS SDK for Java (and the [CreateQueue](http://docs.aws.amazon.com/AWSSimpleQueueService/latest/APIReference/API_CreateQueue.html), [SetQueueAttributes](http://docs.aws.amazon.com/AWSSimpleQueueService/latest/APIReference/API_SetQueueAttributes.html), and [GetQueueAttributes](http://docs.aws.amazon.com/AWSSimpleQueueService/latest/APIReference/API_GetQueueAttributes.html) actions), see the following tutorials:

- Tutorial: Configuring Server-Side Encryption (SSE) for an Existing Amazon SQS Queue
- Tutorial: Configuring Server-Side Encryption (SSE) for an Existing Amazon SQS Queue
- Example 3: Enable Compatibility between AWS Services Such as Amazon CloudWatch Events, Amazon S3, and Amazon SNS and Queues with SSE

SSE encrypts messages as soon as Amazon SQS receives them. The messages are stored in encrypted form and Amazon SQS decrypts messages only when they are sent to an authorized consumer.

Important

All requests to queues with SSE enabled must use HTTPS and Signature Version 4.

Some features of AWS services that can send notifications to Amazon SQS using the AWS Security Token Service [AssumeRole](http://docs.aws.amazon.com/STS/latest/APIReference/API_AssumeRole.html) action are compatible with SSE but work *only with standard queues:*

Auto Scaling Lifecycle Hooks AWS Lambda Dead-Letter Queues Other features of AWS services or third-party services that send notifications to Amazon SQS aren't compatible with SSE, despite allowing you to set an encrypted queue as a target:

AWS IoT Rule Actions For information about compatibility of other services with encrypted queues, see Example 3: Enable Compatibility between AWS Services Such as Amazon CloudWatch Events, Amazon S3, and Amazon SNS and Queues with SSE and your service documentation.

AWS KMS combines secure, highly available hardware and software to provide a key management system scaled for the cloud. When you use Amazon SQS with AWS KMS, the data keys that encrypt your message data are also encrypted and stored with the data they protect.

The following are benefits of using AWS KMS:

- You can create and manage customer master keys (CMKs) yourself.
- You can also use the AWS managed CMK for Amazon SQS, which is unique for each account and region.
- The AWS KMS security standards can help you meet encryption-related compliance requirements.

For more information, see What is AWS Key Management Service? in the *AWS Key Management Service Developer Guide* and the AWS Key Management Service Cryptographic Details whitepaper.

Topics

- What Does SSE for Amazon SQS Encrypt?
- Key Terms
- How Does the Data Key Reuse Period Work?
- How Do I Estimate My AWS KMS Usage Costs?
- What AWS KMS Permissions Do I Need to Use SSE for Amazon SQS?

- Errors

What Does SSE for Amazon SQS Encrypt?

SSE encrypts the body of a message in an Amazon SQS queue.

SSE doesn't encrypt the following:

- Queue metadata (queue name and attributes)
- Message metadata (message ID, timestamp, and attributes)
- Per-queue metrics

Encrypting a message makes its contents unavailable to unauthorized or anonymous users. This doesn't affect the normal functioning of Amazon SQS:

- A message is encrypted only if it is sent after the encryption of a queue is enabled. Amazon SQS doesn't encrypt backlogged messages.
- Any encrypted message remains encrypted even if the encryption of its queue is disabled.

Moving a message to a dead-letter queue doesn't affect its encryption:

- When Amazon SQS moves a message from an encrypted source queue to an unencrypted dead-letter queue, the message remains encrypted.
- When Amazon SQS moves a message from a unencrypted source queue to an encrypted dead-letter queue, the message remains unencrypted.

Key Terms

The following key terms can help you better understand the functionality of SSE. For detailed descriptions, see the *Amazon Simple Queue Service API Reference*.

Data Key
The data encryption key (DEK) responsible for encrypting the contents of Amazon SQS messages.
For more information, see Data Keys in the *AWS Key Management Service Developer Guide* and Envelope Encryption in the *AWS Encryption SDK Developer Guide*.

Data Key Reuse Period
The length of time, in seconds, for which Amazon SQS can reuse a data key to encrypt or decrypt messages before calling AWS KMS again. An integer representing seconds, between 60 seconds (1 minute) and 86,400 seconds (24 hours). The default is 300 (5 minutes). For more information, see How Does the Data Key Reuse Period Work?.
In the unlikely event of being unable to reach AWS KMS, Amazon SQS continues to use the cached data key until a connection is reestablished.

Customer Master Key ID
The alias, alias ARN, key ID, or key ARN of an AWS managed customer master key (CMK) or a custom CMK—in your account or in another account. While the alias of the AWS managed CMK for Amazon SQS is always `alias/aws/sqs`, the alias of a custom CMK can, for example, be `alias/MyAlias`. You can use these CMKs to protect the messages in Amazon SQS queues.
Keep the following in mind:

- If you don't specify a custom CMK, Amazon SQS uses the AWS managed CMK for Amazon SQS. For instructions on creating custom CMKs, see Creating Keys in the *AWS Key Management Service Developer Guide*.
- The first time you use the AWS Management Console to specify the AWS managed CMK for Amazon SQS for a queue, AWS KMS creates the AWS managed CMK for Amazon SQS.

- Alternatively, the first time you use the `SendMessage` or `SendMessageBatch` action on a queue with SSE enabled, AWS KMS creates the AWS managed CMK for Amazon SQS. You can create CMKs, define the policies that control how CMKs can be used, and audit CMK usage using the **Encryption Keys** section of the AWS KMS console or using AWS KMS actions. For more information about CMKs, see Customer Master Keys in the *AWS Key Management Service Developer Guide*. For more examples of CMK identifiers, see KeyId in the *AWS Key Management Service API Reference*.

There are additional charges for using AWS KMS. For more information, see How Do I Estimate My AWS KMS Usage Costs? and AWS Key Management Service Pricing.

How Does the Data Key Reuse Period Work?

Amazon SQS uses a single customer master key (either the AWS managed CMK for Amazon SQS or a custom CMK) to provide envelope encryption and decryption of multiple Amazon SQS messages during the *data key reuse period*. To make the most of the data key reuse period, keep the following in mind:

- A shorter reuse period provides better security but results in more calls to AWS KMS, which might incur charges beyond the Free Tier.
- Although the data key is cached separately for encryption and for decryption, the reuse period applies to both copies of the data key.
- Principals (AWS accounts or IAM users) don't share data keys (messages sent by unique principals always get unique data keys). Thus, the volume of calls to AWS KMS is a multiple of the number of unique principals in use during the data key reuse period:
    - When you send messages using the `SendMessage` or `SendMessageBatch` action, Amazon SQS typically calls the AWS KMS `GenerateDataKey` and `Decrypt` actions once per every data key reuse period. **Note**
    For each data key that AWS KMS generates, SSE calls the `Decrypt` action to verify the integrity of the data key before using it.
    - When you receive messages using the `ReceiveMessage` action, Amazon SQS typically calls the AWS KMS `Decrypt` action once per every data key reuse period.

How Do I Estimate My AWS KMS Usage Costs?

To predict costs and better understand your AWS bill, you might want to know how often Amazon SQS uses your customer master key (CMK).

Note
Although the following formula can give you a very good idea of expected costs, actual costs might be higher because of the distributed nature of Amazon SQS.

To calculate the number of API requests (R) *per queue*, use the following formula:

```
1 R = B / D * (2 * P + C)
```

B is the billing period (in seconds).

D is the data key reuse period (in seconds).

P is the number of producing principals that send to the Amazon SQS queue.

C is the number of consuming principals that receive from the Amazon SQS queue.

Important
In general, producing principals incur double the cost of consuming principals. For more information, see How Does the Data Key Reuse Period Work?
If the producer and consumer have different IAM users, the cost increases.

The following are example calculations. For exact pricing information, see AWS Key Management Service Pricing.

Example 1: Calculating the Number of AWS KMS API Calls for 2 Principals and 1 Queue

This example assumes the following:

- The billing period is January 1-31 (2,678,400 seconds).
- The data key reuse period is set to 5 minutes (300 seconds).
- There is 1 queue.
- There is 1 producing principal and 1 consuming principal.

```
1 2,678,400 / 300 * (2 * 1 + 1) = 26,784
```

Example 2: Calculating the Number of AWS KMS API Calls for Multiple Producers and Consumers and 2 Queues

This example assumes the following:

- The billing period is February 1-28 (2,419,200 seconds).
- The data key reuse period is set to 24 hours (86,400 seconds).
- There are 2 queues.
- The first queue has 3 producing principals and 1 consuming principal.
- The second queue has 5 producing principals and 2 consuming principals.

```
1 (2,419,200 / 86,400 * (2 * 3 + 1)) + (2,419,200 / 86,400 * (2 * 5 + 2)) = 532
```

What AWS KMS Permissions Do I Need to Use SSE for Amazon SQS?

Before you can use SSE, you must configure AWS KMS key policies to allow encryption of queues and encryption and decryption of messages. For examples and more information about AWS KMS permissions, see AWS KMS API Permissions: Actions and Resources Reference in the *AWS Key Management Service Developer Guide*.

Note
You can also manage permissions for KMS keys using IAM policies. For more information, see Using IAM Policies with AWS KMS.
While you can configure global permissions to send to and receive from Amazon SQS, AWS KMS requires explicitly naming the full ARN of CMKs in specific regions in the `Resource` section of an IAM policy.

You must also ensure that the key policies of the customer master key (CMK) allow the necessary permissions. To do this, name the principals that produce and consume encrypted messages in Amazon SQS as users in the CMK key policy.

Alternatively, you can specify the required AWS KMS actions and CMK ARN in an IAM policy assigned to the principals which produce and consume encrypted messages in Amazon SQS. For more information, see Managing Access to AWS KMS CMKs in the *AWS Key Management Service Developer Guide*.

Example 1: Allow a User to Send Single or Batched Messages to a Queue with SSE

The producer must have the `kms:GenerateDataKey` and `kms:Decrypt` permissions for the customer master key (CMK).

```
1 {
2   "Version": "2012-10-17",
3     "Statement": [{
4       "Effect": "Allow",
5       "Action": [
6         "kms:GenerateDataKey",
```

```
7          "kms:Decrypt"
8       ],
9       "Resource": "arn:aws:kms:us-east-2:123456789012:key/1234abcd-12ab-34cd-56ef-1234567890
          ab"
10      }, {
11      "Effect": "Allow",
12      "Action": [
13          "sqs:SendMessage",
14          "sqs:SendMessageBatch"
15      ],
16      "Resource": "arn:aws:sqs:*:123456789012:MyQueue"
17   }]
18 }
```

Example 2: Allow a User to Receive Messages from a Queue with SSE

The consumer must have the kms:Decrypt permission for any customer master key (CMK) that is used to
encrypt the messages in the specified queue. If the queue acts as a dead-letter queue, the consumer must also
have the kms:Decrypt permission for any CMK that is used to encrypt the messages in the source queue.

```
1 {
2    "Version": "2012-10-17",
3       "Statement": [{
4          "Effect": "Allow",
5          "Action": [
6             "kms:Decrypt"
7          ],
8          "Resource": "arn:aws:kms:us-east-2:123456789012:key/1234abcd-12ab-34cd-56ef-1234567890
             ab"
9          }, {
10         "Effect": "Allow",
11         "Action": [
12            "sqs:ReceiveMessage"
13         ],
14         "Resource": "arn:aws:sqs:*:123456789012:MyQueue"
15      }]
16 }
```

Example 3: Enable Compatibility between AWS Services Such as Amazon CloudWatch Events, Amazon S3, and Amazon SNS and Queues with SSE

To allow Amazon CloudWatch Events, Amazon S3 event notifications, or Amazon SNS topic subscriptions to
work with encrypted queues, you must perform the following steps:

1. Create a customer master key (CMK).

2. To allow the AWS service feature to have the kms:GenerateDataKey and kms:Decrypt permissions, add
   the following statement to the policy of the CMK. **Note**
   For Amazon CloudWatch Events, use events For Amazon S3 event notifications, use s3 For Amazon SNS
   topic subscriptions, use sns

```
1 {
2    "Version": "2012-10-17",
3       "Statement": [{
```

```
4          "Effect": "Allow",
5          "Principal": {
6            "Service": "service.amazonaws.com"
7          },
8          "Action": [
9            "kms:GenerateDataKey*",
10           "kms:Decrypt"
11         ],
12         "Resource": "*"
13    }]
14 }
```

3. Create a new SSE queue or configure an existing SSE queue using the ARN of your CMK.

Learn More

- Subscribe to a Topic in the *Amazon Simple Notification Service Developer Guide*
- Creating a CloudWatch Events Rule That Triggers on an Event in the *Amazon CloudWatch Events User Guide*
- Configuring Amazon S3 Event Notifications in the *Amazon Simple Storage Service Developer Guide*

Errors

When you work with Amazon SQS and AWS KMS, you might encounter errors. The following list describes the errors and possible troubleshooting solutions.

KMSAccessDeniedException
The ciphertext references a key that doesn't exist or that you don't have access to.
HTTP Status Code: 400

KMSDisabledException
The request was rejected because the specified CMK isn't enabled.
HTTP Status Code: 400

KMSInvalidStateException
The request was rejected because the state of the specified resource isn't valid for this request. For more information, see How Key State Affects Use of a Customer Master Key in the *AWS Key Management Service Developer Guide*.
HTTP Status Code: 400

KMSNotFoundException
The request was rejected because the specified entity or resource can't be found.
HTTP Status Code: 400

KMSOptInRequired
The AWS access key ID needs a subscription for the service.
HTTP Status Code: 403

KMSThrottlingException
The request was denied due to request throttling. For more information about throttling, see Limits in the *AWS Key Management Service Developer Guide*.
HTTP Status Code: 400

Working with Amazon SQS APIs

This section provides information about constructing Amazon SQS endpoints, making Query API requests using the `GET` and `POST` methods, and using batch API actions. For detailed information about Amazon SQS actions—including parameters, errors, examples, and data types —see the http://docs.aws.amazon.com/AWSSimpleQueueService/latest/APIReference/.

To access Amazon SQS using a variety of programming languages, you can also use AWS SDKs which contain the following automatic functionality:

- Cryptographically signing your service requests
- Retrying requests
- Handling error responses

For command-line tool information, see the Amazon SQS sections in the http://docs.aws.amazon.com/cli/latest/reference/sqs/index.html and the http://docs.aws.amazon.com/powershell/latest/reference/.

Topics

- Making Query API Requests
- Amazon SQS Batch Actions

Making Query API Requests

In this section you'll learn how to construct an Amazon SQS endpoint, make `GET` and `POST` requests and interpret responses.

Topics

- Constructing an Endpoint
- Making a GET Request
- Making a POST Request
- Authenticating Requests
- Interpreting Responses

Constructing an Endpoint

In order to work with Amazon SQS queues, you must construct an endpoint. For information about region-specific Amazon SQS endpoints, see the *Amazon Web Services General Reference*.

Every Amazon SQS endpoint is independent. For example, if two queues are named `MyQueue` and one has the endpoint `sqs.us-east-2.amazonaws.com` while the other has the endpoint `sqs.eu-west-2.amazonaws.com`, the two queues don't share any data with each other.

The following is an example of an endpoint which makes a request to create a queue.

```
1  https://sqs.eu-west-2.amazonaws.com/
2  ?Action=CreateQueue
3  &DefaultVisibilityTimeout=40
4  &QueueName=MyQueue
5  &Version=2012-11-05
6  &AUTHPARAMS
```

Note
Queue names and queue URLs are case-sensitive.
The structure of *AUTHPARAMS* depends on the signature of the API request. For more information, see Signing AWS API Requests in the *Amazon Web Services General Reference*.

Making a GET Request

An Amazon SQS `GET` request is structured as a URL which consists of the following:

- **Endpoint** – The resource that the request is acting on (the queue name and URL), for example: `https://sqs.us-east-2.amazonaws.com/123456789012/MyQueue`
- **Action** – The action that you want to perform on the endpoint. A question mark (?) separates the endpoint from the action, for example: `?Action=SendMessage&MessageBody=Your%20Message%20Text`
- **Parameters** – Any request parameters—each parameter is separated by an ampersand (&), for example: `&Version=2012-11-05&AUTHPARAMS`

The following is an example of a `GET` request that sends a message to an Amazon SQS queue.

```
1  https://sqs.us-east-2.amazonaws.com/123456789012/MyQueue
2  ?Action=SendMessage&MessageBody=Your%20message%20text
3  &Version=2012-11-05
4  &AUTHPARAMS
```

Note
Queue names and queue URLs are case-sensitive.

Because GET requests are URLs, you must URL-encode all parameter values. Because spaces aren't allowed in URLs, each space is URL-encoded as %20. (The rest of the example isn't URL-encoded to make it easier to read.)

Making a POST Request

An Amazon SQS POST requests send query parameters as a form in the body of an HTTP request.

The following is an example of a HTTP header with Content-Type set to application/x-www-form-urlencoded.

```
1 POST /MyQueue HTTP/1.1
2 Host: sqs.us-east-2.amazonaws.com
3 Content-Type: application/x-www-form-urlencoded
```

The header is followed by a [form\-urlencoded](https://www.w3.org/MarkUp/html-spec/html-spec_8.html#SEC8.2) POST request that sends a message to an Amazon SQS queue. Each parameter is separated by an ampersand (&).

```
1 Action=SendMessage
2 &MessageBody=Your+Message+Text
3 &Expires=2020-10-15T12%3A00%3A00Z
4 &Version=2012-11-05
5 &AUTHPARAMS
```

Note
Only the Content-Type HTTP header is required. The AUTHPARAMS is the same as for the GET request. Your HTTP client might add other items to the HTTP request, according to the client's HTTP version.

Authenticating Requests

Authentication is the process of identifying and verifying the party that sends a request. During the first stage of authentication, AWS verifies the identity of the producer and whether the producer is registered to use AWS (for more information, see Step 1: Create an AWS Account and Step 2: Create an IAM User). Next, AWS abides by the following procedure:

1. The producer (sender) obtains the necessary credential.

2. The producer sends a request and the credential to the consumer (receiver).

3. The consumer uses the credential to verify whether the producer sent the request.

4. One of the following happens:

   - If authentication succeeds, the consumer processes the request.
   - If authentication fails, the consumer rejects the request and returns an error.

Topics

- Basic Authentication Process with HMAC-SHA
- Part 1: The Request from the User
- Part 2: The Response from AWS

Basic Authentication Process with HMAC-SHA

When you access Amazon SQS using the Query API, you must provide the following items to authenticate your request:

- The **AWS Access Key ID** that identifies your AWS account, which AWS uses to look up your Secret Access Key.

- The **HMAC-SHA request signature**, calculated using your Secret Access Key (a shared secret known only to you and AWS—for more information, see RFC2104). The AWS SDK handles the signing process; however, if you submit a query request over HTTP or HTTPS, you must include a signature in every query request.

   1. Derive a Signature Version 4 Signing Key. For more information, see Deriving the Signing Key with Java. **Note**
   Amazon SQS supports Signature Version 4, which provides improved SHA256-based security and performance over previous versions. When you create new applications that use Amazon SQS, use Signature Version 4.

   2. Base64-encode the request signature. The following sample Java code does this:

```
1 package amazon.webservices.common;
2
3 // Define common routines for encoding data in AWS requests.
4 public class Encoding {
5
6     /* Perform base64 encoding of input bytes.
7      * rawData is the array of bytes to be encoded.
8      * return is the base64-encoded string representation of rawData.
9      */
10    public static String EncodeBase64(byte[] rawData) {
11        return Base64.encodeBytes(rawData);
12    }
13 }
```

- The **timestamp (or expiration)** of the request. The timestamp that you use in the request must be a `dateTime` object, with the complete date, including hours, minutes, and seconds. For example: `2007-01-31T23:59:59Z` Although this isn't required, we recommend providing the object using the Coordinated Universal Time (Greenwich Mean Time) time zone. **Note**
  Make sure that your server time is set correctly. If you specify a timestamp (rather than an expiration), the request automatically expires 15 minutes after the specified time (AWS doesn't process requests with timestamps more than 15 minutes earlier than the current time on AWS servers).
  If you use .NET, you must not send overly specific timestamps (because of different interpretations of how extra time precision should be dropped). In this case, you should manually construct `dateTime` objects with precision of no more than one millisecond.

Part 1: The Request from the User

The following is the process you must follow to authenticate AWS requests using an HMAC-SHA request signature.

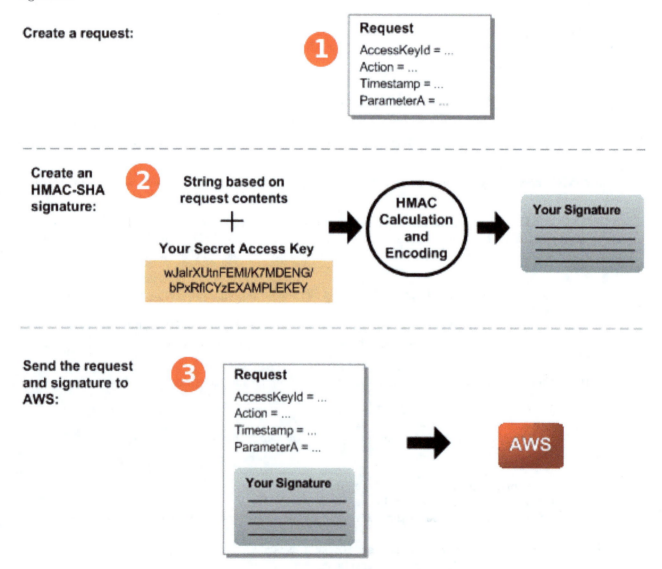

1. Construct a request to AWS.

2. Calculate a keyed-hash message authentication code (HMAC-SHA) signature using your Secret Access Key.

3. Include the signature and your Access Key ID in the request, and then send the request to AWS.

Part 2: The Response from AWS

AWS begins the following process in response.

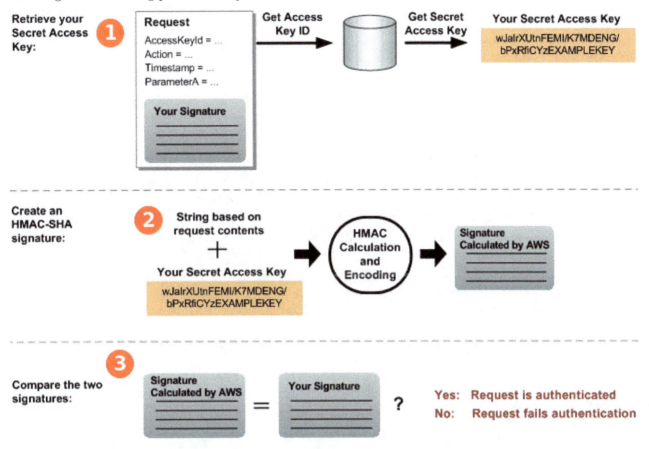

1. AWS uses the Access Key ID to look up your Secret Access Key.

2. AWS generates a signature from the request data and the Secret Access Key, using the same algorithm that you used to calculate the signature you sent in the request.

3. One of the following happens:

   - If the signature that AWS generates matches the one you send in the request, AWS considers the request to be authentic.
   - If the comparison fails, the request is discarded, and AWS returns an error.

Interpreting Responses

In response to an action request, Amazon SQS returns an XML data structure that contains the results of the request. For more information, see the individual actions in the *Amazon Simple Queue Service API Reference*.

Topics

- Successful Response Structure
- Error Response Structure

Successful Response Structure

If the request is successful, the main response element is named after the action, with `Response` appended (`ActionNameResponse`).

This element contains the following child elements:

- `ActionNameResult` – Contains an action-specific element. For example, the `CreateQueueResult` element contains the `QueueUrl` element which, in turn, contains the URL of the created queue.
- `ResponseMetadata` – Contains the `RequestId` which, in turn, contains the UUID of the request.

The following is an example successful response in XML format:

```
1  <CreateQueueResponse
2     xmlns=https://sqs.us-east-2.amazonaws.com/doc/2012-11-05/
3     xmlns:xsi=http://www.w3.org/2001/XMLSchema-instance
4     xsi:type=CreateQueueResponse>
5     <CreateQueueResult>
6        <QueueUrl>https://sqs.us-east-2.amazonaws.com/770098461991/queue2</QueueUrl>
7     </CreateQueueResult>
8     <ResponseMetadata>
9        <RequestId>cb919c0a-9bce-4afe-9b48-9bdf2412bb67</RequestId>
10    </ResponseMetadata>
11 </CreateQueueResponse>
```

Error Response Structure

If a request is unsuccessful, Amazon SQS always returns the main response element `ErrorResponse`. This element contains an `Error` element and a `RequestId` element.

The `Error` element contains the following child elements:

- `Type` – Specifies whether the error was a producer or consumer error.
- `Code` – Specifies the type of error.
- `Message` – Specifies the error condition in a readable format.
- `Detail` – (Optional) Specifies additional details about the error.

The `RequestId` element contains the UUID of the request.

The following is an example error response in XML format:

```
1  <ErrorResponse>
2     <Error>
3        <Type>Sender</Type>
4        <Code>InvalidParameterValue</Code>
5        <Message>
6           Value (quename_nonalpha) for parameter QueueName is invalid.
```

```
7          Must be an alphanumeric String of 1 to 80 in length.
8        </Message>
9      </Error>
10     <RequestId>42d59b56-7407-4c4a-be0f-4c88daeea257</RequestId>
11 </ErrorResponse>
```

Amazon SQS Batch Actions

To reduce costs or manipulate up to 10 messages with a single action, you can use the following actions:

- [SendMessageBatch](http://docs.aws.amazon.com/AWSSimpleQueueService/latest/APIReference/API_SendMessageBatch.html)
- [DeleteMessageBatch](http://docs.aws.amazon.com/AWSSimpleQueueService/latest/APIReference/API_DeleteMessageBatch.html)
- [ChangeMessageVisibilityBatch](http://docs.aws.amazon.com/AWSSimpleQueueService/latest/APIReference/API_ChangeMessageVisibilityBatch.html)

You can take advantage of batch functionality using the Query API, or an AWS SDK that supports the Amazon SQS batch actions.

Note

The total size of all messages that you send in a single SendMessageBatch call can't exceed 262,144 bytes (256 KB).

You can't set permissions for SendMessageBatch, DeleteMessageBatch, or ChangeMessageVisibilityBatch explicitly. Setting permissions for SendMessage, DeleteMessage, or ChangeMessageVisibility sets permissions for the corresponding batch versions of the actions.

The Amazon SQS console doesn't support batch actions.

Topics

- Enabling Client-Side Buffering and Request Batching
- Increasing Throughput using Horizontal Scaling and Action Batching

Enabling Client-Side Buffering and Request Batching

The AWS SDK for Java includes `AmazonSQSBufferedAsyncClient` which accesses Amazon SQS. This client allows for simple request batching using client-side buffering—calls made from the client are first buffered and then sent as a batch request to Amazon SQS.

Client-side buffering allows up to 10 requests to be buffered and sent as a batch request, decreasing your cost of using Amazon SQS and reducing the number of sent requests. `AmazonSQSBufferedAsyncClient` buffers both synchronous and asynchronous calls. Batched requests and support for long polling can also help increase throughput. For more information, see Increasing Throughput using Horizontal Scaling and Action Batching.

Because `AmazonSQSBufferedAsyncClient` implements the same interface as `AmazonSQSAsyncClient`, migrating from `AmazonSQSAsyncClient` to `AmazonSQSBufferedAsyncClient` typically requires only minimal changes to your existing code.

Note

The Amazon SQS Buffered Asynchronous Client doesn't currently support FIFO queues.

Topics

- Using AmazonSQSBufferedAsyncClient
- Configuring AmazonSQSBufferedAsyncClient

Using AmazonSQSBufferedAsyncClient

Before you begin, complete the steps in Setting Up Amazon SQS.

You can create a new `AmazonSQSBufferedAsyncClient` based on `AmazonSQSAsyncClient`, for example:

```
1  // Create the basic Amazon SQS async client
2  final AmazonSQSAsync sqsAsync = new AmazonSQSAsyncClient();
3
4  // Create the buffered client
5  final AmazonSQSAsync bufferedSqs = new AmazonSQSBufferedAsyncClient(sqsAsync);
```

After you create the new `AmazonSQSBufferedAsyncClient`, you can use it to send multiple requests to Amazon SQS (just as you can with `AmazonSQSAsyncClient`), for example:

```
1  final CreateQueueRequest createRequest = new CreateQueueRequest().withQueueName("MyQueue");
2
3  final CreateQueueResult res = bufferedSqs.createQueue(createRequest);
4
5  final SendMessageRequest request = new SendMessageRequest();
6  final String body = "Your message text" + System.currentTimeMillis();
7  request.setMessageBody( body );
8  request.setQueueUrl(res.getQueueUrl());
9
10 final SendMessageResult sendResult = bufferedSqs.sendMessageAsync(request);
11
12 final ReceiveMessageRequest receiveRq = new ReceiveMessageRequest()
13     .withMaxNumberOfMessages(1)
14     .withQueueUrl(queueUrl);
15 final ReceiveMessageResult rx = bufferedSqs.receiveMessage(receiveRq);
```

Configuring AmazonSQSBufferedAsyncClient

AmazonSQSBufferedAsyncClient is preconfigured with settings that work for most use cases. You can further configure AmazonSQSBufferedAsyncClient, for example:

1. Create an instance of the QueueBufferConfig class with the required configuration parameters.

2. Provide the instance to the AmazonSQSBufferedAsyncClient constructor.

```
1 // Create the basic Amazon SQS async client
2 final AmazonSQSAsync sqsAsync = new AmazonSQSAsyncClient();
3
4 final QueueBufferConfig config = new QueueBufferConfig()
5     .withMaxInflightReceiveBatches(5)
6     .withMaxDoneReceiveBatches(15);
7
8 // Create the buffered client
9 final AmazonSQSAsync bufferedSqs = new AmazonSQSBufferedAsyncClient(sqsAsync, config);
```

QueueBufferConfig Configuration Parameters

Parameter	Default Value	Description
longPoll	true	When longPoll is set to true, AmazonSQSBufferedAsyncClient attempts to use long polling when it consumes messages.
longPollWaitTimeoutSeconds	20 s	The maximum amount of time (in seconds) which a ReceiveMessage call blocks off on the server, waiting for messages to appear in the queue before returning with an empty receive result. When long polling is disabled, this setting has no effect.
maxBatchOpenMs	200 ms	The maximum amount of time (in milliseconds) that an outgoing call waits for other calls with which it batches messages of the same type. The higher the setting, the fewer batches are required to perform the same amount of work (however, the first call in a batch has to spend a longer time waiting). When you set this parameter to 0, submitted requests don't wait for other requests, effectively disabling batching.

Parameter	Default Value	Description
maxBatchSize	10 requests per batch	The maximum number of messages that are batched together in a single request. The higher the setting, the fewer batches are required to carry out the same number of requests. 10 requests per batch is the maximum allowed value for Amazon SQS.
maxBatchSizeBytes	256 KB	The maximum size of a message batch, in bytes, that the client attempts to send to Amazon SQS. 256 KB is the maximum allowed value for Amazon SQS.
maxDoneReceiveBatches	10 batches	The maximum number of receive batches that `AmazonSQSBufferedAsyncClient` prefetches and stores client-side. The higher the setting, the more receive requests can be satisfied without having to make a call to Amazon SQS (however, the more messages are prefetched, the longer they remain in the buffer, causing their own visibility timeout to expire). 0 indicates that all message prefetching is disabled and messages are consumed only on demand.
maxInflightOutboundBatches	5 batches	The maximum number of active outbound batches that can be processed at the same time. The higher the setting, the faster outbound batches can be sent (subject to limits such as CPU or bandwidth) and the more threads are consumed by `AmazonSQSBufferedAsyncClient`.

Parameter	Default Value	Description
maxInflightReceiveBatches	10 batches	The maximum number of active receive batches that can be processed at the same time. The higher the setting, the more messages can be received (subject to limits such as CPU or bandwidth), and the more threads are consumed by `AmazonSQSBufferedAsyncClient`. 0 indicates that all message prefetching is disabled and messages are consumed only on demand.
visibilityTimeoutSeconds	-1	When this parameter is set to a positive, non-zero value, the visibility timeout set here overrides the visibility timeout set on the queue from which messages are consumed. -1 indicates that the default setting is selected for the queue. You can't set visibility timeout to 0.

Increasing Throughput using Horizontal Scaling and Action Batching

Amazon SQS queues can deliver very high throughput. Standard queues support a nearly unlimited number of transactions per second (TPS) per action. By default, FIFO queues support up to 3,000 messages per second with batching. To request a limit increase, file a support request. FIFO queues support up to 300 messages per second (300 send, receive, or delete operations per second) without batching.

To achieve high throughput, you must scale message producers and consumers horizontally (add more producers and consumers).

Topics

- Horizontal Scaling
- Action Batching
- Working Java Example for Single-Operation and Batch Requests

Horizontal Scaling

Because you access Amazon SQS through an HTTP request-response protocol, the *request latency* (the interval between initiating a request and receiving a response) limits the throughput that you can achieve from a single thread using a single connection. For example, if the latency from an Amazon EC2-based client to Amazon SQS in the same region averages 20 ms, the maximum throughput from a single thread over a single connection averages 50 TPS.

Horizontal scaling involves increasing the number of message producers (which make [SendMessage](http://docs.aws.amazon.com/AWSSimpleQueueService/latest/APIReference/API_SendMessage.html) requests) and consumers (which make [ReceiveMessage](http://docs.aws.amazon.com/AWSSimpleQueueService/latest/APIReference/API_ReceiveMessage.html) and [DeleteMessage](http://docs.aws.amazon.com/AWSSimpleQueueService/latest/APIReference/API_DeleteMessage.html) requests) in order to increase your overall queue throughput. You can scale horizontally in three ways:

- Increase the number of threads per client
- Add more clients
- Increase the number of threads per client and add more clients

When you add more clients, you achieve essentially linear gains in queue throughput. For example, if you double the number of clients, you also double the throughput.

Note
As you scale horizontally, you must ensure that the Amazon SQS queue that you use has enough connections or threads to support the number of concurrent message producers and consumers that send requests and receive responses. For example, by default, instances of the AWS SDK for Java [AmazonSQSClient](http://docs.aws.amazon.com/AWSJavaSDK/latest/javadoc/com/amazonaws/services/sqs/AmazonSQSClient.html) class maintain at most 50 connections to Amazon SQS. To create additional concurrent producers and consumers, you must adjust the maximum number of allowable producer and consumer threads on an `AmazonSQSClientBuilder` object, for example:

```
1  final AmazonSQS sqsClient = AmazonSQSClientBuilder.standard()
2          .withClientConfiguration(new ClientConfiguration()
3                  .withMaxConnections(producerCount + consumerCount))
4          .build();
```

For [AmazonSQSAsyncClient](http://docs.aws.amazon.com/AWSJavaSDK/latest/javadoc/com/amazonaws/services/sqs/AmazonSQSAsyncClient.html), you also must make sure that enough threads are available.

Action Batching

Batching performs more work during each round trip to the service (for example, when you send multiple messages with a single SendMessageBatch request). The Amazon SQS batch actions are [SendMessageBatch](http://docs.aws.amazon.com/AWSSimpleQueueService/latest/APIReference/API_SendMessageBatch.html), [DeleteMessageBatch](http://docs.aws.amazon.com/AWSSimpleQueueService/latest/APIReference/API_DeleteMessageBatch.html), and [ChangeMessageVisibilityBatch](http://docs.aws.amazon.com/AWSSimpleQueueService/latest/APIReference/API_ChangeMessageVisibilityBatch.html). To take advantage of batching without changing your producers or consumers, you can use the Amazon SQS Buffered Asynchronous Client.

Note
Because [ReceiveMessage](http://docs.aws.amazon.com/AWSSimpleQueueService/latest/APIReference/API_ReceiveMessage.html) can process 10 messages at a time, there is no ReceiveMessageBatch action.

Batching distributes the latency of the batch action over the multiple messages in a batch request, rather than accept the entire latency for a single message (for example, a [SendMessage](http://docs.aws.amazon.com/AWSSimpleQueueService/latest/APIReference/API_SendMessage.html) request). Because each round trip carries more work, batch requests make more efficient use of threads and connections, improving throughput.

You can combine batching with horizontal scaling to provide throughput with fewer threads, connections, and requests than individual message requests. You can use batched Amazon SQS actions to send, receive, or delete up to 10 messages at a time. Because Amazon SQS charges by the request, batching can substantially reduce your costs.

Batching can introduce some complexity for your application (for example, you application must accumulate messages before sending them, or it sometimes must wait longer for a response). However, batching can be still effective in the following cases:

- Your application generates many messages in a short time, so the delay is never very long.
- A message consumer fetches messages from a queue at its discretion, unlike typical message producers that need to send messages in response to events they don't control.

Important
A batch request might succeed even though individual messages in the batch failed. After a batch request, always check for individual message failures and retry the action if necessary.

Working Java Example for Single-Operation and Batch Requests

Prerequisites

Add the aws-java-sdk-sqs.jar, aws-java-sdk-ec2.jar, and commons-logging.jar packages to your Java build class path. The following example shows these dependencies in a Maven project pom.xml file.

```
1  <dependencies>
2      <dependency>
3          <groupId>com.amazonaws</groupId>
4          <artifactId>aws-java-sdk-sqs</artifactId>
5          <version>LATEST</version>
6      </dependency>
7      <dependency>
8          <groupId>com.amazonaws</groupId>
9          <artifactId>aws-java-sdk-ec2</artifactId>
10         <version>LATEST</version>
11     </dependency>
12     <dependency>
13         <groupId>commons-logging</groupId>
```

```
14          <artifactId>commons-logging</artifactId>
15          <version>LATEST</version>
16      </dependency>
17  </dependencies>
```

SimpleProducerConsumer.java

The following Java code example implements a simple producer-consumer pattern. The main thread spawns
a number of producer and consumer threads that process 1 KB messages for a specified time. This example
includes producers and consumers that make single-operation requests and those that make batch requests.

```
1   /*
2    * Copyright 2010-2018 Amazon.com, Inc. or its affiliates. All Rights Reserved.
3    *
4    * Licensed under the Apache License, Version 2.0 (the "License").
5    * You may not use this file except in compliance with the License.
6    * A copy of the License is located at
7    *
8    *   https://aws.amazon.com/apache2.0
9    *
10   * or in the "license" file accompanying this file. This file is distributed
11   * on an "AS IS" BASIS, WITHOUT WARRANTIES OR CONDITIONS OF ANY KIND, either
12   * express or implied. See the License for the specific language governing
13   * permissions and limitations under the License.
14   *
15   */
16
17  import com.amazonaws.AmazonClientException;
18  import com.amazonaws.ClientConfiguration;
19  import com.amazonaws.services.sqs.AmazonSQS;
20  import com.amazonaws.services.sqs.AmazonSQSClientBuilder;
21  import com.amazonaws.services.sqs.model.*;
22  import org.apache.commons.logging.Log;
23  import org.apache.commons.logging.LogFactory;
24
25  import java.math.BigInteger;
26  import java.util.ArrayList;
27  import java.util.List;
28  import java.util.Random;
29  import java.util.Scanner;
30  import java.util.concurrent.TimeUnit;
31  import java.util.concurrent.atomic.AtomicBoolean;
32  import java.util.concurrent.atomic.AtomicInteger;
33
34  /**
35   * Start a specified number of producer and consumer threads, and produce-consume
36   * for the least of the specified duration and 1 hour. Some messages can be left
37   * in the queue because producers and consumers might not be in exact balance.
38   */
39  public class SimpleProducerConsumer {
40
41      // The maximum runtime of the program.
42      private final static int MAX_RUNTIME_MINUTES = 60;
43      private final static Log log = LogFactory.getLog(SimpleProducerConsumer.class);
```

233

```java
44
45    public static void main(String[] args) throws InterruptedException {
46
47        final Scanner input = new Scanner(System.in);
48
49        System.out.print("Enter the queue name: ");
50        final String queueName = input.nextLine();
51
52        System.out.print("Enter the number of producers: ");
53        final int producerCount = input.nextInt();
54
55        System.out.print("Enter the number of consumers: ");
56        final int consumerCount = input.nextInt();
57
58        System.out.print("Enter the number of messages per batch: ");
59        final int batchSize = input.nextInt();
60
61        System.out.print("Enter the message size in bytes: ");
62        final int messageSizeByte = input.nextInt();
63
64        System.out.print("Enter the run time in minutes: ");
65        final int runTimeMinutes = input.nextInt();
66
67        /*
68         * Create a new instance of the builder with all defaults (credentials
69         * and region) set automatically. For more information, see Creating
70         * Service Clients in the AWS SDK for Java Developer Guide.
71         */
72        final ClientConfiguration clientConfiguration = new ClientConfiguration()
73                .withMaxConnections(producerCount + consumerCount);
74
75        final AmazonSQS sqsClient = AmazonSQSClientBuilder.standard()
76                .withClientConfiguration(clientConfiguration)
77                .build();
78
79        final String queueUrl = sqsClient
80                .getQueueUrl(new GetQueueUrlRequest(queueName)).getQueueUrl();
81
82        // The flag used to stop producer, consumer, and monitor threads.
83        final AtomicBoolean stop = new AtomicBoolean(false);
84
85        // Start the producers.
86        final AtomicInteger producedCount = new AtomicInteger();
87        final Thread[] producers = new Thread[producerCount];
88        for (int i = 0; i < producerCount; i++) {
89            if (batchSize == 1) {
90                producers[i] = new Producer(sqsClient, queueUrl, messageSizeByte,
91                        producedCount, stop);
92            } else {
93                producers[i] = new BatchProducer(sqsClient, queueUrl, batchSize,
94                        messageSizeByte, producedCount,
95                        stop);
96            }
97            producers[i].start();
```

```
98          }
99
100         // Start the consumers.
101         final AtomicInteger consumedCount = new AtomicInteger();
102         final Thread[] consumers = new Thread[consumerCount];
103         for (int i = 0; i < consumerCount; i++) {
104             if (batchSize == 1) {
105                 consumers[i] = new Consumer(sqsClient, queueUrl, consumedCount,
106                         stop);
107             } else {
108                 consumers[i] = new BatchConsumer(sqsClient, queueUrl, batchSize,
109                         consumedCount, stop);
110             }
111             consumers[i].start();
112         }
113
114         // Start the monitor thread.
115         final Thread monitor = new Monitor(producedCount, consumedCount, stop);
116         monitor.start();
117
118         // Wait for the specified amount of time then stop.
119         Thread.sleep(TimeUnit.MINUTES.toMillis(Math.min(runTimeMinutes,
120                 MAX_RUNTIME_MINUTES)));
121         stop.set(true);
122
123         // Join all threads.
124         for (int i = 0; i < producerCount; i++) {
125             producers[i].join();
126         }
127
128         for (int i = 0; i < consumerCount; i++) {
129             consumers[i].join();
130         }
131
132         monitor.interrupt();
133         monitor.join();
134     }
135
136     private static String makeRandomString(int sizeByte) {
137         final byte[] bs = new byte[(int) Math.ceil(sizeByte * 5 / 8)];
138         new Random().nextBytes(bs);
139         bs[0] = (byte) ((bs[0] | 64) & 127);
140         return new BigInteger(bs).toString(32);
141     }
142
143     /**
144      * The producer thread uses {@code SendMessage}
145      * to send messages until it is stopped.
146      */
147     private static class Producer extends Thread {
148         final AmazonSQS sqsClient;
149         final String queueUrl;
150         final AtomicInteger producedCount;
151         final AtomicBoolean stop;
```

```
152        final String theMessage;
153
154        Producer(AmazonSQS sqsQueueBuffer, String queueUrl, int messageSizeByte,
155                    AtomicInteger producedCount, AtomicBoolean stop) {
156            this.sqsClient = sqsQueueBuffer;
157            this.queueUrl = queueUrl;
158            this.producedCount = producedCount;
159            this.stop = stop;
160            this.theMessage = makeRandomString(messageSizeByte);
161        }
162
163        /*
164         * The producedCount object tracks the number of messages produced by
165         * all producer threads. If there is an error, the program exits the
166         * run() method.
167         */
168        public void run() {
169            try {
170                while (!stop.get()) {
171                    sqsClient.sendMessage(new SendMessageRequest(queueUrl,
172                            theMessage));
173                    producedCount.incrementAndGet();
174                }
175            } catch (AmazonClientException e) {
176                /*
177                 * By default, AmazonSQSClient retries calls 3 times before
178                 * failing. If this unlikely condition occurs, stop.
179                 */
180                log.error("Producer: " + e.getMessage());
181                System.exit(1);
182            }
183        }
184    }
185
186    /**
187     * The producer thread uses {@code SendMessageBatch}
188     * to send messages until it is stopped.
189     */
190    private static class BatchProducer extends Thread {
191        final AmazonSQS sqsClient;
192        final String queueUrl;
193        final int batchSize;
194        final AtomicInteger producedCount;
195        final AtomicBoolean stop;
196        final String theMessage;
197
198        BatchProducer(AmazonSQS sqsQueueBuffer, String queueUrl, int batchSize,
199                        int messageSizeByte, AtomicInteger producedCount,
200                        AtomicBoolean stop) {
201            this.sqsClient = sqsQueueBuffer;
202            this.queueUrl = queueUrl;
203            this.batchSize = batchSize;
204            this.producedCount = producedCount;
205            this.stop = stop;
```

```java
                    this.theMessage = makeRandomString(messageSizeByte);
                }

    public void run() {
        try {
            while (!stop.get()) {
                final SendMessageBatchRequest batchRequest =
                        new SendMessageBatchRequest().withQueueUrl(queueUrl);

                final List<SendMessageBatchRequestEntry> entries =
                        new ArrayList<SendMessageBatchRequestEntry>();
                for (int i = 0; i < batchSize; i++)
                    entries.add(new SendMessageBatchRequestEntry()
                            .withId(Integer.toString(i))
                            .withMessageBody(theMessage));
                batchRequest.setEntries(entries);

                final SendMessageBatchResult batchResult =
                        sqsClient.sendMessageBatch(batchRequest);
                producedCount.addAndGet(batchResult.getSuccessful().size());

                /*
                 * Because SendMessageBatch can return successfully, but
                 * individual batch items fail, retry the failed batch items.
                 */
                if (!batchResult.getFailed().isEmpty()) {
                    log.warn("Producer: retrying sending "
                            + batchResult.getFailed().size() + " messages");
                    for (int i = 0, n = batchResult.getFailed().size();
                            i < n; i++) {
                        sqsClient.sendMessage(new
                                SendMessageRequest(queueUrl, theMessage));
                        producedCount.incrementAndGet();
                    }
                }
            }
        } catch (AmazonClientException e) {
            /*
             * By default, AmazonSQSClient retries calls 3 times before
             * failing. If this unlikely condition occurs, stop.
             */
            log.error("BatchProducer: " + e.getMessage());
            System.exit(1);
        }
    }
}

/**
 * The consumer thread uses {@code ReceiveMessage} and {@code DeleteMessage}
 * to consume messages until it is stopped.
 */
private static class Consumer extends Thread {
    final AmazonSQS sqsClient;
    final String queueUrl;
```

```
260        final AtomicInteger consumedCount;
261        final AtomicBoolean stop;
262
263        Consumer(AmazonSQS sqsClient, String queueUrl, AtomicInteger consumedCount,
264                AtomicBoolean stop) {
265            this.sqsClient = sqsClient;
266            this.queueUrl = queueUrl;
267            this.consumedCount = consumedCount;
268            this.stop = stop;
269        }
270
271        /*
272         * Each consumer thread receives and deletes messages until the main
273         * thread stops the consumer thread. The consumedCount object tracks the
274         * number of messages that are consumed by all consumer threads, and the
275         * count is logged periodically.
276         */
277        public void run() {
278            try {
279                while (!stop.get()) {
280                    try {
281                        final ReceiveMessageResult result = sqsClient
282                                .receiveMessage(new
283                                        ReceiveMessageRequest(queueUrl));
284
285                        if (!result.getMessages().isEmpty()) {
286                            final Message m = result.getMessages().get(0);
287                            sqsClient.deleteMessage(new
288                                    DeleteMessageRequest(queueUrl,
289                                    m.getReceiptHandle()));
290                            consumedCount.incrementAndGet();
291                        }
292                    } catch (AmazonClientException e) {
293                        log.error(e.getMessage());
294                    }
295                }
296            } catch (AmazonClientException e) {
297                /*
298                 * By default, AmazonSQSClient retries calls 3 times before
299                 * failing. If this unlikely condition occurs, stop.
300                 */
301                log.error("Consumer: " + e.getMessage());
302                System.exit(1);
303            }
304        }
305    }
306
307    /**
308     * The consumer thread uses {@code ReceiveMessage} and {@code
309     * DeleteMessageBatch} to consume messages until it is stopped.
310     */
311    private static class BatchConsumer extends Thread {
312        final AmazonSQS sqsClient;
313        final String queueUrl;
```

```
314      final int batchSize;
315      final AtomicInteger consumedCount;
316      final AtomicBoolean stop;
317
318      BatchConsumer(AmazonSQS sqsClient, String queueUrl, int batchSize,
319                    AtomicInteger consumedCount, AtomicBoolean stop) {
320          this.sqsClient = sqsClient;
321          this.queueUrl = queueUrl;
322          this.batchSize = batchSize;
323          this.consumedCount = consumedCount;
324          this.stop = stop;
325      }
326
327      public void run() {
328          try {
329              while (!stop.get()) {
330                  final ReceiveMessageResult result = sqsClient
331                          .receiveMessage(new ReceiveMessageRequest(queueUrl)
332                              .withMaxNumberOfMessages(batchSize));
333
334                  if (!result.getMessages().isEmpty()) {
335                      final List<Message> messages = result.getMessages();
336                      final DeleteMessageBatchRequest batchRequest =
337                          new DeleteMessageBatchRequest()
338                              .withQueueUrl(queueUrl);
339
340                      final List<DeleteMessageBatchRequestEntry> entries =
341                          new ArrayList<DeleteMessageBatchRequestEntry>();
342                      for (int i = 0, n = messages.size(); i < n; i++)
343                          entries.add(new DeleteMessageBatchRequestEntry()
344                                  .withId(Integer.toString(i))
345                                  .withReceiptHandle(messages.get(i)
346                                      .getReceiptHandle()));
347                      batchRequest.setEntries(entries);
348
349                      final DeleteMessageBatchResult batchResult = sqsClient
350                              .deleteMessageBatch(batchRequest);
351                      consumedCount.addAndGet(batchResult.getSuccessful().size());
352
353                      /*
354                       * Because DeleteMessageBatch can return successfully,
355                       * but individual batch items fail, retry the failed
356                       * batch items.
357                       */
358                      if (!batchResult.getFailed().isEmpty()) {
359                          final int n = batchResult.getFailed().size();
360                          log.warn("Producer: retrying deleting " + n
361                                  + " messages");
362                          for (BatchResultErrorEntry e : batchResult
363                                  .getFailed()) {
364
365                              sqsClient.deleteMessage(
366                                      new DeleteMessageRequest(queueUrl,
367                                          messages.get(Integer
```

239

```
368                                                    .parseInt(e.getId()))
369                                                    .getReceiptHandle())));
370
371                          consumedCount.incrementAndGet();
372                      }
373                  }
374              }
375          }
376      } catch (AmazonClientException e) {
377          /*
378           * By default, AmazonSQSClient retries calls 3 times before
379           * failing. If this unlikely condition occurs, stop.
380           */
381          log.error("BatchConsumer: " + e.getMessage());
382          System.exit(1);
383      }
384  }
385  }
386
387  /**
388   * This thread prints every second the number of messages produced and
389   * consumed so far.
390   */
391  private static class Monitor extends Thread {
392      private final AtomicInteger producedCount;
393      private final AtomicInteger consumedCount;
394      private final AtomicBoolean stop;
395
396      Monitor(AtomicInteger producedCount, AtomicInteger consumedCount,
397              AtomicBoolean stop) {
398          this.producedCount = producedCount;
399          this.consumedCount = consumedCount;
400          this.stop = stop;
401      }
402
403      public void run() {
404          try {
405              while (!stop.get()) {
406                  Thread.sleep(1000);
407                  log.info("produced messages = " + producedCount.get()
408                          + ", consumed messages = " + consumedCount.get());
409              }
410          } catch (InterruptedException e) {
411              // Allow the thread to exit.
412          }
413      }
414  }
415 }
```

Monitoring Volume Metrics from the Example Run

Amazon SQS automatically generates volume metrics for sent, received, and deleted messages. You can access those metrics and others through the **Monitoring** tab for your queue or on the CloudWatch console.

Note

The metrics can take up to 15 minutes after the queue starts to become available.

Related Amazon SQS Resources

The following table lists related resources that you might find useful as you work with this service.

Resource	Description
Amazon Simple Queue Service API Reference	Descriptions of actions, parameters, and data types and a list of errors that the service returns.
Amazon SQS in the *AWS CLI Command Reference*	Descriptions of the AWS CLI commands that you can use to work with queues.
Regions and Endpoints	Information about Amazon SQS regions and endpoints
Product Page	The primary web page for information about Amazon SQS.
Discussion Forum	A community-based forum for developers to discuss technical questions related to Amazon SQS.
AWS Premium Support Information	The primary web page for information about AWS Premium Support, a one-on-one, fast-response support channel to help you build and run applications on AWS infrastructure services.

Amazon SQS Release Notes

The following table lists Amazon SQS feature releases and improvements. For changes to the *Amazon Simple Queue Service Developer Guide*, see Amazon SQS Document History.

Date	Feature Release
May 24, 2018	Server-side encryption (SSE) for Amazon SQS is available in all commercial regions where Amazon SQS is available, except for the China Regions. For more information on server-side encryption and how to get started using it, see Protecting Data Using Server-Side Encryption (SSE) and AWS KMS .
March 20, 2018	Amazon CloudWatch Events can use Amazon SQS FIFO queues as targets. For more information, see Automating Notifications from AWS Services to Amazon SQS using CloudWatch Events.
January 23, 2018	Amazon S3 Event Notifications are compatible with Amazon SQS SSE. For more information, see the updated Example 3: Enable Compatibility between AWS Services Such as Amazon CloudWatch Events, Amazon S3, and Amazon SNS and Queues with SSE section.
January 2, 2018	The following features of AWS services are compatible with Amazon SQS SSE: [See the AWS documentation website for more details]
October 19, 2017	You can track cost allocation by adding, updating, removing, and listing metadata tags for Amazon SQS queues using the [TagQueue](http://docs.aws.amazon .com/AWSSimpleQueueService/latest /APIReference/API_TagQueue.html), [UntagQueue](http://docs.aws. amazon.com/AWSSimpleQueueService/ latest/APIReference/API_UntagQueue .html), and [ListQueueTags](http://docs.aws.amazon.com/ AWSSimpleQueueService/latest/ APIReference/API_ListQueueTags.html) actions and the AWS Management Console. For more information, see Amazon SQS Cost Allocation Tags and the Adding, Updating, and Removing Tags from an Amazon SQS Queue tutorial.
September 1, 2017	The complete set of Amazon SQS actions is displayed in the **Actions** list on the **Add a Permission to *MyQueue*** dialog box. For more information, see the Tutorial: Adding Permissions to an Amazon SQS Queue tutorial.

Date	Feature Release
June 14, 2017	FIFO (First-In-First-Out) queues are available in the US East (N. Virginia) Region, in addition to the EU (Ireland), US East (Ohio), and US West (Oregon) Regions. For more information about how FIFO queues work and how to get started using them, see Amazon SQS FIFO (First-In-First-Out) Queues.
June 8, 2017	FIFO (First-In-First-Out) queues are available in the EU (Ireland) Region, in addition to the US East (Ohio) and US West (Oregon) Regions. For more information about how FIFO queues work and how to get started using them, see Amazon SQS FIFO (First-In-First-Out) Queues.
May 23, 2017	Server-side encryption (SSE) for Amazon SQS is available in the US East (N. Virginia) Region, in addition to the US East (Ohio) and US West (Oregon) Regions. For more information about server-side encryption and how to get started using it, see Protecting Data Using Server-Side Encryption (SSE) and AWS KMS .
May 19, 2017	[See the AWS documentation website for more details]
May 1, 2017	AWS has expanded its HIPAA compliance program to include Amazon SQS as a HIPAA Eligible Service.

Date	Feature Release
April 28, 2017	Server-side encryption (SSE) for Amazon SQS is available in the US East (Ohio) and US West (Oregon) Regions. SSE lets you protect the contents of messages in Amazon SQS queues using keys managed in the AWS Key Management Service (AWS KMS). For more information about server-side encryption and how to get started using it, see Protecting Data Using Server-Side Encryption (SSE) and AWS KMS . For tutorials, see the following:[See the AWS documentation website for more details]SSE adds the KmsMasterKeyId and KmsDataKeyReusePeriodSeconds attributes to the `[CreateQueue](http://docs.aws.amazon.com/AWSSimpleQueueService/latest/APIReference/API_CreateQueue.html)`, `[GetQueueAttributes](http://docs.aws.amazon.com/AWSSimpleQueueService/latest/APIReference/API_GetQueueAttributes.html)`, and `[SetQueueAttributes](http://docs.aws.amazon.com/AWSSimpleQueueService/latest/APIReference/API_SetQueueAttributes.html)` actions.Some features of AWS services that can send notifications to Amazon SQS using the AWS Security Token Service `[AssumeRole](http://docs.aws.amazon.com/STS/latest/APIReference/API_AssumeRole.html)` action are compatible with SSE but work *only with standard queues:* Auto Scaling Lifecycle Hooks AWS Lambda Dead-Letter Queues Other features of AWS services or third-party services that send notifications to Amazon SQS aren't compatible with SSE, despite allowing you to set an encrypted queue as a target: AWS IoT Rule Actions For information about compatibility of other services with encrypted queues, see Example 3: Enable Compatibility between AWS Services Such as Amazon CloudWatch Events, Amazon S3, and Amazon SNS and Queues with SSE and your service documentation.
April 24, 2017	[See the AWS documentation website for more details]
March 28, 2017	AWS CloudFormation lets your create FIFO queues. Added the AWS CloudFormation tutorial.

Date	Feature Release
November 17, 2016	FIFO (First-In-First-Out) queues or standard queues (another name for existing queues) are available in the US West (Oregon) and US East (Ohio) Regions. For more information about how FIFO queues work and how to get started using them, see the following:[See the AWS documentation website for more details]For revised Amazon SQS tutorials, see the following:[See the AWS documentation website for more details]FIFO queues add the following API functionality:[See the AWS documentation website for more details] As of November 17, 2016, Amazon SQS no longer publishes a WSDL. The Amazon SQS Buffered Asynchronous Client doesn't currently support FIFO queues. Some AWS or external services that send notifications to Amazon SQS might not be compatible with FIFO queues, despite allowing you to set a FIFO queue as a target. The following features of AWS services aren't currently compatible with FIFO queues: Auto Scaling Lifecycle Hooks AWS IoT Rule Actions AWS Lambda Dead-Letter Queues For information about compatibility of other services with FIFO queues, see your service documentation. FIFO queues don't support timers on individual messages.
August 31, 2016	The ApproximateAgeOfOldestMessage CloudWatch metric lets you find the approximate age of the oldest non-deleted message in the queue. For more information, see Available CloudWatch Metrics for Amazon SQS.
February 12, 2016	You can view CloudWatch metrics from the Amazon SQS console for up to 10 of your queues at a time. For more information, see Monitoring Amazon SQS Queues Using CloudWatch.
October 27, 2015	The Amazon SQS Extended Client Library for Java lets you manage Amazon SQS messages with Amazon S3. For more information, see Managing Large Amazon SQS Messages Using Amazon S3 in the Amazon Simple Queue Service Developer Guide.
December 29, 2014	Amazon SQS lets you use JMS (Java Message Service) with Amazon SQS queues. For more information, see Working with JMS and Amazon SQS in the *Amazon Simple Queue Service Developer Guide.*

Date	Feature Release
December 8, 2014	Amazon SQS lets you delete the messages in a queue using the `PurgeQueue` action. For more information, see PurgeQueue in the *Amazon Simple Queue Service API Reference*.
July 16, 2014	Amazon SQS lets you log actions using AWS CloudTrail. For more information, see Logging Amazon SQS Actions Using AWS Cloud-Trail.
May 6, 2014	Amazon SQS provides support for message attributes. For more information, see Amazon SQS Message Attributes.
January 29, 2014	Amazon SQS provides support for dead-letter queues. For more information, see Amazon SQS Dead-Letter Queues.
November 21, 2012	You can subscribe an Amazon SQS queue to an Amazon SNS topic using the Amazon SQS console. For more information, see Tutorial: Subscribing an Amazon SQS Queue to an Amazon SNS Topic.
November 5, 2012	The 2012-11-05 API version of Amazon SQS adds support for Signature Version 4, which provides improved security and performance. For more information about Signature Version 4, see Basic Authentication Process with HMAC-SHA.
November 5, 2012	The AWS SDK for Java includes a buffered asynchronous client, `AmazonSQSBufferedAsyncClient`, for accessing Amazon SQS. This client allows for easier request batching by enabling client-side buffering, where calls made from the client are first buffered and then sent as a batch request to Amazon SQS. For more information about client-side buffering and request batching, see Enabling Client-Side Buffering and Request Batching.
November 5, 2012	The 2012-11-05 API version of Amazon SQS adds long polling support. Long polling allows Amazon SQS to wait for a specified amount time for a message to be available instead of returning an empty response if one isn't available. For more information about long polling, see Amazon SQS Long Polling.

Amazon SQS Document History

The following table lists changes to the *Amazon Simple Queue Service Developer Guide*. For Amazon SQS feature releases and improvements, see Amazon SQS Release Notes.

Date	Documentation Update
June 11, 2018	[See the AWS documentation website for more details]
June 5, 2018	In addition to GitHub, HTML, PDF, and Kindle, the *Amazon MQ Developer Guide* release notes are available as an RSS feed.
May 29, 2018	[See the AWS documentation website for more details]
May 24, 2018	Updated the Protecting Data Using Server-Side Encryption (SSE) and AWS KMS section.
May 22, 2018	[See the AWS documentation website for more details]
May 15, 2018	Clarified the information in the Processing Messages in a Timely Manner section.
May 10, 2018	[See the AWS documentation website for more details]
May 9, 2018	Rewrote the Amazon SQS Message Timers section.
May 8, 2018	[See the AWS documentation website for more details]
May 3, 2018	[See the AWS documentation website for more details]
May 2, 2018	[See the AWS documentation website for more details]
May 1, 2018	Corrected and clarified the information in the Limits Related to Queues section.
April 25, 2018	[See the AWS documentation website for more details]
April 24, 2018	[See the AWS documentation website for more details]
April 23, 2018	Rewrote the Processing Messages in a Timely Manner section.
April 11, 2018	[See the AWS documentation website for more details]
April 10, 2018	[See the AWS documentation website for more details]
April 9, 2018	[See the AWS documentation website for more details]
April 6, 2018	[See the AWS documentation website for more details]
April 5, 2018	[See the AWS documentation website for more details]

Date	Documentation Update
April 4, 2018	[See the AWS documentation website for more details]
March 29, 2018	Added the following note to the Calculating the MD5 Message Digest for Message Attributes section: Always include custom data type suffixes in the MD5 message-digest calculation.
March 27, 2018	[See the AWS documentation website for more details]
March 26, 2018	[See the AWS documentation website for more details]
March 23, 2018	[See the AWS documentation website for more details]
March 22, 2018	[See the AWS documentation website for more details]
March 20, 2018	[See the AWS documentation website for more details]
March 19, 2018	Clarified in the Limits Related to Policies and Tutorial: Adding Permissions to an Amazon SQS Queue sections that an Amazon SQS policy can have a maximum of 7 actions.
March 14, 2018	[See the AWS documentation website for more details]
March 13, 2018	Clarified the batched and unbatched throughput for FIFO queues throughout this guide.
March 7, 2018	Updated the New and Frequently Viewed Amazon SQS Topics section.
March 2, 2018	[See the AWS documentation website for more details]
February 28, 2018	Corrected image display in GitHub.
February 27, 2018	In addition to HTML, PDF, and Kindle, the Amazon Simple Queue Service Developer Guide is available on GitHub. To leave feedback, choose the GitHub icon in the upper right-hand corner.
February 26, 2018	[See the AWS documentation website for more details]
February 23, 2018	[See the AWS documentation website for more details]
February 21, 2018	[See the AWS documentation website for more details]
February 20, 2018	[See the AWS documentation website for more details]
February 19, 2018	Optimized the example Java code and corrected pom.xml prerequisites in the following sections: [See the AWS documentation website for more details]

Date	Documentation Update
February 16, 2018	Simplified the example Java code and added pom.xml prerequisites to the following sections: [See the AWS documentation website for more details]
February 15, 2018	Updated the Related Amazon SQS Resources section.
February 14, 2018	[See the AWS documentation website for more details]
February 13, 2018	[See the AWS documentation website for more details]
February 9, 2018	[See the AWS documentation website for more details]
February 8, 2018	Rewrote the Java example in the Working Java Example for Single-Operation and Batch Requests section.
February 7, 2018	Rewrote the following sections: [See the AWS documentation website for more details]
February 6, 2018	Rewrote the following sections: [See the AWS documentation website for more details]
February 5, 2018	Clarified the information in the Tutorial: Configuring an Amazon SQS Dead-Letter Queue section.
February 2, 2018	Created the New and Frequently Viewed Amazon SQS Topics section.
February 1, 2018	[See the AWS documentation website for more details]
January 31, 2018	Clarified the information in the following sections: [See the AWS documentation website for more details]
January 30, 2018	Rewrote the following sections: [See the AWS documentation website for more details]
January 29, 2018	Rewrote the following sections: [See the AWS documentation website for more details]
January 25, 2018	[See the AWS documentation website for more details]
January 24, 2018	Clarified the wording for Amazon SQS actions throughout this guide.
January 22, 2018	Added the Example 3: Enable Compatibility between AWS Services Such as Amazon CloudWatch Events, Amazon S3, and Amazon SNS and Queues with SSE section.
January 19, 2018	Clarified the information in the How Do Dead-Letter Queues Work? section.
January 18, 2018	[See the AWS documentation website for more details]
January 17, 2018	[See the AWS documentation website for more details]
January 16, 2018	[See the AWS documentation website for more details]
January 15, 2018	[See the AWS documentation website for more details]
January 3, 2018	Further clarified the throughput for FIFO queues throughout this guide.

Date	Documentation Update
December 7, 2017	[See the AWS documentation website for more details]
December 6, 2017	[See the AWS documentation website for more details]
December 1, 2017	Clarified and reorganized the information in the Monitoring Amazon SQS Queues Using CloudWatch section.
October 30, 2017	[See the AWS documentation website for more details]
October 27, 2017	Clarified the explanation of throughput for FIFO queues in the Amazon SQS FIFO (First-In-First-Out) Queues section.
September 29, 2017	Added a note about the Amazon SQS Buffered Asynchronous Client to the Increasing Throughput using Horizontal Scaling and Action Batching section.
September 19, 2017	Corrected the diagrams in the Using Amazon SQS and IAM Policies section.
August 29, 2017	Clarified the information in the Changing the Visibility Timeout for a Message section.
August 17, 2017	Clarified the permissions for the SendMessage and SendMessageBatch actions in Amazon SQS API Permissions: Actions and Resource Reference.
August 15, 2017	Updated information about dead-letter queues in the Recommendations for Amazon SQS Standard and FIFO (First-In-First-Out) Queues section.
August 9, 2017	[See the AWS documentation website for more details]
July 27, 2017	Changed the deprecated `AmazonSQSClient` constructor to `AmazonSQSClientBuilder` and revised the corresponding region specification in the Working Java Example for Standard Queues section.
July 25, 2017	Clarified the throughput for standard and FIFO queues throughout this guide.

Date	Documentation Update
July 20, 2017	Clarified the compatibility between Amazon SQS SSE queues and AWS and third-party service features throughout this guide: Some features of AWS services that can send notifications to Amazon SQS using the AWS Security Token Service `[AssumeRole](http ://docs.aws.amazon.com/STS/latest/ APIReference/API_AssumeRole.html)` action are compatible with SSE but work *only with standard queues:* [See the AWS documentation website for more details] Other features of AWS services or third-party services that send notifications to Amazon SQS aren't compatible with SSE, despite allowing you to set an encrypted queue as a target: [See the AWS documentation website for more details] For information about compatibility of other services with encrypted queues, see Example 3: Enable Compatibility between AWS Services Such as Amazon CloudWatch Events, Amazon S3, and Amazon SNS and Queues with SSE and your service documentation.
June 23, 2017	Corrected the information in the Limits Related to Messages section.
June 20, 2017	Clarified the information in the Amazon SQS Dead-Letter Queues section.
June 2, 2017	[See the AWS documentation website for more details]
June 1, 2017	Updated the What is Amazon Simple Queue Service? section.
May 24, 2017	[See the AWS documentation website for more details]
May 23, 2017	Server-side encryption (SSE) for Amazon SQS is available in the US East (N. Virginia) Region, in addition to the US East (Ohio) and US West (Oregon) Regions. For more information about server-side encryption and how to get started using it, see Protecting Data Using Server-Side Encryption (SSE) and AWS KMS .
May 19, 2017	[See the AWS documentation website for more details]
April 25, 2017	Restructured and updated the Amazon SQS Long Polling section.
February 6, 2017	Updated the Authentication and Access Control section.
December 16, 2016	Retired the Amazon Simple Queue Service Getting Started Guide and incorporated some of its content into the following sections of this guide:[See the AWS documentation website for more details]

Date	Documentation Update
December 2, 2016	Restructured and updated the Authentication and Access Control section.
November 2, 2016	Renamed the Walkthroughs section to Amazon SQS Tutorials.
May 27, 2016	Added the Best Practices for Amazon SQS section.
May 12, 2016	Added the Amazon SQS Limits section.
December 7, 2015	Updated Amazon SQS console screenshots.
August 4, 2014	Updated information about access keys. For more information, see Authenticating Requests.

AWS Glossary

For the latest AWS terminology, see the AWS Glossary in the *AWS General Reference*.

www.ingramcontent.com/pod-product-compliance
Lightning Source LLC
LaVergne TN
LVHW081445070326
R19240600001B/R192406PG832904LVX00001B/1